The
Making
of
Meaning

The
Making
of
Meaning

Metaphors, Models, and Maxims
for Writing Teachers

Ann E. Berthoff

Boynton/Cook Publishers, Inc.

The proprietors of the following copyrighted works have kindly given us permission for their use:

Sylvia Ashton-Warner, from *Teacher*: Copyright © 1963 by Sylvia Ashton-Warner. Reprinted by permission of Simon & Schuster, a division of Gulf & Western Corporation.

Emil Jaques-Dalcroze, from *Rhythm, Music, and Education*: Reprinted by Benjamin Blom Inc. Distributed by Arno Press Inc. Reprinted by permission of the publisher.

Paulo Freire, from *Education for Critical Consciousness*: Copyright © 1973 by the Author. Reprinted by permission of the Continuum Publishing Corporation.

Paul A. Freund, "The Law and the Schools": Copyright © 1966 by President and Fellows of Harvard College.

Northrop Frye, from *Design for Learning*: Copyright © 1962 by University of Toronto Press. Reprinted by permission of the author.

I.A. Richards, from *How to Read a Page:* Copyright © 1942 by W. W. Norton & Company, Inc. Copyright renewed © 1969 by I.A. Richards. Reprinted by permission of W. W. Norton & Company, Inc.

Schoolboys of Barbiana, from *Letter to a Teacher*: Translated by Nora Rossi and Tom Cole. Copyright © 1970 by Random House, Inc. Reprinted by permission of the publisher.

Bob Sievert, "Bugs: One Insect Leads to Another": Copyright © 1976 by Teachers & Writers Collaborative. Reprinted from *Teachers and Writers*, Vol. 7, No. 2, by Bob Sievert by permission of Teachers & Writers Collaborative, 84 Fifth Avenue, New York, N.Y. 10011.

Alfred North Whitehead, from *The Aims of Education*: Copyright © 1929 by Macmillan Publishing Co., Inc., renewed 1957 by Evelyn Whitehead. Reprinted with permission of Macmillan Publishing Company, Inc.

Library of Congress Cataloging in Publication Data

Berthoff, Ann E.
   The making of meaning.

   Bibliography: p.
   1. English language—Rhetoric—Study and teaching—Addresses, essays, lectures.
I. Title
PE1404.B47   808'.042'071073   81–9948
ISBN 0–86709–003–0   AACR2

For information address Boynton/Cook Publishers, Inc., P.O. Box 860, Upper Montclair, NJ 07043

Printed in the United States of America

86 87 88 89 90 10 9 8 7 6 5 4 3

11-10-93

Preface

This book gathers together talks and articles I have written in the past few years on the challenge, as I see it, of teaching people how to write. It includes casual harangues and serious polemic, as well as straightforward discussions of such matters as the role of the teacher as researcher, the definition of pedagogy, theories of meaning and meaning-making, the nature of perception, images of composing, models of process, writing across the curriculum, and writing as a way of knowing and a mode of learning. All of that constitutes Part II. In Part I, I've discussed ways in which metaphors, models, and maxims can keep theory accessible so that we can convert it to method.

The audiences have been school teachers, college teachers, and teachers of teachers. I have done some cutting so that my obsessions will not prove tiresome, but there are many formulations of those principles I am trying to make clear to myself and others. I've left the texts pretty much the way they were delivered in the hope that the particular occasions can be recreated by readers. If the tone is now and then magisterial, I hope that will not be offensive: I lay down the law when I think I've found it. I enjoy argument, though I try to remember I. A. Richards' warnings that disputation can be hazardous, that since "the disputant's energies are controlled by immediate specific purposes, he is commonly too busy making points to see what they are."

The case I've tried to make in almost every one of these pieces is that if we are to teach writing as a process of making meaning, we will need a philosophy of language that can account for meaning not as "a can that has been filled or a lump of clay that has been moulded," as Richards puts it in *The Philosophy of Rhetoric*, but as a plant that has grown. Interpretation is a branch of biology, in this view. *Forming* and *imagination* have provided my chief "speculative instruments," as Richards calls the ideas we think with. From Richards and from Susanne K. Langer I have learned most about what I am trying to do as an English teacher—to see *that* as a philosophical enterprise. I want to do everything I can to persuade teachers, K–35, to become philos-

ophers—to remind them that that is, indeed, what they are when they
consider language and thought, theory and practice, intending and
realizing, writing and rewriting; when they think about thinking or
consider the meanings of meaning; when, in Coleridge's wonderful
phrase, they seek *to know their knowledge.*

In Part III, "Up to the Classroom," I've selected passages, and in
a few cases, entire essays that I've found instructive in my own teaching. I subscribe wholeheartedly to Sylvia Ashton-Warner's notion that
the end of "the education story" can't be told unless we know the beginning. These selections concern, for the most part, the teaching of
youngsters. Just as metaphor provides a focus for the study of meaning, so, I think, considering how children learn is the best way to
learn to teach writing as a process of forming. As Gordon Allport has
said: "Whatever else it might be, learning is certainly a disposition to
form structures." Part III is, of course, a restricted sample: I have not
included many writers whose work is full of interest for anyone teaching or learning to teach composing. In a forthcoming volume, *Reclaiming the Imagination,* I have collected essays—from artists,
scientists, philosophers, historians, and others—that provide a philosophical framework for thinking about the composing process; but for
the time being I have focused on comment by some of the great
teachers of our century.

I appreciate the friendly welcome I've had from those who have in-
vited my participation in seminars, institutes, and conferences: James
Broderick, Patricia Burnes, Leslie Chard, Joseph Check, James Day,
Michael Flanigan, Robert Foulke, Norma Kahn, James Lee, Sandra
Stotsky, and Seymour Yesner. And at various Non-Conferences, I've
enjoyed long conversations with friends and colleagues and students.
They have all given me invaluable feedback and feedforward. I want
to thank especially Patricia Bizzell, Neal Bruss, Jane Christensen, William E. Coles, Jr., Rosemary Deen, Florence S. DeVecchi, Angela
Dorenkamp, Mary K. Healy, Janet Kotler, Ann Raimes, Rosamond
Rosenmeier, and Taylor Stoehr. George and Loretta Slover first introduced me to Paulo Freire's work and I have since enjoyed exploring his pedagogy with them and with Joseph Summers. Fran Morris
told me about Dalcroze; Brenda Engel made me read Tolstoy and
opened my mind to new ideas about what research can mean. Dixie
Goswami, who has used this collection in her seminar at the Breadloaf
School of English for two summers running, has encouraged me in
my belief that we teachers have more to learn from one another than
all the psychologists in the world have to tell us.

Bob Boynton had the idea that I should collect my talks to teachers
along with certain essays from which I have learned in thirty years of

trying to teach composing as a matter of making meaning. I am grateful to him, again, for his thoughtful guidance, as I am to Bill Cook for the care and imagination with which he has designed this book.

Contents

The
Making
of
Meaning

Part I

Method

Method: Metaphors, Models, and Maxims

It's often said that people learn to write by writing—and this is true, if it's said in rejection of the idea that people learn to write by drilling for skill or by reading what rhetoricians have to say about invention, arrangement, style; surface features and deep structure; narration, definition, description; problem solving, tagmemic heuristics, getting into your left hemisphere and getting out again. But writing can't teach writing unless it is understood as a nonlinear, dialectical process in which the writer continually circles back, reviewing and rewriting: certainly, the way to learn to do that is to practice *doing* just that. If we leave unexamined what we mean by "writing" and assume simply that all students who do it will learn to do it better, I think we are failing to take into account an important factor. Students, when they have been taught anything at all about writing, have often been taught some very wrongheaded things, such as outlining as a first step; not writing at all "until you know what you want to say"; avoiding generalizations, always *making it vivid;* casting so-called thesis statements in the form of simple assertions; combining artificially fragmented mini-statements into one large, less-fragmented but still piecemeal statement. It is far easier, I think, to teach those who have had no training in writing than it is to unteach the anticomposing that so many have learned.

The chief purpose of a theory of composition is to provide teachers with ways to present writing so that it can indeed be learned by writing. Many teachers are, however, impatient with theory—not an irrational attitude, given the fact that most compositional theory is ill-conceived, ill-founded, and ill-argued. Others find it irrelevant, on the assumption that since practice is practical, theory must be impractical. But theory is not the antithesis of practice and, in fact, can only serve an authentic purpose if it is continually brought into relationship with practice so that each can inform the other. There is no point in "theory for theory's sake" in rhetoric or composition, despite the claim of one distinguished rhetorician that a discipline is mature only when it can find room for such study.[1]

Without the perspective that theory provides, there is no way of maintaining a genuinely critical attitude towards assignments and courses. Without theory, practice can become cut and dried—which

is just the way many people want it. Teaching composition is famously tedious, so that composition pedagogy is often developed according to principles like these: (1) teaching writing comes down to
making theme assignments and evaluating the results; (2) it doesn't
matter why something works, so long as it works; (3) if you can get
things worked out once and for all, you won't have to waste time on
replanning the course every year. In between recipe swapping, which
is the result of rejecting theory, and the collocation and manipulation
of data, which is the result of theory for theory's sake, there is a third
way. It requires no special training; it invites us to use everything we
know about language and learning. This third way is best named *method*.

Like all the other words we must depend on in thinking about the
composing process and how to teach it, *method* is ambiguous. It can
and usually does mean, simply, a procedure, a sequence of activities
undertaken for one or another often unexamined purpose. There are
methods, in this sense, for doing everything from dieting to climbing
Mt. Everest. But *method* has important meanings in philosophy which
I think we can usefully reclaim. A method is a way of bringing together what we think we are doing and how we are doing it: *meta + hodos*
= about the way; the way about the way.

Throughout my talks I have commented on this circularity or dialectic that is characteristic of all critical study of language: interpreting our interpretations, thinking about thinking, arranging our
techniques for arranging, knowing our knowledge. The most interesting challenge is to take advantage of the fact that we can't step outside language in order to study it. Rather, we must use language to
study what language is doing. This is what Vygotsky means in claiming that the study of concept formation must begin with meaning.
And it is the basis for I. A. Richards' claim that "all studies are language studies, concerned with the speculative instruments they employ." Ideas in any field are not only what we think *about;* they are
what we think *with.* Method raises our consciousness of just what our
ideas are and how they are working for us—or against us.

The most powerful speculative instrument English teachers have is
imagination. If we can reclaim the imagination, seeing it as a name for
the active mind, we can use it to think with when we come to teach
writing as the composing process. Its power lies in the fact that it
makes possible so many fruitful analogies between writing and all
other acts of mind whereby we make sense of the world. *Imagination*
can help us form the concept of forming. Forming depends on abstraction, symbolization, selection, "purposing"; it requires or enables us to coordinate and subordinate, to amalgamate, discard, and

expand; it is our means of giving shape to content. Forming is the mind in action. It is what we do when we learn; when we discover or recognize; when we interpret; when we come to know. Forming is how we make meaning.

Now the point is this: how do we make the theory that "composing is forming" work for us? how can it guide our practice? how can we make of it a method? Theory must be accessible; it must be there when we need it, or we will find that our theoretical interest wanes and, with it, the intellectual energy needed for teaching composition. In my opinion, the best way to keep theory lively and practice responsive is to have *in mind* models and metaphors to *remind* us and our students of what is involved in learning and teaching the composing process.

For instance, because forming entails sorting and gathering, composing as forming can be represented by the gathering hand. Here is my attempt to use that image as a way of explaining paragraphs; it comes from my textbook, *Forming/Thinking/Writing*, pp. 157–58:

> . . . Paragraphing is both an effect—it results from the way you have grouped your sentences—and a means, a form that bundles your sentences. The paragraph is the product of composing, but it is also the means of composing. Like concepts, paragraphs are gatherers and gatherings. They are often described metaphorically in terms of shape—funnels and pyramids, chiefly. A funnel paragraph begins with an assortment of particularizations that undergo classification and are finally narrowed down to a generalization, at which narrow point the paragraph ends. A pyramid paragraph begins with the assertion of a generalization that is then analyzed and demonstrated, given a foundation of fact and detail. There are variations, such as the hourglass, which combines funnel and pyramid. I used to try to explain the gathering action of a paragraph by drawing an analogy with the triangular frame that organizes the balls for a game of pool. But none of these images, I now think, can suggest the dialectic of the relationship of the structure and its parts. They are all faulty, since they concentrate on either the product (you can't build a pyramid from the top) or the producing (what happens to what goes through the funnel?) and thus do not adequately represent the way the sentences build the paragraph, which in turn shapes the sentences. If you think of the paragraph simply as a mold to pour sentences into, you lose the chance to learn its forming powers.

That's why it's useful, I think, to keep in mind that a paragraph gathers like a hand. Note that the gathering hand operates in different ways: the hand that holds a couple of eggs or tennis balls works differently from the hand that holds a bridle or a motorbike handle. When you measure out spaghetti by the handful, scoop up water by the handful, hold a load of books on your hip, knead bread, shape a stack of papers, build a sand castle, your hands move in different planes and with different motions, according to the nature of the material being gathered. But in any case, the hand can gather because of the *opposable* thumb. (The thumb of the human hand can be brought into *opposition* with the fingers.) A paragraph gathers by opposing a concept and the elements that develop and substantiate it. The kind of gathering a paragraph makes is thus dependent on both the kind of elements and the way in which they have been gathered.

Now, the way to use the paragraph as a rhetorical form that can gather and shape sentences—and form the substance of what you are saying—is to assure that there is an "opposable thumb." If you consider a certain cluster of sentences as parts that can be gathered together into a whole and if you then *name* that whole, you will have a title for the proto-paragraph. We will call this title a *gloss*. Compose it in the form of an opposition or of a shorthand sentence that identifies the *who* or *what* and the *does*. This will give you what journalists call a "lead" and the substance for what English teachers and rhetoricians call a "topic sentence."

To represent the character of the composing process as one in which everything happens at once—forming/thinking/writing—I have often used the metaphor of the rheostat, which I understand better as a metaphor than I do as a mechanism. Any analogy can be faulty or misleading if it is carried too far, of course, but some are more dangerously unstable than others. Metaphors derived from computer technology are extremely hazardous, not only because the difference between brain and mind is obscured by talking about mental operations in terms properly used to describe brain function, but also because certain words have entirely different meanings as terms in information theory than they have in rhetoric. For instance, *information* in information theory has nothing (repeat: nothing) to do with substance or content, nothing to do with anything that in common parlance we might mean by the word. To speak of the way the brain *processes information* as an analogy for the way the writer *processes infor-*

mation is to confuse a neurological function with a psychological operation. Nevertheless, all metaphors, if used as speculative instruments, can be valuable as we continue to find out what we are trying to do.

I've been claiming that metaphors are ways of seeing the implications of theory. Metaphoric images such as Vygotsky's of meaning as a living cell can bring to mind all that is involved in thinking of the making of meaning as a natural, organic process. They bring to mind, in the sense of *reminding,* but also in the sense of encouraging us to discover relationships and how they might be articulated. Metaphors are thus heuristic[2] in function.

Like metaphors and images, models are picturable analogies that are aids to reflection—speculative instruments. (Psychologists call their metaphors "models" in the belief that that makes them "scientific.") There are differences between images and models[3], but both are analogies and should not be mistaken for anything other than representations of ideas, which (like all symbols) require interpretation.

After reading several accounts of the discovery of the structure of the DNA molecule, I constructed for my own amusement a model of the composing process as a double helix, trying to let the relationships articulated in that form help me discover those of composing. I had heard Francis Crick remark that you know a model is working for you when you get more out of it than you had put in—and I was delighted to see this happen. Although the process begins at the bottom and works its way upward, in each of the units, the four acts of mind, whether perceptual, conceptual, or rhetorical, can be read from top down as well as from bottom up. *Naming, opposing, defining* I have identified as acts of mind, which are continuous in all phases of the composing process. (See *Forming/Thinking/Writing,* pp. 70–79 and pp. 218–20.)

Maxims, like images, metaphors, and models, can make theory accessible; they provide a way to keep our speculative instruments handy. They have always found a place in rhetorical theory because rhetoricians like to claim that certain procedures and modes have the status of self-evident propositions. Although maxims are often set down as imperatives—"keep to the point," "use coordination," "use the active voice"—they should be understood as carrying the sense of "everybody agrees that it is best to/not to. . . ." This kind of confusion is a fact of human life: not just rhetoricians say, "This is the way it is," when what they mean is, "This is the way I think it should be."

I can't imagine that anybody ever learned by means of maxims, but they can serve a pedagogical function: by assembling and formulating important concepts in a minimalist way—the mostest in the leastest—

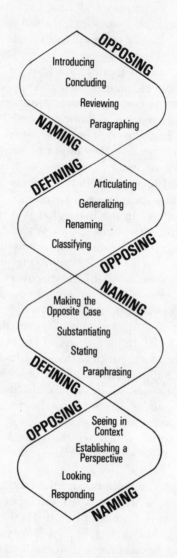

Composing As A Double Helix

they can encourage us to explore what is implied. A good maxim is like a fable in little: expanding and interpreting maxims is very good mental (and moral) exercise. The terms should be problematic but easily translatable. An example of a bad maxim is this one from current rhetorical theory: "Units of experience are hierarchically structured systems." "Units" seems to be equated with "systems," which surely can't be correct; "structured" is a redundant qualifier; and "system" has a range of meanings that is impossible to narrow without contextual clues. What you have when you're through unpacking might not be worth the trouble. Handbook maxims such as "make it vivid" or "use transitional devices in paragraphs" needn't be unpacked: their worthlessness is self-evident.

If maxims are to operate heuristically—if they are not simply exhortations masquerading as rules (or tautologies pretending to be definitions)—then they must suggest by antithesis or the logic of metaphor what the options are. In Coleridge's observation, "The shortest way gives me the knowledge best; the longest way makes me more knowing," we not only have a memorable formulation; we have a double opposition, which is something to think about—and to think with. A Chinese manual of painting tells the apprentice: "Splash ink; spare ink." That maxim is about style, genre, taste, and judgment, by way of a teasing contradiction that reminds the painter of the art of matching means and ends.

I've tried my hand at formulating maxims that can be instructive if they are unpacked. I can't claim that they're wise or witty, but they have, perhaps, a touch of surprise that invites speculation about the relationship of theory and practice. For the ones I've borrowed from Piaget and Tolstoy, I will claim both wit and wisdom.

∽∽∽ Begin with where they are.

This is a maxim reclaimed from those who mean by it, "Begin with where they are—as dummies, incapable of understanding anything that isn't factored and reduced to manageable bits." It was for a time the motto of those who favored *relevance;* they tried to make a virtue of deprivation: "If they can't read, don't waste time with books. Show films. Just talk—never mind about what." I first saw that it didn't have to mean that when a teacher said to me, "They've been there long enough!"

It can mean: "Begin with where they are as language animals, endowed with the form-finding and form-creating powers of mind and language." Then the maxim can help us redefine just who "they" are in philosophical terms. This is what Paulo Freire did. He began his literacy training with Brazilian peasants by having them name their world—by naming tools, places, jobs, people in their lives. These "generative words" provided the means of making meaning. He began with where the peasants were—as peasants; but he also began with the peasants as culture-makers, historical subjects, and children of God.

〜〜〜 **How you construe is how you construct.**

Anything we can do to make composing not entirely different from anything else our students have ever done will be helpful. If we are to teach writing as the composing process, we should be able, ourselves, to form the concept of composing as a continuum of forming, as consonant with all those acts of mind whereby we make sense of the world. Hundreds of research projects in reading are funded by the federal government but only a handful in writing: what would happen if we composition teachers could make the point first to ourselves, then to our students, then to the funders, that what we do when we read is fundamentally analogous to what we do when we interpret any situation, event, state of affairs (or feeling or mind); that that construing is in all respects analogous to what we do when we construct lists, formulas, statements—when we compose? We need research projects in teaching reading and writing together. Because literature tends to crowd out writing, some have exiled it from the composition classroom. This is a solution that creates further problems. We need teachers who know how to relate critical reading to composing—not by finding topics to write about in the assigned reading, but by identifying how forming is central to both reading and writing.

〜〜〜 **To understand is to invent.**

[Jean Piaget]

If we can learn to teach reading and writing together as construing and constructing, both as modes of interpreting, then we can the more easily see the justification for teaching creative and critical writing together at least some of the time. Of course, they can be differentiated by the sound principle that they serve different purposes. But they are usually differentiated only in terms of the affective-cognitive opposition. I have zealously preached against this doctrine in several of the talks printed here, so I won't argue the case now. Piaget's maxim is better than argument anyway, since his paradox simultaneously destroys the false opposition of the creative and the critical and declares their interdependence.

"To observe what varies with what" is as good a characterization of scientific method as any I know; isn't it also at the heart of composing a poem? I. A. Richards wrote a lengthy essay early in his career entitled *Science and Poetry*. When he came to revise it, he changed the title to *Poetries and Sciences*. If we remember that *science* means a kind of knowledge and that *poetry* means a kind of making, we have a better chance of seeing that defining what they have in common is as important to us in teaching the composing process as identifying how they are different.

~~~~~ **Elements of what we want to end with must be present in some form from the start.**

The abyss that opens up between the fall semester and the spring semester, between English 101 and 102, between personal writing and expository writing, between "free writing" and "guided structured writing"—all these gaps result inevitably when we try to teach according to some linear model in which something allegedly simple must come before something allegedly complex. Pedagogy always echoes epistemology: the way we teach reflects the conception we have of what knowledge is and does, the way we think about thinking. Using the categories of the Old Rhetoric as models for theme assignments keeps us from showing our students the essential acts of mind that are necessarily involved, no matter what kind of writing is being done. By categorizing in this way—narrative, compare-contrast, definition, description, etc.—we separate in an artificial way what should be kept together. Narrative is the oldest, and sometimes the best, mode of description; it is impossible to define without "compare-contrast"; description without the aim of definition is certainly tiresome and probably pointless. The simplest description can be assigned so that it involves more complex aims than "Make it Vivid" can suggest. Most "Engfish" (Macrorie) and "Themewriting" (Coles) results directly from the kind of assignments we make.

The New Rhetoric is no more helpful, with its deconstruction of a process that must be dialectical from the start. The notion, for instance, that there is a "writer-based prose" and *then* a "reader-based prose" is radically faulty, since constraints to be developed heuristically can come *first of all* from an awareness of how one or another audience can shape our purposes. The composition of arguments, as of short stories and poems, can begin anywhere, even with a "reader-based" final sentence.

If meaning is what we want to end with, meaning must be there from the start. Vygotsky makes the point in explaining that we can not understand how concepts are formed unless we begin not with "language" or "thought" but with verbal meaning.

〰〰〰〰   **To the teacher the simplest and most general appears as the easiest, whereas for a pupil only the complex and living appears easy.**

[Leo Tolstoy]

This is the maxim of maxims—the *maxim maximus*. It challenges the idea found at all levels of education that complexity must wait, that those "first things" that come first must always be bits and pieces rather than wholes, that we must walk before we can run, that we must have the skills before we can perform. All these counter-maxims are based on the completely misleading notion that forming, thinking, and writing are all best modeled by *motor behavior*. But language is not just *verbal behavior*, and when we make sense of the world, we do not do so by assembling little bits, by adding up elements, by pasting together impressions retrieved from our LTM's. Rather, we are making meaning, and that is a dialectical process, not a linear one. All the selections in "Up to the Classroom" illuminate what it means to say that teachers, in beginning with the complex and living, are beginning *naturally*. It's what Sylvia Ashton-Warner means by *organic teaching*. The challenge is not to get rid of complexity or to put it off, but to clear away distractions so that structure can be apprehended, to assure that the natural processes of forming by means of which we make sense of the world can take place when students are learning to read and write.

Metaphors, models, and maxims help remind us of what we are trying to do and can thereby help us discover how to do it. No mere statement of aims, goals, or objectives is likely to serve this purpose of bringing the *what* and the *how* to bear on one another. To assure that nexus is the motive of method; only method can guide our thinking about thinking.

Notes

[1]This odd notion is easily understood once it is seen as an instance of a widespread attitude towards the ranking of the sciences. As explained to me by Dr. Mina J. Bissell of the Lawrence Berkeley Laboratory, theoretical physics is often regarded as being at the top of a hierarchical order descending from physics to physical chemistry, organic chemistry to molecular biology, to biochemistry and biology—and, underneath a very heavy ledger line, psychology. Any scientist tends to think that he or she is thoroughly qualified to speak to any issue involving any fields "below" his or her own. Thus the physical chemist believes he can rightfully take all of chemistry for his territory and all of biology; in turn, he will be beholden to physicists. This model

explains a great deal about the pretensions of psychology, the need to claim scientific status by aping the natural sciences. (The habitual defense of psychologists against criticism is that it comes from those who fear Science.) Of course, there is a role for pure research and for pure theory in logic and mathematics, but it is an absurd misconception to characterize rhetorical theory on the analogy of "pure" science in contradistinction to classroom practice as "applied" science—or engineering.

[2]A heuristic is any form or procedure that leads to knowledge.

[3]Here is Susanne K. Langer's analysis from *Mind: An Essay on Human Feelings,* I. p. 68: "An image is not a model. It is a rendering of the appearance of its object in one perspective out of many possible ones. It sets forth what the object looks or seems like, and according to its own style it emphasizes separations or continuities, contrasts or gradations, details, complexities or simple masses. A model, on the contrary, always illustrates a principle of construction or operation; it is a symbolic projection of its object which need not resemble it in appearance at all, but must permit one to match the factors of the model with respective factors of the object, according to some convention. The convention governs the selectiveness of the model; to all items in the selected class the model is equally true, to the limit of its accuracy, that is, to the limit of formal simplification imposed by the symbolic translation."

More Maxims

I have depended on certain formulations in trying to make the case for reclaiming the imagination in order to teach the composing process as a matter of making meaning. Throughout the talks and articles that constitute Part II, I have cited a few statements repeatedly. They are indicated in the text by this sign: △ For convenience's sake, I've gathered them here with bibliographic data.

Whatever else learning may be, it is clearly *a disposition to form structures.*

[Gordon Allport, *Becoming* (New Haven: Yale University Press, 1955), p. 27.]

I think that the educational story from the infant room to the university is like the writing of a novel. You can't be sure of your beginning until you have checked it with your ending. What might come of infant teachers [Kindergarten teachers] visiting the university and professors visiting the infant room?

[Sylvia Ashton-Warner, *Teacher* (N.Y.: Simon and Schuster, 1963), p. 98.]

If philosophy is the study of beginnings, how is it to be taught without patient fresh starts? In the realm of mind, to begin is to know one has the right to begin again.

[Gaston Bachelard, *The Right to Dream* (N. Y.: Grossman, 1971), p. 203.]

Implied in the use of the negative, there is both the ability to generalize and the ability to specify. That is, you cannot use the negative properly without by the same token exemplifying the two basic dialectical resources of merger and division. For you can use "no" properly insofar as you can classify under one head many situations that are, in their positive details, quite distinct from one another. In effect, you group them under the head of "Situations all of which are classes in terms of the negative." And in the very act of so classifying, you distinguish them from another class of situations that are "*not* No-Situations."

[Kenneth Burke, *Language as Symbolic Action* (Berkeley: University of California Press, 1968), p. 425.]

14

Though all organisms are critics in the sense that they interpret the signs about them, the experimental speculative technique made available by speech would seem to single out the human species as the only one possessing an equipment for going beyond the criticism of experience to a criticism of criticism. We not only interpret the characters of events (manifesting in our responses all the gradations of fear, apprehension, assurance, for which there are rough behavioristic counterparts in animals—we may also interpret our interpretations.

[Kenneth Burke, *Permanence and Change* (1935; rpt. N.Y.: Bobbs-Merrill, 1965), p. 6.]

The primary IMAGINATION I hold to be the living Power and prime Agent of all human Perception, and as a repetition in the finite mind of the eternal act of creation in the infinite I AM.

[Samuel Taylor Coleridge, *Biographia Literaria,* Chap. XIII.]

The educator [who helps learners arrive at a more and more critical view of their reality] is a knowing subject, face to face with other knowing subjects. He can never be a mere memorizer, but a person constantly readjusting his knowledge, who calls forth knowledge from his students. For him, education is a pedagogy of knowing.

[Paulo Freire, "The Adult Literacy Process as Cultural Action for Freedom," *Harvard Educational Review* (40), 1970, 217.]

Questioner: Like a whole composition, then, a word is a bundle of parts?
Speaker: A bundle, a life, with a life history. . . .

[Josephine Miles, "English: A Colloquy; or, How What's What in the Language," *California English Journal*, 2 (1966), 3–14.]

Language . . . is an organ—the supreme organ of the mind's self-ordering growth.

Corresponding to all these studies [Mathematics, Physics, Chemistry, Biology, Sociology, Anthropology, Poetics, Dialectic] are characteristic uses of language. Poetics, I suggest, is faced by the most complex of them. Above Poetics I would put only Dialectic as being concerned with the relations of Poetics with all other studies and with their relations to one another. Dialectics would thus be the supreme study, with Philosophy as its Diplomatic Agent. All of them are *both* subject matter and language studies. That is the chief point here: there is no study which is not a language study, concerned with the speculative instruments it employs.

[I. A. Richards, *Speculative Instruments* (N.Y.: Harcourt, 1955), p. 9; pp. 115–16.]

A particular impression is already a product of conscrescence. Behind, or in it, there has been a coming together of *sortings*. When we take a number of particular impressions—or a number of white things, say—and abstract from them an idea of whiteness, we are explicitly reversing a process which has been implicitly at work in our perception of them as all white. Our risk is to confuse the abstractness we thus arrive at intellectually with the primordial abstractness out of which these impressions have already grown— before ever any conscious explicit reflection took place.

[I. A. Richards, *The Philosophy of Rhetoric* (1936; rpt. N.Y.: Harcourt, 1964), p. 36.]

[Literacy training requires] not so much some improved philosophic and psychological doctrine, though no one should despise that, as sets of sequenced exercises through which . . . people could explore, for themselves, their own abilities and grow in capacity, practical and intelligential, as a result. In most cases, perhaps, this amounts to offering them *assisted invitations* to attempt to find out what they are trying to do and thereby how to do it.

[I. A. Richards, *Design for Escape* (New York: Harcourt, 1968), p. 111.]

In general we will find that the more important a word is, and the more central and necessary its meanings are in our pictures of ourselves and the world, the more ambiguous and possibly deceiving the word will be. Naturally these words are also those which have been most used in philosophy. But it is not the philosophers who have made them ambiguous; it is the position of their ideas, as the very hinges of all thought. Our archproblem . . . has been "What should guide the reader's mind?" Our answer was "Our awareness of interdependence, of how things hang together, which makes us able to give and audit an account of what may be meant in a discussion—that highest activity of REASON which Plato named "Dialectic."

[I. A. Richards, *How to Read a Page* (1942; rpt. Boston: Beacon Press, 1959), p. 24; p. 240.]

Not the chemical composition of water but its molecules and their behavior are the key to the understanding of the properties of water. The true unit of biological analysis is the living cell, possessing the basic properties of the living organism.

When the process of concept formation is seen in all its complexity, it appears as a movement of thought within the pyramid of concepts constantly alternating between two directions, from the particular to the general, and from the general to the particular.

[L. S. Vygotsky, *Thought and Language* (Cambridge: MIT Press, 1962), pp. 4–5; p. 80.]

Part II

Talks
to
Teachers

In the course of the five or six years since the earliest of these papers was written, I have changed my mind about the relative importance of certain principles and criticisms and strategies, but the argument throughout is of a piece: to teach composition is to teach the process of making meaning. That requires an understanding of the kind of process composing is, which in turn necessitates an understanding of the forming power of mind and the heuristic powers of language itself. This is what I have meant by calling for a theory of imagination: imagination is the most important idea we could have to think *with*. We should reclaim imagination from those who have identified it with ill-conceived notions of "creativity" and make of it our chief speculative instrument. △ (Throughout Part II, this sign follows key words and phrases from maxims for which the full text may be found in Part I, pp. 14–16.)

My title—"Talks to Teachers"—is unassuming enough, but I have borrowed it from William James and am thus open to charges of pretension. I claim only to have been inspired by his example. James was able to define pedagogical problems in philosophical terms, to subject the stereotypes and unexamined assumptions of his day to an analysis that usefully revealed false premises, cleared away illogical arguments, and redefined what was worth keeping. James set about to de-mystify psychology so that teachers would see that they had no reason to be intimidated by the "methods" and special terminology of the practitioners of what he called "brass instrument" psychology. Jargon is never just a list of special terms; it has both aggressive and defensive uses and only insofar as we are alert to the character of such language are we genuinely free to undertake critical thinking about matters in question. James sought to help teachers trust their classroom experience, considering it in the light of a few sound principles of psychology. For instance, he called their attention to the fact that the various mental faculties, though their operations could be isolated and measured, do not work in isolation from one another. Such caveats are important in our own time.

I believe that college and university teachers must talk to—or, more accurately, *with*—school teachers, not because solutions to "problems" are to be sought higher up, but because dialogue is essential to the understanding we must develop in order to define and confront illiteracy. We should carry on that dialogue in the interest of bringing theory to bear on practice and in order to keep ourselves honest, those of us who are interested in theory. No one is better qualified to put theory to the test than the classroom teacher: I passionately share I. A. Richards' conviction that the classroom is the philosophical laboratory.

1. Theory and Practice

*What we think we are doing and how we are doing it: when
theory and practice are brought to bear on one another, the nexus
is method. Method, so conceived, is philosophically complex and
is much too important to be left to educationists willing to reduce
it to a matter of procedure, or to psychologists and rhetoricians
who prefer to ignore it in the interest of a clinical analysis of
"writing behaviors" or the development of Theory for Theory's
Sake. By documenting what happens in their classrooms, in the
light of a theory of language and learning, especially when the
practice itself includes thinking about thinking, teachers can carry
out the research that is most needed: they can develop an
authentic "pedagogy of knowing."* △

What We Teach

What we teach when we teach composition will depend on our
views of the nature of learning and of language. If we think of learning as a matter of digesting information, then teaching composition
will be simply a matter of assigning topics and correcting the resulting work. But the fact is that teaching composition by arbitrarily setting topics and then concentrating on the mechanics of expression
and the conventions governing correct usage does not guarantee that
students will learn to write competently, and it certainly does not encourage the discovery of language either as an instrument of knowing
or as our chief means of shaping and communicating ideas and experience. On the other hand, if we consider learning as primarily "a
disposition to form structures," △ then we can teach composition as
a mode of learning: composing is preeminently a matter of forming
structures.

This is the draft of a position paper, prepared for, but not used by, the NCTE Com-
mission on Composition.

19

As a working definition, we can think of composition as "a bundle of parts" △ This can encourage us to teach ways and means of finding, inventing, rediscovering, selecting, shaping, and assembling parts into bundles of several kinds. The composer develops and organizes ideas, makes statements, and creates images by way of discovering the parts he or she wants to assemble and, in the process, invents and orders an assembly to suit purpose and audience. If we teach composing as a mode of learning, a way of thinking, then we will be teaching it as a process.

Composing is not a process like playing a game of tennis or cooking a meal; there are no hard and fast rules, and it does not proceed in one direction—in a straightforward manner. Composing is not a linear process, though what it creates has linear form. That's why it's easy to mistake the methods appropriate to teaching the product as being equally appropriate to teaching the process. Thus conventional textbooks describe a sequence in which you "get" your idea; develop it by means of the appropriate rhetorical strategies; outline the hierarchical order in which comparisons, allusions, definitions, examples are to be presented; and then write it up. The final stage of composition, then, is going over the paper to "catch" any errors. But nobody writes this way—not even the authors of conventional textbooks.

Any process has phases and so does composing, but they interact with one another in a complex way. Compositions do not just grow from particular examples to generalizations or from preformed generalizations to examples. The beginning of an essay, for instance, may be written last; a poet may have composed the concluding couplet before the "argument" of the poem has been worked out; we may have an idea that gets the writing started, but which is itself discarded. Composing—in contradistinction to filling in the slots of a drill sheet or a preformed outline—is a means of discovering what we want to say, as well as being the saying of it.

We can best help students develop their own powers by assuring that they have occasions to discover that composing is itself a process of discovery and interpretation, of naming and stating, of seeing relationships and making meanings. Here are four aspects of the composing process, which students can and should be taught.

1. Invention

Classical rhetoric is largely concerned with *commonplaces* or topics, the writer's points of departure. Modern rhetoric has added problem-solving strategies, various formulas that can generate critical questions, and other devices—heuristics—for getting started in composition. Students can learn to take an inventory, no matter what they are writing: accounting for what you already have in the way of facts, "data," comparisons, definitions, examples, and so forth is the best way to determine what you need to find out, to formulate, to invent. The other chief means of getting started writing (and of keeping at it) is to return continually to the question of what it is that the reader needs to know. Writers who learn how to let the *what* help them discover the *how* are learning the use of limits. And it is by keeping the audience in mind that the writer is reminded of the kind of writing he or she is doing and to use the limits that form provides, whether it's a personal essay or a memorandum, a critical summary or an exam answer, a book report or a narrative.

2. Specification

Insofar as the composing process involves forming concepts, it is essential for student writers to practice specifying. Frequently, students are told not to generalize, but what is meant is that they should not do so without making clear the grounds for generalizing. A writer continually moves back and forth between examples and particular cases and general ideas by specifying, saying what kinds and classes are involved. Concept formation is not something that is finished before writing is begun ("Don't write until you know what you want to say!") but is in progress throughout the entire composing process. (That's why writing is a way of thinking.) Learning how—remembering how—to "be specific" is an important challenge to all writers, no matter how practiced they are.

3. Developing and deploying syntactical resources

In other times and places, students coming to study composition have often brought with them a repertory of sentence patterns and syntactical structures, developed by virtue of having been read to or of having read, of having been continuously talked to and with, especially in the early years. For many reasons that are important for English teachers to understand, modern culture does not foster literacy. Our students, generally speaking, do not have their heads full of patterns and ways of articulating thought, which could provide the armature for their own style.

The challenge is first of all to teach our students to listen, a skill that sometimes has to be relearned in medical and law schools. Much about the composing process can be learned in the practice of taking notes on lectures and talks and informal small group discussions. And by careful study of complex, well-built sentences and by exercises in imitation, paraphrase, and sentence composing, students can develop a repertory of sentence patterns and syntactical structures. Teachers should remember, however, that "syntactical maturity" without conceptual maturity is likely to yield "Engfish," empty statements written in an inflated and pretentious manner and symptomatic of a faulty understanding of the logic of statement.

4. Revising and editing

We can usefully differentiate editing, which is aimed at the identification and correction of error, from revising, which is an integral part of the composing process. Committing ourselves to teaching process does not require that we ignore the product, only that we see it as a dynamic result, a coming-into-being. Modern rhetoric, drawing on certain studies in linguistics, has developed new descriptions for the ways in which a writer works to assure that paragraphs have unity, coherence, and emphasis. Students can learn that the sound design of a piece of writing, by analogy with a highway, depends not on road signs or markers but on the articulation of the structural elements. The means of achieving "cohesion" can be taught as a way of understanding the interaction of thinking and writing.

Perhaps the most difficult aspect of teaching writing as process and of considering the result as something that is nurtured and brought along, not mechanically produced, is that our students do not like uncertainty (who does?); they find it hard to tolerate ambiguity and are tempted to what psychologists call "premature closure." They want the writing to be over and done with; unfortunately, much composition teaching encourages those feelings. We can encourage our students, instead, in learning techniques of revision only if we forego treating false starts, unfruitful beginnings, contradictions, and dead ends as mistakes, and see them, rather, as tentative steps, stages in a process.

Composing involves the writer in making choices all along the way and thus has social and political implications: we aren't free unless we know how to choose. Teaching composition as a process can put students in touch with their own minds; it can give them back their language. It is not too much to claim that the composition classroom is a place where students can discover their humanity in both a moral and political sense.

Reclaiming the Imagination

I'm glad to know that there are school teachers in the audience and that I am sharing the platform with teachers concerned with different kinds of writing. I think we have to begin to talk not only across the curriculum but up and down the grades, K-35. I fervently agree with Sylvia Ashton-Warner, who has observed that you can't tell the end of the education story until you know the beginning.△ The university teacher, she wrote, must visit the "infant room"—New Zealandese for "kindergarten"—and the elementary school teacher must visit the seminar.△ I was asked several weeks ago in Washington at the Conference on College Composition and Communication what recommendation I had for doctoral programs in rhetoric, one which would offset the heavy emphasis on statistics, protocol analysis, psycholinguistics, and other approaches sanctioned by rhetoricians. My reply was that all candidates for the Ph.D. in rhetorical theory should be required to teach in the third grade for a year.

That conference made me pretty gloomy because I came away convinced that not many people realize how serious a challenge the literacy crisis is. Certainly, the rhetoricians don't: their talk gets more and more abstruse as their ideas get more and more simpleminded. Of course the public's apprehension of the literacy crisis is equally feeble: it isn't just that your students and mine don't know the rules governing the use of the comma or that they can't spell *parallel, only,* and *rhythm.* It's that they can't hear what is said; they can't read with the normal expectations of an experienced reader; they don't talk with any sense of continuity—everything is in the eternal present, including the narration of past events. If our students can't talk, can't listen, can't read with the resources, experience, and flexibility that we generally presuppose, why should we be surprised when they don't write very well?

I want to consider this evening what is required if we are to raise critical questions about literacy training and what it means to say that

"Reclaiming the Imagination" is an all-purpose title I've used on several occasions; it's also the title of a forthcoming collection of essays and passages from the writings of scientists, artists, philosophers, as they are concerned about composing, or matters of interest to those who are. Here, it is the title of a conference for high school and college teachers of writing sponsored by the English Department of the University of Maine at Orono in April, 1980. The other panelists were Peter Elbow and Thomas Williams.

I have incorporated passages from the keynote address I delivered to a conference on the teaching of writing sponsored by the Pennsylvania Department of Education and the Bucks County Intermediate Unit #22, March, 1980, as well as from talks to English teachers of the Brookline (MA) Public Schools.

we should teach writing in the context of these other language activities, what it means to say that we should teach writing as a matter of making meaning. To do that—to teach the composing process—requires, I think, a theory of imagination. We have to have some ideas—very strong, well-founded ideas—about the power of the human mind and the power of language. Only a theory of imagination can help us get rid of certain misconceptions that continually make us prey to fads and panaceas—misconceptions that make it impossibly difficult to make the case against going back to basics, narrowly conceived, as they generally are, as rules and regulations. A theory of imagination can help us argue the fact of the matter, which is that drill can teach youngsters—and college freshmen—how to correct faulty sentences in workbooks, but it cannot teach them to write substantial, readable sentences. If we want our students to compose their sentences, and not just to combine somebody else's pretend subsentences, we will have to know something about language as a form, an instrument, a means of making meaning. A theory of imagination can do that by reminding us that language is not a code, merely, but, as I. A. Richards once put it, "the supreme organ of the mind's self-ordering growth." △

Let me identify some of the misconceptions that make it difficult for us to address the problem of illiteracy, and then I will return to the imagination and how it can help us.

The first misconception (or misapprehension) is that by talking about "the composing process" we are doing something about teaching it. How many textbooks are there that can help us develop a pedagogy appropriate to teaching the composing process? *Pre-writing* is on everybody's lips, but I see little evidence that people understand that "pre-writing" is *writing*. In the manual that one writing lab put out for tutors, in a section called "Pre-writing," I read that the best thing to do if a freshman has trouble organizing (which is like saying "if water is wet") is to teach him to outline! But of course an outline, like a blueprint, comes not first but last. Some friends of mine recently hired an architect to build a house for them, one to replace a well-loved farmhouse, which had burned down. They began specifying what they wanted and where they wanted it: "The kitchen should lead into the living room and we'd like a little doorway here, but be sure that there's access to the porch so the door should be. . . ." But the architect said: "Tell me how you live and then I'll design the house." That's what an architect is for: to know how to translate your purposes, to realize your intentions; blueprints can't do that job. Most rhetorics, guides, and manuals speak of four (or three or five or ten) "distinct phases" of composing. The very rhetoricians who talk *process* and *discovery* are frequently the ones who recommend procedures that run counter to these ideas, procedures presupposing that we think out what we say and then write it up; that we think and then we express; that there is, as one puts it, "a battle to clothe the insight in symbolic form." In other words, composing is seen to be analogous to a linear process like laundering, in which you have to separate the socks from the shorts *first,* set the dials *first,* put in the soap *first*—and *then* do this and *then* that. The phases of the composing process are not distinct: they are dialectical; they are on again-off again. Revising, for instance, can, and I think should, continue right up until the last; introductions are seldom written first.

Underlying this misconception of distinct, linear phases is the idea that language is a muffin tin; that we *have* meanings, a kind of batter we then pour into molds. What we need, instead, are ways of thinking of language as an instrument, a means of seeing and articulating relationships.

A second misconception is that writing is a skill, that it can be factored into subskills. The father of a fifth grader told me recently that his son does no writing: he's too busy with his subskills. Further, the notion of "single skill correction" is seen as the best solution to several problems. Principals are delighted with this pedagogy, which generates charts showing the growth and development of the comma-using skill and the pronoun reference skill; they have something to show the parents who come charging in, declaring that they want their children to know The Basics. In one manual I have seen, prepared by teachers for their own guidance, the final chapter includes this sentence: "Unfortunately, the students don't seem to understand the process: we get trivial papers which are error-free and papers of substance which show no evidence that single-skill correction has remedied faulty English." This refreshing honesty will, I hope, lead those conscientious teachers (they spent three years on the manual) to discover that the reason students don't understand this process is that it is not, in any real sense, a process at all.

One response to this kind of failure with teaching writing as a skill, once it is honestly confronted, is to add substantial items to the list of "subskills." Thus Professor Hirsch, for instance, includes "organization" in his list. But if the concept of subskills includes both mechanics and organization, it is worthless as a critical term. Sometimes, of course, "skill" is a kind of shorthand expression for a well-defined concept. ESL teachers, for instance, speak of "social skills," meaning not how to introduce a young man to an elderly lady or where to put the soup spoon but those habits whereby certain linguistic conventions are deployed to serve the communication process. These conventions are not just a matter of words in the right order but of knowing which words in which order come when. Thus a student from the Middle East needs to learn the social skill of interrupting: "Yes, I understand, but isn't it also true that. . . ." (A schematic representation of an Iranian conversation with pauses between each comment or observation, little plateaus of silence, will not resemble a model of a Hispanic conversation! Nor do we need a course in pauseology to see the point.) ESL teachers realize that these so-called social skills involve matching judgments and idioms: "social skills" are taught in the context of actual conversation because it is recognized that they are acts of interpretation, ways of making meaning.

Generally speaking, however, there is no such awareness of how complex the activity is which has been called a "skill." To model writing on motor skills is hazardous. Consider playing the piano: motor skill is absolutely essential, of course. You have to do five-finger exercises in order to liberate that fourth finger, in order to stretch the muscles so you can reach a good interval, so that your fingers will "know" where the keys are. But those exercises will not produce music: skill is, in the logicians' formula, necessary but not sufficient. To play even a little minuet from the practice book Bach compiled for his wife (presumably to cheer the idle hours of her twenty-one pregnancies), you must be able to hear the music—to hear the phrase, the cadence, the dynamics, the rhythmic pattern. To make music requires, in addition to motor skill, the auditory imagination.

Underlying this misconception of writing as a skill is the idea of language as verbal behavior. Of course it's behavior, but it is not *just* behavior: language is an *activity*. Speaking, listening, reading, and writing are acts of mind by which we make meaning.

The third misconception that forestalls our coming to grips with illiteracy is that creative and critical writing are entirely different, that they require different brain halves, different skills, different "behaviors," different cognitive processes, different slots in the English curriculum. Now poems are not bank statements, and the specifications for an engine overhaul do not constitute a novel—not yet—but differentiating the aims and modes of discourse is a far more complex task than you would ever guess from studying, say, James Kinneavy's attempt to do so. When something called "personal writing" is differentiated from something called "expository writing," do we really know what we're differentiating? A young colleague of mine once remarked that it wasn't until he found himself in a graduate seminar on Defoe that he discovered how much narrative and exposition have in common. (I discover that bureaucrats call "narrative" anything that's sequential and uses personal pronouns.) I understand that expository writing is called in the schools "guided structured writing": in contradistinction to what, I wonder? I like to quote Allen Tate's definition of a poet: "A poet is a man [sic] willing to come under the bondage of limitations—if he can find them." Separating some kinds of writing and calling them "structured" leaves other kinds to be pushed into the creativity corner.

Here's the kind of thing that happens, as many of you will recognize. A friend of mine has a nine-year-old son who is vitally interested in "governance" problems at school. He sees them as moral dilemmas, and at the dinner table he gives full and passionate accounts: "And do you know what *he* said? *He* said. . . ." But none of this is taken up in his English class, which must have had guided structured writing last year because this year it's narrative. He must write up "an interesting incident." He writes: "The boy took his dog for a walk." Then he thinks: "Oh my goodness! That isn't vivid." So he rewrites: "The blond boy took his dog Shadow for a walk." We can teach the use of detail—the conceptual, emblematic, intellectual, symbolic, substantiating role of detail only if we do so in the course of developing authentic occasions for writing. The prose I get from my freshmen is an adjective swamp with little hummocky Thesis Statements. It is a style which results directly from having been taught in courses in which the functions of writing have been separated in this absurd manner. Something of the same thing happens in college when students, never having had the opportunity to write and revise a poem, have no means of knowing that poems are made, composed, or that literature is a form of knowledge, much less to know what might be meant by "the poetry of science."

The underlying misconception in this case is fundamental to the positivist philosophy that informs current rhetorical theory and practice. I mean the idea that "the cognitive" and "the affective" reside in *Domains,* separate domains. I used to think that this all-pervasive doctrine was something in the air—the way people used to think that malaria was caused by a miasma. Recently, I've discovered the mosquito, at least as far as pedagogy is concerned: it is called Bloom's Taxonomy. When I made the case to the members of my seminar in the teaching of composition that this was a very wrongheaded notion given credence because of the spurious use of research in hemisphere dominance, one teacher urgently asked for help. She told us that her principal had called her in, saying, "Ginny, you're off the map in The Affective, but what are you doing in The Cognitive?" "How can I explain to him," she asked us, "that when I have my students writing poems it's not a matter of marshmallows and butterflies?"

In their sneaky way, cognitive psychologists have taken over the term "domain" from the neurologists: there are areas and domains in the brain, and they control certain mental activities in rather defi-

nite ways. An aphasic suffering brain damage in one area can't interpret facial expressions; damage in another area will mean that a
patient can't construe body language. Syntax seems to be handled in
one area, semantics in another. But these fascinating studies are being used to legitimize differentiations of quite another sort: the Sunday Supplements and current rhetorical theory claim that "emotion"
is limited to one hemisphere of the brain and cognition to the other;
that the right side controls "insight" and the left, "cognition."

The emphasis on differentiating creative and critical writing, as if
they were symptoms of different brain functions, has meant that
we've lost the advantages that are there to be enjoyed if we concentrate instead on what they have in common. The emphasis on subskills and single skill correction in the hope of making things easier
for everybody means that we forego the one sure way of teaching anything, which is to define and nourish a need. Skills are learned—really
learned—only when there is a reason to use them. And reasons and
purposes are no more reducible to *positive reinforcement* than concept
formation can be seen accurately as an accumulation of subskills.

The emphasis on "process," unsupported by an accurate, substantial conception of the kind of process composing is, has done very little to advance our understanding of how to teach writing, to say
nothing of how to understand the literacy crisis. If a sound pedagogy
is what we're after, we will have to discard the positivist notions of
language as a muffin tin or a code to be dialed or plugged in, of language as a set of behaviors. If we are to conceive of literacy as a fa-
cility in making meaning in reading and writing, we will need to
understand the heuristic powers of language itself. The chief speculative instrument—that is, a powerful idea to think *with* as well as
about—is, I believe, the imagination. It has to be *reclaimed* because it
has been consigned to The Affective Domain. Imagination must be
rescued from the creativity corner and returned to the center of all
that we do.

Reclaiming the imagination begins with recognizing it as a name
for the active mind. It's always useful in philosophical definitions to
begin not with essence but with function. Instead of asking, "What *is*
imagination?" we can ask, "What does imagination do?" We have a
great answer from Coleridge who wrote in one of the most famous
passages in the literature of criticism that "Imagination is the living
power and prime agent of all human perception."[△] The imagination
is a doer, an agent; it is active. What it does in perception it does in
all acts of mind: it forms. *Imagination* is a name for the form-finding
and form-creating power. Such a theory of imagination can help us
teach writing as a process because it can guide us in seeing how writing is analogous to all other forming.

If we can reclaim imagination as a speculative instrument, there's a good chance we can think our way through and beyond the misconceptions of language and learning that currently abound. In that process, we will be moving towards what Paulo Freire has called a "pedagogy of knowing," [Δ] a method of teaching that recognizes the human need and ability to shape, discriminate, select: the mind's power to form. That's an education story worth telling.

The Teacher as REsearcher

I'm happy and proud to be here: your association exemplifies in all its activities the kind of involvement that makes our profession so lively. In my experience, it's the affiliates of the NCTE rather than the parent organization that are more likely to know how to engage in dialogue, real dialogue—not university personnel handing down the theory and school teachers working out the practice; not education schools doing the research and teachers providing the data. The Bay Area Writing Project is a superb example of such dialogue. What I want to suggest in these remarks is that real teachers in dialogue with one another can find directions for excellence as they work out their own theory. I will conclude with some observations about a theory of the composing process and how it can guide our teaching of writing.

My favorite text on this notion of an exchange between teachers comes from Sylvia Ashton-Warner. "The educational story," she writes in *Teacher*, "is like the writing of a novel. You can't be sure of your beginning until you have checked it with your ending. What might come of infant teachers visiting the university and professors visiting the infant room?"△ What can come of it, what has come of such visits is not "research," but useful questions and answers that can provide directions. I want to claim that what we need is not what is called "research," but the kind of theory that is generated in dialogue among teachers. When we real teachers get together, we ask one another real questions: "If language capacities are innate, why is it so hard to teach kids to write sound sentences?" "How can you teach the use of *however* if they don't understand the however relationship?" I don't think real teachers ask questions like "what is the T-unit average among your o10 students?" I promise you I will be polemical for only a few minutes, but I want to rock the boat a little: finding directions always entails rocking the boat, doesn't it? (The way I handle a canoe it does.)

The notion that "research" can provide directions is absurd—I mean the kind of research supported, for instance, by the National Institute of Education. The institute guidelines explicitly state that NIE has no interest whatsoever in practical application: no proposals for curriculum, course design, or sequences of assignments will be enter-

An address delivered at the annual meeting of the California Association of Teachers of English, San Diego, 1979. The conference theme was "Directions for Excellence."

tained; attempts to define implications for the classroom are unwelcome. Instead, the guidelines announce, the institute is concerned with establishing scientific understanding by gathering fresh data on, say, the effects of home environment on literacy. The social scientists who prepared these guidelines argue this way: basic research is essential to the advancement of learning in physics; therefore, basic research is essential to an understanding of education. That analogy is fraudulent because education is not comparable to the natural sciences. Why? Because education profoundly and essentially involves language—and language is not a natural process but a symbolic form and a social process, though it's contingent on natural processes. The people who call language "verbal behavior" are the ones who call literature "literary material," just as they are the ones who call making mud pies "earthplay." They are not our allies.

Let me end my polemic with this assertion: educational research is nothing to our purpose, unless we formulate the questions; if the procedures by which answers are sought are not dialectic and dialogic, that is to say, if the questions and the answers are not continually REformulated by those who are working in the classroom, educational research is pointless. My spies tell me that it's becoming harder and harder for researchers to get into the schools: I rejoice in that news because I think it might encourage teachers to become researchers themselves, and once that happens, the character of research is bound to change.

It helps to pronounce "research" the way southerners do: REsearch. REsearch, like REcognition, is a REflexive act. It means looking—and looking again. This new kind of REsearch would not mean going out after new "data," but rather REconsidering what is at hand. REsearch would come to mean looking and looking again at what happens in the English classroom. We do not need new information; we need to think about the information we have. We need to interpret what goes on when students respond to one kind of assignment and not to another, or when some respond to an assignment and others do not. We need to interpret things like that—and then to interpret our interpretations. There is nothing in the NIE guidelines to suggest that anybody in Washington has ever heard of the idea of thinking about thinking. Maybe they'd listen if we reminded them of what Piaget once observed (Piaget is, of course, a hot item just now). Piaget remarked that "to understand is to invent." What we need is not research designed for us by the National Science Foundation, as Professor Hirsch is suggesting, but questions we can invent about what we think we are doing, questions that will help us, too, in devising the criteria for evaluating what we are getting. Inventing as a way of understanding is a truth known to poets as well as to cognitive psychologists. A version of that dialectic is the one we all know concerning the composing process: you can't really know what you mean until you hear what you say. In my opinion, theory and practice should stand in this same relationship to one another, a dialectical relationship: theory and practice need one another.

The way to get them together is to begin with them together. Only that way will we be able to judge the degree to which what we meant to do is matched by what we did. The primary role of theory is to guide us in defining our purposes and thus in evaluating our efforts, in realizing them. How can we know what we're doing, how can we find out where we're going, if we don't have a conception of what we think we're doing? This is not, however, the same thing as stating behavioral objectives. They can forestall our ideas by constraining us too soon, too rigidly. But to be wary of behavioral objectives is not to settle for the visionary. Of course we must have plans, but they should not be narrowly defined in ways meant to make it easy for the researchers to quantify.

The trouble with behavioral objectives is that they are not meant to be modified by our practice; they control what we do (three sentence patterns by October). Rather, the primary use of theory should be to define what our purposes and aims are and thereby how to evaluate our efforts in reaching them: what and thereby how. I don't think there's anything more important for us to remember than that connector *thereby:* we have to keep the what and the how together—the what are we doing? together with the how do we do it? and the how did it go? and the how did it work? Evaluation, in other words, should be considered an aspect of method. Let me tell you about the experience of a friend of mine, Brenda S. Engel, of Lesley College. The question was how to evaluate the then new program of the Cambridge Alternative Schools by appropriate criteria. If you're doing something new and different, you shouldn't expect to evaluate it in terms appropriate to what it's supposed to supplant. The emphasis was on observation in the classroom so as to determine what was being learned how: Brenda worked out ways of coding kinds and modes of learning so that what was actually going on could be documented. Charts could then be prepared showing, for instance, how much time a particular child spent working by himself and how much with others. Or, one could tell at a glance how much independent work was going on, typically, in a particular teacher's classroom.

Theory can help us judge what's going on, and it can also explain why something works. Suppose you look at a particular exercise that has been very successful and you say, "Terrific! Now I'll do this."

And you follow X with Y, which seems appropriate, and it doesn't work. If you don't have a theory about why X worked, you won't have any way of defining the real relationship of X to Y, logically or psychologically. Taking my cue from Sylvia Ashton-Warner, let me tell you about an incident described by Patricia Carini, a teacher and researcher in New England.

She tells of how a teacher in a rural school observed her class of youngsters at the sand table as they filled coffee cans and strawberry boxes with wet sand, inverting them to make, as she thought, towers and houses, sheds and factories. "Aha! They're making cities!" So, as a followup, she organized a field trip to a nearby town—but the children were bored, unimpressed, and uninterested. Patricia Carini's analysis was as follows: those kids weren't making towns; they weren't into architecture! They were forming: they were playing with shapes, moulded shapes, and what should have followed that—and what did follow successfully, after consultation with the teacher—was playing in empty packing cases. The children went from compact, thingy shapes to empty, explorable shapes with different kinds of limits; they went from one kind of forming to another, from manipulating a shape to being shaped.

Theory can help us figure out why something works so we can repeat it, inventing variations. A theoretical understanding of cognitive development in this case, of how learning involves forming, can help us figure out our sequences of assignments. The centrally important question in all teaching is, "What comes next?" We must learn continually how to build on what has gone before, how to devise what I. A. Richards calls "the partially parallel task." Of course, we follow something with something else like it, but we can't do that authentically unless we can identify that first something: what is really going on? Theory can help us see what act we're trying to follow.

Theory gives us perspective; just as it allows us to determine sequences, it saves us from too much particularity. Teachers have to be pragmatic; they have to be down-to-earth, but being down-to-earth without knowing the theoretical coordinates for the landscape is a good way to lose your sense of direction. We English teachers are given to recipe swapping—and that can be hazardous. In my ideal commonwealth, the first thing that would happen—of course ideal commonwealths are really dictatorships—in my ideal commonwealth, *I* would order the closing down of the Exercise Exchange; the NCTE would not be allowed to operate it unless they instituted a Theory Exchange. And you couldn't get a recipe unless you also went there. I have a friend in the Denver schools who does just that. When her colleagues say, "Oh, that sounds wonderful! Can I have that exercise?"

she says, "Sure—but you have to take the theory too." And the exercise comes typed up with a little theoretical statement at the top, an explanation of whatever aspect or function of learning the assignment is meant to exercise. That combination of theory and practice can help prevent what so often happens: you know how it is; it has certainly happened to me. You hear something described that sounds good; it's obviously foolproof; you try it, and it doesn't work. So you feel terrible because this great exercise is a proved success—and you flubbed it. By reminding us that reading and writing happen in contexts—social, political, psychological—that can set up static ruinous to the reception of the very best assignments, theory can save us from wasting time blaming ourselves or our students.

By reminding us of contexts, theory can free us from an overdependence on preparation, reminding us, too, that the alternative to the immutable lesson plan is not the bull session. Those of you who have taught more than a year—or maybe more than a week—know about this. But there is nothing more typical of the inexperienced teacher—is there?—than total preparation in which every five minutes is scheduled. Anxiety overloads the circuit. Overpreparation forecloses the possibility of responding to what John Donne calls "emergent occasions." The publishers and the educational establishment want to allay that anxiety, but their prescription is a medicine that's worse than the trouble it's meant to cure. Tight schedules, leakproof syllabi, the instructor's manual, and the gilt-edged study guide are all agencies by which "extension" supplants "communication": those are Paulo Freire's terms. In *Education for Critical Consciousness,* Freire speaks of the agricultural *extension* service in Brazil as being antithetical to the communication by which learning is truly effected. The peasants don't learn from someone *extending* a service to them. Nor do students. I remember, as a most depressing experience indeed, being shown the way literature is taught in the Boston high schools. The head of the English Department showed me proudly the guide that was provided for every teacher—a loose-leaf notebook designed so it could lie flat unobtrusively in front of the teacher, out of sight of the class, between the teacher and the text: the same principle as reading a comic book with *The Return of the Native* propped up in front. For each poem there was provided a page of questions—all variations on the primeval query: "What is the author trying to say?" And with answers! Nothing can kill a class sooner than to ask a question to which there is a prefabricated answer. Of course, using somebody else's list of questions and answers is worse, but I think asking your own, without being able to accommodate the response you get, is almost as bad. I'm not telling you anything you don't know; I simply want to restate the home truths in the context of remarks on the uses of theory.

But the fear of losing control is very real: having an agenda is, after all, a pretty good defense, if that's what we want. When I first taught, I certainly wanted a defense against the possibility that the class or the text would get out of control, or out of my control. And, of course, there were very important facts about *Beowulf* that I wanted them to have. When somebody would ask a question that got me off the track, I was very upset. But back I would go to the agenda, my security blanket. Within a week I had discovered that what was really interesting was what happened when we talked with one another about emergent questions. I learned to come to class, not thinking of a territory to be covered, but with a compass—a metaphor, or a juxtaposition, or a question from the class before. In my experience, that's a lesson that is never finally learned; I have to learn it all over again every time I design a new course. I want to say, *"Listen* to all this fascinating stuff I've just learned about linguistics—" and I proceed with my own order. Only when I really start hearing the questions or eliciting the real ones does the class take on direction— whether towards excellence or not is problematic, but the point is that the show is on the road.

You probably know the story of the first years of Bruner's curriculum, *Man: A Course of Study.* Teachers were prepared to teach the new course by studying the scientific background implicit in the lessons. The course was enormously interesting to students who raised dozens of questions, the answers to which the teachers did not have. They complained to the course designers who then offered a refresher course (*"Do* flies have muscles?"). They returned to their classrooms—and to dozens of new questions! And finally everyone saw that what we needed was to learn a stance, a way of handling any question in dialogue.

That's a good example, I think, of how theory and practice and evaluation can all work together, can all be brought together: unless this happens, practice gets gimmicky and theory becomes dogmatic and evaluation stays in the hands of the Board of Education. The initiation of the teacher as REsearcher could be the ritual burning of all instructors' manuals, and the students could ceremoniously toss on the bonfire their study guides and their yellow felt marking pens. I tell my students that my course is an anti-Evelyn Wood course in how to slow down your reading in order to speed it up eventually.

I've reached the point now at which Cicero suggests that the orator should begin to say *in conclusion:* I'm two-thirds through. I want to spend the rest of my time suggesting how theory can help us teach composition.

The theory we need in that endeavor is a theory of the imagination. Imagination is the conceptual bridge from English to the real world because it is, in Coleridge's resonant phrase, "the prime agent of all human perception."△ Constructing and construing, writing and reading and perceiving are all acts of interpretation. In my textbook I have experimented with ways in which we might reclaim the imagination as a concept to help us get the affective and the cognitive together, not partitioned in their separate domains or in their separate brain halves. Educators tend to associate imagination with Friday afternoon projects and courses not in the core, with the unintellectual, the noncognitive, the merely personal expression of merely personal experience. But imagination is properly a name for the active mind, the mind of the child making forms in sand, the artist making forms in granite: Dame Barbara Hepworth, the British sculptor, speaks of her left hand as her "thinking" hand; the right is only the motor hand, the hand that holds the mallet. Her thinking hand finds the form in the stone—not her "inspirational" or her genius hand or her "creative" hand: her *thinking* hand. Thinking is not the province of the logician alone. If we can keep thinking and creating together, I don't think there will be any difficulty finding directions. A theory of imagination could guide us in teaching critical and creative writing together, reading and writing together; and most important, it could help us understand what it really means to speak of the composing *process*.

Composing is forming: it is a continuum; it goes on all the time. Composing is what the mind does by nature: composing is the function of the active mind. Composing is the way we make sense of the world: it's our way of learning.

Here's what Gordon Allport has to say about learning: "Whatever else learning may be, it is surely a disposition to form structures."△ Our chief resource as teachers of composition is right there: it is the mind's disposition to form structures, to compose.

Now what are the pedagogical implications? If composing begins with birth, if composing is making sense of the world and that's what the mind does, and if this composing is a continuum, then whatever is fundamental to perception is also fundamental to conception, to concept formation: a theory of imagination would remind us to provide occasions for lots of perception, for lots of looking at things, for observation. Perception is the other side of concept formation. We don't have to teach that, thank the Lord; thank the Lord for that, because the human mind is created as a composer: by means of language we construe each particular thing as a symbol for that kind of thing. When we see a lamb, we simultaneously see *that* lamb and that lamb as a *kind* of thing. That's what it means to say that man is the *animal symbolicum*, the symbol-making animal. When we teach perception—but of course we don't do that: when we encourage observation, looking and looking again, we're not teaching some merely preliminary thing. (When do we get to "real" writing?) When we offer what I call, after I. A. Richards, "assisted invitations"△ to students to use their minds in looking at things, we're also exercising the capacity to form concepts. Perception is not something that comes first and then we get to ideas; perception is itself a construing, an interpretation, a making of meaning, a composing.

We let students of composition do a lot of looking—not because we want detail for detail's sake, not because we are committed to "show, don't tell," but because *looking, seeing, turns on the mind.* When we encourage our students to look and look again, we are not differentiating creative and critical writing, which should be kept together, just as composing and editing should be kept apart. In practicing close observation and critical response, students of composition can raise their consciousness of themselves as composers—that process, which Paulo Freire calls "conscientization," a process involving a community of observer-critics, of responsive audiences and purposeful writers. Students of composition who do a lot of looking will learn that perspective and context are essential to interpretation. In short, they will learn habits of mind essential to critical and creative thinking. I do not think these habits should be labeled "cognitive skills"; they have an importance which that label of the educationists cannot suggest.

A theory of imagination helps us invent assignments appropriate to one or another phase of the composing process. It can do that by reminding us that composing is forming and that forms don't come out of the air. Now English teachers have recently rediscovered that fact. In the past seven or eight years, with the help of Peter Elbow and Ken Macrorie especially, we have learned to recognize the role of free writing in the forming that is composing. But I've been noticing recently that as this fundamental idea becomes accepted more widely, it becomes less well-defined; as it is institutionalized, free writing is often just a faddish name for the old method it was meant to replace. In the preface to a writing lab manual for tutors we read that the chief purpose of pre-writing is for the student to get his thesis statement and to learn to outline! Quote from the section called "Pre-writing": "The standard outline is still the best method to help students overcome organizational problems." Of course, if students knew how to outline, they wouldn't have any organizational problems to overcome! And if they can outline right off the bat, then they don't need pre-writing because they will already know what they have to say. Someone who knows exactly what he wants to say without any preliminary forming: that's a fair definition of a *hack.*

The concept of pre-writing as a necessary phase in the composing process is disappearing before our very eyes because there has been no theoretical understanding of the role it plays; I mean any philosophical understanding. The psychological rationale is obvious: it relaxes you; it gives you something other than the blank page to confront and thus can allay anxiety; it can explode one kind of writer's block. The philosophical rationale for pre-writing is not often articulated. Let me try:

Learning to make pre-writing a phase of the composing process and not just a five-finger exercise, a warm up—though it is that too—means learning the uses of chaos. The reason that free writing, listing, and other modes of pre-writing can lead to something else is that the seemingly shapeless, seemingly random words, the images and phrases and fragments are stand-ins for fuller statements, for relationships, for assertions and questions. They are protosentences and paragraphs-in-utero. The conventional wisdom of most schools of psychology cannot explain that: no theory of verbal behavior can account for that power of words, but a philosophy of language as symbolic form can, and so can a theory of imagination as the forming power.

Our students, because they are language animals, because they have the power of naming, can generate chaos; they can find ways out of chaos because language creates them. Language is itself the great heuristic: words come into being as verbal generalization: any name implies generalization; and as students look again at chaos they can see it happen. Words cluster because they belong together—and sentences can be composed that name that relationship. Clusters of words turn into syntax: it is the discursive character of language, its tendency to "run along"—and that's what discourse means—language's tendency to be syntactical brings thought along with it. It is the discursive, generalizing, forming power of language that makes meanings from chaos, which makes pre-writing not *just* preliminary.

Jean Pumphrey's scatter poems demonstrate this power of language to shape meanings. Kenneth Koch's syntactic structures and "poetry ideas," as he calls his rhetorical forms, are what generate the poetry he gets from his youngsters. Any transforming exercise can demonstrate the power of language to make new meanings. Here's a passage from a report written for the Materials and Soils Program of the Division of Highways in Pierre, South Dakota. It's written as a poem called "Observations":

> Some areas of the upper depositions
> of Pierre Shale are fractured
> and lie in jointed platy layers.

Surface water tends
to accumulate
and build up perched water tables in the roadbeds.
The platy layers are dyked off
by impervious shale beds
and have no free drainage outlets.
A large water-fed slide
on old U.S. 16
required many thousands of yards of material
to hold the toe of a berm.
On the interstate near Wasta, South Dakota
water problems developed which caused
much differential heaving.

I think this represents something of what I. A. Richards meant when he spoke once of poetry as "an instrument of research."

Students can learn to write by learning the uses of chaos, which is to say, rediscovering the power of language to generate meanings. Our job is to design sequences of assignments that let them discover what language can do, what they can do with language.

Our students can learn to write only if we give them back their language, and that means playing with it, working with it, using it instrumentally, making many starts. We want them to learn the truth of Gaston Bachelard's observation that "in the realm of the mind, to begin is to know you have the right to begin again."△ If our students are to learn the uses of chaos, we will have to learn ways of teaching them to tolerate ambiguity and to be patient with their beginnings— which should never be graded: identifying mistakes is irrelevant when we are teaching how to begin the process of making meanings. And when we do come to respond to compositions, our comments should continue the dialogue that has been formed in the writer's mind, transformed in his dialogue on paper. As Josephine Miles has suggested, our comments can most usefully take the form of a question: "The main point seems to be *X*; your supporting statements are here, here, and here; if this is so, why is that paragraph where it is?" "The main idea of this paper is *X*; the main steps of its development are here, and here, and here: how then does paragraph 4 fit in, and what transitional connective term would be helpful?"

A theory of the imagination, I've been arguing, can guide us in teaching composition as a dialectical *process*—not a linear, one-way street. In my book, I compare the composer to a sheep dog. A colleague who's using the book told me that nobody knew what a sheep dog was like, but the fact that it was *not* like a tractor got across! Our assignments should be appropriate to all that running about, that hithering and thithering of the sheep dog: short papers, long papers, throw away papers, one sentence written ten different ways—ten different intentions written in one sentence pattern; papers written out of class, papers in class, papers to be forgotten, papers to be revised and edited. Surely, teaching from the perspective of a theory of imagination could help us separate composing and editing. Keats couldn't spell for a hot egg!

In conclusion, I want you to hear a paragraph written by a seventh grader in a remedial class. His teacher, my student, Mrs. Paula Girouard-McCann, who'd been reading George Hillocks' little NCTE pamphlet, "Observing and Writing," brought in a bag of marbles and told her class that they could write whatever they wanted about how the marble looked to them, and that they were not to worry about grammar and spelling.

> A marble is round and made out of glass. When you drop it, it makes a trickle sound. Inside there are little marbles that look like bubbles from a splash in the water. If you think hard enough while your looking in, you can see what you are thinking. Most marbles are see-through. If you whip it down on the ground, it might smash into tiny little pieces. When you put a marble up to a window, you can see your image upside down instead of right side up. It is like an eye whithout a mirror or diaphragm. It looks like there are tiny scratches all over it; but when you feel it, it feels like there are none at all. When you think of it in science terms, you can see parameciums and many other different microrganisms. If you think of it in social science terms, you think of who invented glass and who thought of marbles. If you think of it in math terms, you notice how perfectly round it is. If you think of it in English terms, you can write about it and tell of all the ways it was made, the roundness of it, the science about it, and how you can tell all the ways about a little marble and all the wonders.

I had planned to end with a long passage from Coleridge on the imagination, but I think the seventh grader looking at the marble is better: everything we need to know about composing as a continuum of forming, thinking, and writing is in the boy's sentence:

> If you think hard enough while your looking in, you can see what you are thinking.

A Curious Triangle and the Double-Entry Notebook; or, How Theory Can Help Us Teach Reading and Writing

Criticism is a tricky word, as tricky as any we depend on when we talk about how to teach reading and writing. I suggest that we think of criticism as the point where theory and practice meet: Criticism is knowing what you're doing and thereby how to do it. Criticism is method; it is practicing what you preach. One reason the teaching of English is stymied is that the sense of method as theory brought to bear on practice has been lost. Theory is considered as either irrelevant, because it's abstract, or important, for precisely the same reason. The result is that instead of guidance for our pedagogy, we have, on the one hand, recipe-swapping ("I tried this last week and it worked—never mind why.") and, on the other, abstruse collocations of "data" concerning such ill-defined concepts as "syntactical maturity." If teachers have no interest in theory, it becomes the province of social scientists, psycholinguists, behavioral and cognitive psychologists, or anybody else who can be funded to do "research." Criticism in the classroom could make researchers of all teachers: research in our field ought to mean studying the relationship of the *what* and the *how*.

By assuring a place for criticism in the classroom, we are reclaiming method. Becoming critical, developing a method, is the best way, I think, for teachers and students to learn from one another. If we are all continually discovering, recognizing what it is we are doing, we'll have many more ways of finding out how to do it. In other words, criticism in the classroom could help us get rid of rigid lesson plans so that we would be able to take advantage of what John Donne called "emergent occasions." We could get rid of study questions, refusing to order textbooks that include them; refusing the Instructor's Manual that has the answers, asking for a refund of the money added onto the cost of the textbook so that the manual could be "provided free of charge." Out would go prefabricated units and tests and assignments. A ritual bonfire of those pink and yellow markers used to make pastel islands out of "important passages" would close this introduc-

This essay appeared in the Winter, 1981, issue of *Focus: Teaching English Language Arts*, a journal published by the Southeastern Ohio Council of Teachers of English and the Department of English, Ohio University.

tory phase of criticism in the classroom. We would then be free to undertake what I. A. Richards considered central to all learning, "the continuing audit of meaning."[1]

It is often argued that we should encourage spontaneous response to literature rather than intervening with theory and abstract questions. I want to suggest in the following comment that our pedagogical choices are not limited to fostering unthinking "gut" reactions or encouraging anxious answers from our students about why they "feel" as they do, or tirelessly asking, "What is the author trying to say?" The essential significance of criticism in the classroom is that it enables us to teach reading for meaning and writing as a way of making meaning.

Criticism requires a theory of language that can account for meaning, which does not set it aside as a "mentalistic" matter or treat it as "the semantic component," a spark plug that you insert in the language machine. How we think of language will, of course, determine how we think of literature. If we think of language as a set of slots to be filled, literature will be simply a fancy set of such slots; and we will teach, alternately, the slots and the slotted: "form" and "content." If our idea of language is that it is simply a "communication medium," then our energies in the literature class will go to finding "the message" that's being sent over the wires. If language is a veil that obtrudes between us and reality, there will be no way to suggest revisions or reconsiderations of one or another attempt to pierce it, boring or wild as the foray might be.

If we are to teach our students to read for meaning—to construe and interpret and appreciate literary texts—the meaning of *meaning* most useful to us is that it is a means: speaking and writing, listening and reading all engage us in the making of meaning by means of language. If we can learn to think of language not as a tool, a single-purpose facilitator, but as an instrument that lets us see in many different ways—as both microscope and telescope, X-ray and radar—then we can better discover how to make room at the center of all our courses for interpretation, for the study of meaning.

When we read critically, we are reading for meaning—and that is not the same thing as reading for "message." Meanings are not things, and finding them is not like going on an Easter egg hunt. Meanings are relationships: they are unstable, shifting, dynamic; they do not stay still nor can we prove the authenticity or the validity of one or another meaning that we find. But that does not imply a necessary solipsism; it doesn't mean that the only thing we can say is, "To me it means *X*—and that's that!" Rather, when teachers and students, in constructing and construing, cultivate the attitude that the philosopher C. S. Peirce called a "contrite fallibilism," the need for making a careful case to support our interpretations becomes evident. Isn't that what we want to teach? If students see that we can't prove we're absolutely correct, interpretations not being amenable to that kind of demonstration, then the task of making the best possible case gains an authenticity it might have lacked. If we aren't gods who have perfect knowledge, we are nonetheless powerful creatures who can describe and define; argue and tell stories, encouraging, persuading, entertaining: *rhetoric* is what we have instead of *omniscience.*

Before turning to the practical aspects of method, let me suggest how we might keep in mind the nature of meaning as a means, a way to remember that meaning is dynamic and dialectical, that it depends on context and perspective, the setting in which it is seen and the angle from which it is seen. The model I'm thinking of is a triangle, but of a radically different sort from the familiar "triangle of discourse," which looks like this:

Sometimes, *speaker/ reality/ audience* are at the three points, with *language* or *text* occupying the field enclosed. In this model there is no way of telling the relationship of *message* to either its sources or to the speaker or the form in which it is expressed. As we know, "messages" are continually sent in the real world without being understood, but there is nothing in this model to explain why, or what we, as teachers of reading and writing, might do about failures of "communication."

The triangle I'm suggesting as a model helps on that score; it looks like this:

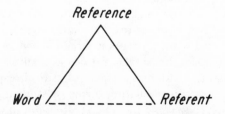

This diagram represents the "sign," or what I've been calling the "meaning relationship." What the word stands for—the referent—is known in terms of the reference. The dotted line stands for the fact that there is no immediate, direct relationship between words and things (including other words); we interpret the word or symbol by means of the idea it represents to us. It takes an idea to find an idea. We know reality *in terms of* our ideas of reality. This curious triangle with the dotted line can help us remember that what we know, we know by means of mediating form. The triangle represents mediation, the interdependence of interpreter (what he already knows), the symbol (image or word), and the import or significance it has. Ironically, by not being quite a triangle, this triangle represents the *triadicity* of meaning relationships. It can help us keep in mind that we must include the beholder, the interpreter, in our account of texts; that texts require contexts and that contexts depend on perspective.[2]

If criticism is supported by such a theory of language as mediating form, what are the pedagogical implications? How can the curious triangle help us teach reading and writing? First of all, it can clarify how being conscious of what we are doing is the way to find out how to do it. Critical awareness is consciousness of *consciousness* (a name for the active mind). Minding the mind, being conscious of consciousness, is not the same sort of thing as thinking about your elbows when you're about to pitch a baseball; nor is it *self*-consciousness. Consciousness in meaning-making activity always involves us in interpreting our interpretations; thinking is a matter of "arranging our techniques of arranging"; criticism is a matter of coming to "know our knowledge." These circular formulations (they can make you dizzy at first) are, like the triangle with the dotted line, emblems of the fact that we can't get under the net of language. The point is that we can learn to take advantage of that fact, making the raising of consciousness about the making of meaning our chief strategy in teaching the circularity of all knowledge and in developing a "pedagogy of knowing."[3]

And, second, the curious triangle can help us focus on ways to bring students to see texts as the intermediary form of a process of making meaning that began in mysterious and unknowable ways, unfolding in sometimes predictable ways and sometimes in surprising ways, and which continues as texts are construed and reconstructed. (The faddish term for this process is *deconstruction,* but that word suggests to me *demolition,* the breaking down of analysis without the synthesis that constitutes the other aspect of critical response.) Students can learn to see texts as mediating forms by studying evidence of the process by which they came into being. Reading in the notebooks of poets and novelists; seeing the rough drafts of a single poem; tracing the growth and development of a story from a scribbled note, a single image, a pair of terms; watching the meanings shift and change in the course of revising—all such study of literary work in progress will help make the point of "technique as discovery," in a well-known phrase.[4] It's a good idea too, I think, to cultivate the habit of watching and listening to rehearsals and practice sessions of musicians and dancers, of watching artists at work. There is as much to be learned in the studio and the practice room about the composing process, the making of meaning, as there is in the library.

The most useful way to raise consciousness of texts as intermediary forms and to develop a method of critical reading is, simply put, to have students write continuously in a double-entry notebook, which I will shortly describe. Writing in the literature class is usually limited to taking notes on lectures and composing critical appreciations, critical essays, or book reports. But writing can help develop a critical method of reading by, first of all, providing for students an example of a text coming into being—their own. And, second, by encouraging habits of reflective questioning in the process of reading, chiefly by means of interpretive paraphrase, writing can help students replace the nonquestion, "What is the author trying to say?" with the critical question, "How does it change the meaning when I change the text and put it this way?" The double-entry notebook, by offering the chance to practice interpreting in such a way that whatever is learned about reading is something learned about writing, can teach that how we construe is how we construct. *Languaging,* as some like to say, is our means of making meaning.

I ask my students (all of them: freshmen, upperclassmen, teachers in graduate seminars) to furnish themselves with a notebook, spiral-bound at the side, small enough to be easily carried around but not so small that writing is cramped. (School teachers who have tried this idea tell me, however, that their students insist on a notebook that will fit into the back pocket of their jeans.) What makes this notebook different from most, perhaps, is the notion of the double entry: on the right side reading notes, direct quotations, observational notes, fragments, lists, images—verbal and visual—are recorded; on the other (facing) side, notes about those notes, summaries, formulations, aphorisms, editorial suggestions, revisions, comment on comment are written. The reason for the double-entry format is that it provides a way for the student to conduct that "continuing audit of meaning" that is at the heart of learning to read and write critically. The facing pages are in dialogue with one another.

The double-entry notebook is for all kinds of writing, creative or critical; any assignment you can think up can be adapted so that it can teach dialectic, another name for the continuing audit.[5] Suppose you want your students in the seventh grade (or the eleventh: in between, *self*-consciousness tends to overpower conscientization) to read some nature poems. The writing assigned could be a record of ten minutes of observation and meditation carried out daily over a week—descriptions and speculations in response to a seashell, a milkweed pod, a chestnut burr, or any natural object (the odder the better) that can serve as "text": *reading the book of nature* is probably the oldest writing assignment in the world. Each day should begin with rereading the notes from the day before and writing a recapitulation on the facing page. At the week's end, two paragraphs are assigned: (1) a description of the object, based on the right-hand side entries; (2) a comment on the process of observing and interpreting, based on the left-hand side—but in either case, the writer is free to move back and forth from notes to recapitulation.

But assignments need not be so highly structured: any writing assignments that encourage students to look and look again will be teaching critical reading and critical thinking. Perception is one of the best models for the process of making meaning. A few strategies like transformation or a simple heuristic such as, "What is it the opposite of?" can be quickly learned and put to use by all students, no matter what their level of proficiency. Designing a poster to advertise a play, for instance, could be a process of constructing that would use the right-hand page for notes on lettering, visual design, suggestions of scenes to be depicted, and so forth. The left-hand page could be a rough sketch or instructions to the artist. This is not an "affective" pleasantry but an exercise in translating, the most basic form of interpretation. Writing mini-versions of novels and plays exercises the powers of generalizing, summary and definition.[6] Expanding or expatiating or parodying is an excellent way to practice drawing out implications. Thus working towards narrative from photographs in Edward Steichen's *Family of Man* can teach as much about the strategies of characterization as students would get in fifty pages of study questions about how Hardy makes his characters plausible.

The essential point of the double-entry notebook is that meaning is being made from the first: the reason that we find it so hard to move from personal writing to expository writing in our teaching is that we do not always define what they have in common. The chief pedagogical use of the curious triangle with the dotted line is to remind us that students, in whatever they write and with whatever they read, are interpreting and composing: they are making meaning.

Notes

[1]Richards, one of the founders of modern literary criticism, is the only critic to have devoted his time principally to elucidating the ways in which

theory and practice can be mutually beneficial. English teachers at all levels have more to learn from him than from anyone else, I believe. *Speculative Instruments* (N.Y.: Harcourt, 1955) and *How to Read a Page* (N.Y.: Norton, 1942; rpt. 1965) are good places to begin.

[2]The "triadic" triangle comes from *The Meaning of Meaning,* C. K. Ogden and I. A. Richards (N.Y.: Harcourt, 1946). For an interesting discussion of the two triangles and "triadicity," see Walker Percy, *The Message in the Bottle* (N.Y.: Farrar, Straus, Giroux, 1975). I have tried to suggest some of the pedagogical implications of triadicity in "Towards a Pedagogy of Knowing," *Freshman English News* (Spring 1978). (See pages 48–60.)

[3]"Pedagogy of knowing" and "conscientization" are terms of critical importance (they are both theoretical and practical) in the thinking of Paulo Freire, from whose work in literacy training we all can learn. *Education for Critical Consciousness* (N.Y.: Seabury Press, 1973) is a good introduction. I have included a chapter here: see pages 159–173.

[4]The essay with this title by Mark Schorer is an important document in modern criticism. It appeared in the first issue of the *Hudson Review* (1948) and has been widely reprinted.

[5]*Dialogue* and *dialectic* are cognate: I call it a "dialectical notebook" in my textbook, *Forming/Thinking/Writing: The Composing Imagination* (Hayden, 1978), where it is described in some detail.

[6]Morris Sagoff's *ShrinkLits* (N.Y.: Workman, 1980) offers some amusing examples.

Towards a Pedagogy of Knowing

Our anxieties can be incapacitating when we discover that what we probably have to do in teaching reading and writing is "what should have been done in the fifth grade." But once we get past blaming the victim or social and political forces beyond our control; once we undertake to learn to teach the new student, defined either as actually illiterate or culturally deprived by the fact of having been reared in an exclusively suburban or inner-city environment; once we admit that neither recipes nor harangues are what we need, we find ourselves interested in pedagogy. The word is fashionable once again, though the concept is not well-formed. An uncle of mine with a lifetime's experience of the Mississippi once explained engineering to me this way: "Any fool can build a bridge that might stand up against a flood, but an engineer is supposed to make sure that it does." Pedagogy is not, alas, engineering and it can't possibly offer that kind of assurance, but it can help us be less foolish about what can be done in the English classroom.

Pedagogy can mean simply the old normal schools' "materials and methods" or it can name the means to a profoundly political awakening, as in Paulo Freire's "pedagogy of the oppressed"; it can be unconscious or it can be factored into lesson plans. I doubt that there are any cases in which it is as minimal as it once frequently was: Robert Frost remarked that the only thing his Latin teacher ever said to the class was "Next!" At Radcliffe in the late '40s, graduate students heard a series of lectures on pedagogy, disquisitions by some very distinguished professors on ways of telling how long 50 minutes is and what to do when students fall asleep; only I. A. Richards seemed to know that the topic was complex. As I remember, he used mountaineering metaphors to persuade us to teach to the top of the class because otherwise we would surely lose them, and probably the middle too—and we might not reach the bottom third in any case. The point was that, in the ascent, everybody needed to feel the rope in tension. Nowadays, when we may well be persuaded that the whole class is, as it were, in the bottom third, that pedagogical advice would need revising: we should teach to the *top* of *everybody's* sensibility and capacity. Modern pedagogy should, I believe, help us determine how to identify and encourage the innate powers of our students' minds; to

This essay appeared in *Freshman English News*, Spring, 1978.

nurture what is native; to explore what it can mean to say, "Begin with where they are."

Any pedagogy is properly constituted by a method, models, and a theory. Insofar as a pedagogy is concerned with teaching reading and writing, a concern for language will be central to all three. The province of rhetoric, which is the structure and function of language, is thus coterminous with the boundaries of an English pedagogy. I propose here to describe certain inadequacies in the conception and realization of methods, models, and theories that make a critical assessment of what we are doing in teaching English virtually impossible, and to suggest, then, the character of a different sort of pedagogy that might be developed.

What Is a Method?

True to the spirit of the age, English pedagogues—I use the term to name all those who are concerned with methods, models, and theories—have sought to be scientific, but with very ill-formed notions of what constitutes scientific inquiry. They are generally still content with variations on "What is English?"—the question raised at the Dartmouth Conference a decade ago, and a very poor question it is. (As Oppenheimer observed, Einstein did not develop his theory of relativity by asking, "What is a clock?") Scientific or not, we need a method that encourages critical questions about goals in conjunction with ways and means: a method that does not allow for the continual exploration of purposes and premises as well as procedures will soon become doctrinaire.

Such questions should be directed both to what we are doing as teachers and to what our students are doing, and they should include questions about what is going wrong. But asking what's wrong with a course of study or an approach is rare in our field; the primary mode of critical review is denial that it is necessary ("Students have always written badly") or, alternately, "innovation." Comparably, asking what is wrong with a composition is often taken metonymically for asking what's wrong with the composer. But to make a student feel rotten is bad teaching, not the necessary outcome of a method that uses the analysis of mistakes, misconceptions, and misstatements. "A good way to study auto mechanics is to study auto breakdowns," as Walker Percy puts it. "Vapor locks, short circuits, transmission failures may be the best evidence that there are such things as carburetors, electrical systems, and gears—especially if the mechanic can't lift the hood."[1]

The primary lesson of modern scientific inquiry has not been learned by those English pedagogues who claim that a method is "neutral."[2] What we are looking for determines, up to a point, how we seek; the ways of searching will control, up to a point, what we find. Call it dialectics, complementarity, the hermeneutic circle: the mutual dependence of ends and means is a principle of critical inquiry shared by scientists and students of language; it should be a commonplace for anyone setting up as theoretician. Methods are no more neutral than ideologies are value-free.

A method may require specialized language for its explication, but having a lexicon doesn't insure that we have a method. We can't expect jargon to do the work of instruction. In a new textbook we read, "The idea is to internalize the principles upon which these patterns are based so that when you use them they become intuitive rather than self-conscious." The Piagetian term *internalize,* which is neither explained nor used elsewhere in this passage, is metaphoric and memorable, but what are we remembering? What does *internalize* mean here in juxtaposition with *self-conscious?* That relationship is centrally important to an understanding of the composing process, but mere assertion of a point—especially when it's vague: the idea of the *intuitive* is a notorious catch-all—cannot serve as the statement of a method, as this purports to be.

We are trapped over and over by the language we have borrowed from psychology, heedless of the fact that the social sciences, in an attempt to resolve an identity crisis suffered from birth, have themselves borrowed the language of other disciplines; in our hands, these terms are at an even further remove from physics, communication theory, neurology, molecular biology, etc. Here's a psycholinguist discussing what he calls "the student's ability to store meaningful [sic] semantic units and to encode these units in syntactic form." Changes are due, he says, "not to central effects, that is, changes in linguistic ability of students, but to peripheral effects, that is, changes in certain skills that students utilize in the writing process."[3] The sly importation of "central" and "peripheral" is meant to substantiate this entirely problematic assertion *(linguistic? ability? effects? skills? utilize? writing process?)* by lending it the rigor of neurological description. This language also tends to distract us from considering the absurdity of trying to separate what we do with language (if "linguistic ability" means something other than getting case endings right) from how we think.

Methods of scientific inquiry cannot be adapted by aping the language of the laboratory. That strategy has not helped psychology become a science, nor can we bring "English" up to date by taking over psychology's second-hand language or, indeed, its pseudo-concepts.

Psychologists imagine that they are being scientific when they speak of persons as "hominid individuals"; English pedagogues are peculiarly susceptible to this kind of self-delusion. If we want to speak of "scribal fluency," we should know that the term can have as much to do with skywriting as it does with the composing process.

Although a method can take the form of a list of steps, such a list is not necessarily a method. Like language itself, method is reflexive; it is dialectical by definition: *meta + hodos, about the way.* Method is a way of relating ends and means, and that is a dialectical process. Method lets us discover how *X* in conjunction with *Y* becomes *Z*, which in turn may convert *Y* to *W.* Discovery procedures should be dialectical; that is to say, methods of invention should keep the *what* and the *how* together, should continually relate the *why* and the *what* and the *how*. More often than not, however, such methods are presented as something to be applied mechanically to some preexistent subject matter. Heuristic procedures are frequently conceived of as directions for thawing out frozen, prebaked topics on a tagmemic grid. Rhetoricians are now intoning *pentad,* paying no attention to Burke's dialectic—the calculus of the five dramatistic terms. Dialectic is, as Richards has it, paraphrasing Plato, "the continuing audit of meaning." △ Without an understanding of dialectic as the heart of a method, we are doomed to see one after another promising technique disappear without ever having been given a fair chance.

Models—or Muddles?

The same sort of misconception is evident in the way English pedagogues use what they call "models." The term is borrowed from psychologists who borrowed it from natural scientists who use models to conceptualize and represent functional relationships. A model represents a mode of operation; it allows us to see the structure of a process, a system in action. A model is an analogy, a representation of one form by another.[4] My guess is that our faddish interest in "models" derives from a McLuhanesque notion that "linear" representations are misleading. Scientists don't worry about the linearity of their equations; they build models to represent those equations, not to abrogate them. Models also serve heuristic functions for scientists: "You know it's working," Francis Crick has remarked in an interview, "when you get more out of it than you put in."

What does the concept of "model" mean when it is used in discussing rhetoric and pedagogy? What, for instance, is a "communication skills model" of the composition course, which is often set in opposition to a "personal growth model"? *Communication* I will return to in a moment; as for *skills*—another problematic word that has been taken over from educational psychology—they are identified by one who has written of such a model as "organization, unity, coherence, development"—those sound remarkably like characteristics of discourse, not of a discourser. (Is a logical error what we get out of this model?) The pseudo-concept of "skills" breeds one poorly-formed idea after another. We read, for instance, that "the act of writing . . . engages behavioral as well as mental skills." But wherever language is concerned, there is no "behavior" that is not also "mental." Do we not continually find it said that if we add up "the basic skills" we will reach a total that can be recognized as "improvement in the ability to write"—or, as it is likely to be put, "an increase in performance capability"? Learning to compose is only in rather limited respects like learning to hit a tennis ball or to flip an omelet; there are skills involved in composing, but composing is something other than the sum of basic skills and some super-skills; otherwise we could teach it by means of drill. In any case, neither *skills* nor *model* seems a well-formed concept, with the results that *skills model* is an obscure and muddling phrase.

Nor is the other half of the opposition any clearer—that "personal growth model" or "self-awareness model," which is generally described in language that bespeaks exactly the same presuppositions about learning as those underlying the skills model. Thus "expression" is considered another kind of "response," and encouraging self-awareness is seen as a matter of getting the right stimuli. It is remarkable that the more highly behaviorist and positivistic the conceptual framework of the model builder, the more likely it is that, sooner or later, the Self will make an appearance. Gordon Allport (a literate and humane psychologist who can be read with profit and delight, but I have never seen his work cited in any essay by an English pedagogue) has the following observation: "Many psychologists reinvent self when they find no coherence in positivistic analysis. This self is the obscurantist's homunculus."[5] *Self* is certainly a more difficult concept to form than *skills,* but as Allport suggests, when it is used in this way, "self" is little more than the ghost in the positivist machine.

Everything that makes it difficult to apprehend the relationship between language and thought makes it difficult to explain to ourselves what we should do in teaching composition, or even what we think we are doing. We are not helped in that endeavor by a pair of models that separate precisely what we should be aiming to keep together from the start. As the author of this particular formulation observes (in a typical sentence): "The whole area of getting from students' needs to content in the more traditional sense is a sticky one."

And one reason is that the concept relied on most frequently to articulate the relationship between the writer and his writing, between

both and an audience, is *communication.* Its obvious failings as a critically useful concept, whether deployed in devising methods or in
model building (What is communicated? Why? How?), have been ignored because, I think, "communication" is protected by its presumed scientific status. Communication (or information) theory is, of
course, a scientific construct of central importance to computer engineers, but when others use them, the chief terms of the theory are
extremely hazardous. Despite the warnings of engineers and logicians
that *information* has nothing to do with *meaning,* that word is used continually as a synonym for *meaning.* We should continually be defining
the meaning of meaning, but instead we consider that there is no
need since we are using a scientific term.

Consider the use to which Roman Jakobson's diagram of "the communication situation" has been put. This schematic representation
has been widely reproduced in rhetorics: an *addresser* encodes a *message,* which is decoded by an *addressee;* the message has a *context* (reference), a *code,* and a *contact* (channel, a physical means of being
realized). His friend I. A. Richards has analyzed Jakobson's diagram
many times and in "Towards a Theory of Comprehending" has devised his own schema to represent other factors in "transmission."[6]
Let me summarize his objections: what is between speaker and hearer
in the diagram is not *message* but *signal,* and it is with signals that communication (or information) theory is concerned. Distinguishing signal and message is a central issue in any study of language, but,
applying the Crick test, what we get out of this model is not a clari-
fication of that relationship but a conception of language as, in Richards' metaphor, a verbal butterfly net for catching nonverbal
butterflies.

The Jakobson model perpetuates the inept separation of "form"
and "content" that seems to legitimate teaching "the message," a
term which even Jakobson's wiring diagram can't demystify. But the
model is popular with those who would like to conceive of interpretation as a straightforward, scientific procedure, as in this explanation
by a rhetorician who knows better: "The next step is to see if we can
translate the literal meaning, the surface meaning, into a code other
than the one the poet uses and still keep the bare ideas that were in
the original." Anyone guiding students in reading Marvell—the poem
whose bare ideas students are contemplating here is "To his Coy Mis-
tress"—should be wary of assuming that "literal" is a term with self-
evident meaning. In Jakobsonian terms, the message is *decoded,* not
"translated" into another code. Chomsky doesn't speak of "surface
meaning," but the Chomskyist term "surface" (from "surface features") is used to dignify the empty concept of "the words on the
page." Such jargon is not needed to legitimize paraphrase, which is

essential to critical reading; our task, however, is to teach students *how* to paraphrase, not to pretend that it's a matter of "decoding." What we have here is not a new model but only another version of "What is the author trying to say?"

Jakobson's diagram of "the communication situation" presupposes a positivist epistemology according to which we process "the raw data of experience." This model encourages us to teach that there is an immediate (i.e., unmediated) response or recording, as distinct from "reflection about the moment." But unless we understand that there is no immediate experience, no reality known to us formlessly, we won't be able to get from "experience" to "reflection," or from "skills" to "personal growth": we won't be able to get from here to there.

Know That/Know How

If it is to be more than a collection of recipes, an English pedagogy will be, necessarily, theoretical. But theoreticians in the field of English have shown little interest in *pedagogical* theory, devoting their energies instead to theories of the aims, elements, and modes of *discourse.* These theories are often little more than taxonomies and sometimes they are illogical, at that. It is not instructive to be told, for instance, that the essay is a linguistic principle or that "literary discourse embraces the genres [sic] of literature, songs, puns, the limerick, jokes, and the TV drama." A more hopeful point of departure for developing a theory for an English pedagogy is the study of how we learn.

All theories of learning (and language) must give an account of knowing. The formulation offered by John Warnock differentiates two kinds of knowing but begs the question of how they are related.[7] The opposition of *know that* and *know how,* a contribution of the British philosopher Gilbert Ryle, has that beguiling positivist character of seeming to make rigorous distinctions in ordinary language, but like Moffett's spurious distinction of "English" (not *language,* as in Wittgenstein's formulation) as a "subject" and an "activity," it muddles rather than clarifies. *Know-how* gives Warnock no trouble. He explains it by the example of bicycle riding; *know-how* is a skill that can be exercised without the intervention of *knowing that.* ("Who's Afraid," 19) Earlier, however, Warnock has told us that it is, epistemologically speaking, impossible "to have practice without theory." How is "having practice" different from "practicing"? Who "has" this "practice"? As for "theory," he means, I think, that presuppositions and assumptions are logically unavoidable, and that theory can always be adduced from practice. But is *knowing that* presupposition, then, or theory? Is *knowing that* contingent on theoretical formulation? What the ordinary language philosophers leave out must be put back in by anyone trying to use their concepts.

Warnock has a hard time not only explaining what he means by *knowing that* but also describing the place it should have in the composition course and the role it should play for the composer. To help him out, he calls in Peter Elbow, citing his differentiation of producing and editing as stages of writing. Warnock then comments: "One might also call them the performative and the critical stages or . . . the operating and testing stages." ("Who's Afraid," 19) I have no wish to cavil, but this interpretation surely confuses the issue. Producing can continue—it does continue—until the final stages of revision. Whatever research has been done corroborates what every experienced writer knows, that the form of what is being written helps discover the substance; that intention and representation are mutually contingent. Editing is what editors (or writers-as-editors) do; it is not an integral part of the composing process. To call producing *performance* and editing *criticism* falsifies the distinction Elbow is making.

What is gained by calling any phase of the composing process a *performance?* Is *performance* a synonym for a "behavior"? And what is that? (Is it a "subject" or an "activity"?) Is *performance* something we can talk about as a "real" as opposed to an "abstract" matter? Is the term *performance* intended to remind us of *performative* speech acts? Are we meant to think of a Chomskyist *performance,* in contradistinction to *competence?* When Warnock remarks that "after performance, theory can help us get a view of what the writing is finally trying to do," ("New Rhetoric," 20) does he mean that the writer performs and the performance then has the intention? (That sounds like the stomach talking to the body in the Alka Seltzer ad—an interesting kind of dialogue; but I don't really know what Warnock means by "what the writing is finally trying to do.") "Theory," he goes on, "can help consolidate the enterprise and give it a sense of direction." You bet it can—but why do we have to wait until "after the performance" for this beneficence? I see circus horses getting their sugar.

As for separating "performance" from "criticism," that is the oldest of the new pedagogies.[8] But sooner or later—"after the performance" is one occasion—theory and practice have to be brought together, preferably by the practitioner, but at least by the theoretician. Since positivist models are fueled by behaviorist concepts, it is not surprising to find this passage in Warnock's disquisition on the relationship of *know how* and *know that:* "In non-reflective behavior, *know-how* implies first of all an organism's ability to know that it has encountered an unsatisfactory state of affairs . . . and, after operation, that it has achieved a satisfactory one." ("New Rhetoric," 3) If this "organism" is acting "non-reflectively," it is not a specimen that can provide analogies for an English pedagogy (Warnock is describing instinctual reaction, presumably); nor is it a specimen that a zoologist would know how (sic) to categorize, since, though it is allegedly non-reflective, it nevertheless *knows that.* There ain't no such animal; nevertheless, "it" functions as a model, for in the next paragraph Warnock writes: "Assuming now that we are dealing with non-reflective writing . . ." But there's no such thing as "non-reflective" writing, if "non-reflective" means what an organism does instinctually. This is what happens when pedagogues take "verbal behavior" seriously: it allows them to concoct pseudo-concepts like "non-reflective" writing. Warnock, I suppose, is trying to be rigorous about "uncritical" writing by renaming it "non-reflective" by analogy with instinctual animal behavior. It's a maneuver comparable to calling conceptual acts of mind "mental skills," by analogy with playing softball or riding a bicycle.

The notion of "non-reflective writing" makes it seem feasible to isolate criticism as a factor, but this won't do—and Warnock belatedly realizes the basic absurdity of a conception of writing dichotomized as *performance* and *criticism.* He uses the prime positivist strategy of smuggling back into the model what has just been removed as a component. Thus *know how* reenters (rather surreptitiously) as "heuristic procedures" that can be learned "in advance"; they are a way "to enhance the chances of intuiting a solution to a particular problem." ("Who's Afraid," 19, 20) Now intuition is, as a logical concept, simply the capacity to discover analogies, and that is an operation of mind that is not beyond the pale of reason. (A syllogism, as Langer has remarked, is a device for getting from one intuition to another.) Intuition is neither mystical nor mysterious, but in the hands of positivists, who can't accommodate nonpropositional logic, it *becomes* mysterious and vague. The same sort of thing happens when tagmemic theorists (who, by the way, provide those heuristic procedures to be learned in advance), realizing that problem solving is likely to become prescriptive or rule-governed, rename it "creative problem solving."

In any case, the writer using these heuristic procedures will be no closer to *know how* because he will not know in advance just what the "particular problem" is. Indeed, I would say that is a shortcoming of most of our students: they do not easily recognize particular problems because they do not have a method, that is, a means of formulating critical questions. Heuristic procedures should, of course, be carried out, not just "in advance," but in continuation, throughout the composing process. It is also certainly true that the writer must learn to intuit, to grasp relationships, to see how things are related; he must *form concepts.* And that has nothing to do with non-reflective or instinctual behavior; it is an operation of mind and it requires thinking *with* concepts and not just *about* them. To intuit means to see the relationship of parts to the meaning of a whole. In composing, that whole is coming into being: the question of questions for the writer is—or should be—"How can I make the whole until I have the parts—how can I find the parts until I know the whole?" The paradox of intuition can only be resolved by a dialectical method of composing in which the whole is hypothesized and the parts identified, created, and gathered accordingly; in which the parts can be seen tentatively as representative of the meaning of the whole.

That method maintains *knowing that* and *knowing how* in a dialectical relationship. For instance, knowing that chaos affords the materials of composition *(ex nihilo nihil fit)* is a way of knowing how to begin by naming, by proceeding without a concern for "thesis statements" and all the claptrap that goes with the irrational maxim, "Don't write until you know what you want to say!" *Knowing that* chaos is the source is the condition of *knowing how* to use it. Learning the uses of chaos is a method for learning to intuit the relationship of parts in a whole that is coming into being, which in compositional terms means coming to *mean:* the juncture of thought and language is the making of meaning. That is to say, the answer to the writer's most important question comes by way of another question: "How do I know what I mean until I hear what I say?" It is language itself that is the indispensable heuristic. It is language that enables us to know that we know that, and to know how to know how. It is language that allows us, as Coleridge put it, *to know our knowledge.*

John Warnock has come further than most in recognizing the philosophical character of the issues involved in pedagogical theory. But since he tries to work with the concepts of a positivist epistemology, there is no way for him to avoid begging the questions we must raise if we are to understand the relationship of the several kinds of knowing. Without that understanding, I can't see how it will be possible to conceptualize "a grammar of pedagogy," new or old.

Towards a Pedagogy of Knowing

If the only thing we can count on these days is the power of the human mind, then we should have a theory that can account for that power in its own terms, not in those appropriate to the study of snails and chimpanzees. As my references to Richards here and elsewhere attest, I believe that it is from him that we have most to learn. Having recently freed himself from the bonds of behavioral psychology and logical positivism with the help of Mencius and Coleridge, Richards knew that the new rhetoric for which he called in 1936 would have to be philosophical. The "contextual theorem of meaning" really was new and *The Philosophy of Rhetoric* became one of the charters of the New Criticism, providing as it did a conceptual framework in which metaphor could be the focus of a study of meaning; ambiguity could be seen as a resource; and the "interinanimation" of words be understood as the dynamic of meaning. With *Interpretation in Teaching* two years later, Richards turned to an exploration of the pedagogical implications of a philosophical rhetoric. That search has continued through half a dozen books, in one of which he recently described a pedagogy that would provide "sets of sequenced exercises through which millions of people could explore, for themselves, their own abilities and grow in capacity, practical and intelligential, as a result." The "millions" referred to are the illiterate peoples of the world who could benefit from a model that does not oppose skills and personal growth but makes them contingent upon one another, a method that would amount to offering "assisted invitations to attempt to find out just what they are trying to do and thereby how to do it."[9] We learn *how* by means of reflecting on the *what:* that method is consonant with the dialectical character of thought and language and with what teachers continually rediscover (if they are really watching) about how their students learn.

This dialectical method is also consonant with Paulo Freire's dialogical "pedagogy of knowing." Perhaps it is not just coincidence that this other model from which we have most to learn is the creation of another teacher devoted to the adult literacy process.[10] The Archimedean points we need in order to undertake a critical inquiry into our teaching of reading and writing in college are provided, I believe, by the pedagogy of ESL (English as a second language), literacy training, and the teaching of reading to youngsters.

Freire's *conscientization,* like Richards' *design for escape* (i.e., an escape from the dangers of planlessness and the merely self-centered), is based on a philosophy of language that takes full advantage of the critical character of language—we interpret our interpretations, as Kenneth Burke puts it; it depends on a psychology in which all acts of learning are at once creative and critical; it points to a pedagogy in which knowing subjects encounter one another in dialogue mediated by the world of common experience.

I close with a passage from Freire's *Pedagogy of the Oppressed,* in which method, model, and theory are all consonant with the idea that to begin with where our students are is to learn to trust the power of the human mind.

> Human existence cannot be silent, nor can it be nourished by false words, but only by true words, with which men transform the world. To exist, humanly, is to *name* the world, to change it. Once named, the world in its turn reappears to the namers as a problem and requires of them a new *naming*. Men are not built in silence, but in word, in work, in action-reflection. But while to say the true word—which is work, which is praxis—is to transform the world, saying that word is not the privilege of some few men, but the right of every man. Consequently, no one can say a true word alone—nor can he say it *for* another, in a prescriptive act which robs others of their words. Dialogue is the encounter between men mediated by the world, in order to name the world.[11]

Notes

[1] *The Message in the Bottle* (New York: Farrar, Straus, Giroux, 1975), p. 166.

[2] Here are two examples of this thinking: "The concept of problem solving . . . is totally neutral" (W. Ross Winterowd, in *Contemporary Rhetoric* [New York: Harcourt Brace Jovanovich, 1957], p. 90). "Some English teachers respond to words such as 'cybernetics' and 'overdetermination' as if they represented all the evil advances that communication programs have made, often at the expense of traditional English programs, over the past few decades. The words themselves are neutral, however." (Joseph Comprone, "Cybernetics and Rhetoric: Freshman English in an Overdetermined World," *ADE Bulletin*, Sept. 1975.)

Problem solving is not comparable to O in mathematics about which we need not entertain a belief; it is a method whose presuppositions are themselves problematical. For instance, to decide to convert an issue to a problem is to pass a kind of judgment that may or may not be called for. A critique of problem solving should always include this question: "In whose interest is it to pose the issue as such and such a problem?" In problem solving, as developed by technologists who are given problems to solve, there is certainly a prejudice towards quantification and sequencing according to rather rigidly defined conceptions of causality. Like every other method, problem solving comes with certain philosophical assumptions about purpose and aim; it would be useless if it didn't.

By "advances" made by "communications programs" over "traditional English programs," Comprone presumably means substituting audiovisual "experience" for "print media." In any case, concepts, not words, are the proper subjects of critical inquiry; words are always "neutral" in the dictionary.

[3] James W. Ney, "Notes towards a Psycholinguistic Model of the Writing Process," *Research in the Teaching of English* (Summer 1974): 168.

[4] There are scale models and theoretical models, as well as analogue models. For a thorough and lively discussion of the logic of models, see Max

Black, *Models and Metaphors* (Ithaca: Cornell University Press, 1962), especially Chapter XIII.

[5]*Becoming* (New Haven: Yale University Press, 1955), p. 38.

[6]In *Speculative Instruments* (New York: Harcourt Brace World, 1955).

[7]"Who's Afraid of Theory?" *College Composition and Communication* (February 1976): 16–20; "New Rhetoric and the Grammar of Pedagogy," *Freshman English News* (Fall 1976): 1–22.

[8]Some models of the composition course quite deliberately keep students in the dark about what they are doing, for shorter or longer periods of time. In the famous Amherst course, for instance, puzzling assignments were given without explanation. However, with criticism coming on the heels of each performance, and with performances every week, it soon became possible to think of the criticism as coming "before" the performance. For a careful analysis of the philosophical foundations of this course, see James H. Broderick, "A Study of the Freshman Composition Course at Amherst: Action, Order, and Language," *Harvard Educational Review* (Winter 1958): 44–57.

In other instances, the separation of two allegedly different phases of composing has been instituted in order to encourage the unspoiled reaction or, more accurately I think, to rationalize the deplorable practice of requiring students to produce terrible writing before instruction can begin.

[9]*Design for Escape* (New York: Harcourt Brace World, 1968), p. 11.

[10]Richards' long career as a critic encompasses everything from neurology to the study of textual variants, but the pedagogical dimension is there in almost everything he has written. Adult literacy is a recurring topic of *So Much Nearer* (New York: Harcourt Brace World, 1968) and *Design for Escape.*

[11]*Pedagogy of the Oppressed* (New York: Herder and Herder, 1970), p. 76. Freire's critical language is an odd mixture of Christian and Marxist idiom. His exposition is turgid; repetition is virtually his only means of emphasis; his terms can be found very confusing. However, the struggle to read him is worthwhile: no one else writing on literacy (one of the meanings of "English") has so profound a philosophical foundation. The best introduction to his work is "The Adult Literacy Process as Cultural Action for Freedom," *HER* (May 1970): 205–25.

2. Composing Is Forming

> *For all the talk about "process," there is virtually no*
> *institutional understanding of the kind of process composing is.*
> *At the heart of the matter is the need for an understanding that*
> *forming is abstraction and that it is carried out in two modes: by*
> *means of successive generalization and by means of direct insight.*
> *By forming the concept of abstraction, we can make the case for*
> *dialogue and perception as the two most promising models for the*
> *composing process, each representing primarily one of the two*
> *modes of abstraction. And we can better justify the differentiation*
> *of composing and editing.*

The Intelligent Eye
and the Thinking Hand

It is inspiriting to participate in a conference of teachers addressing themselves unabashedly to mind, not problem-solving; daring to speak of *the writer's mind,* not competence or performance; of *writing as a mode of thinking,* not as verbal communication. It is a pleasant change to find the emphasis on *mind* rather than on information processing or signal detectability or protocol analysis. To speak of mind could represent an unembarrassed recognition of the fact that everything we deal with in composition theory is fundamentally and unavoidably philosophical. I believe that it is only by being philosophical that rhetoric can "take charge of the criticism of its own assumptions." That was the way I. A. Richards put it in 1936 in *The Philosophy of Rhetoric,* a book that we composition teachers should return to, if only to rinse our minds of the effects of another book, curiously called *The Philosophy of Composition.* Let me say right away that

This paper was read at a conference co-sponsored by the New York College English Association and the Department of English, Skidmore College, October, 1980. The conference was called "The Writer's Mind: Writing as a Mode of Thinking."

61

what Professor Hirsch means by "philosophy," though obscure, is in any case not what Dr. Richards meant or what, in my opinion, teachers of composition should concern themselves with: *The Philosophy of Composition* gives philosophy, to say nothing of composition, a bad name.

Professor Hirsch has, interestingly enough, chosen as an epigraph for his book a statement of Herbert Spencer, the English father of Positivism. Positivist presuppositions are everywhere to be found in current rhetorical theory, and they are the chief cause of all our woe. Let me offer a polemical summary. Positivism is a philosophy whose epistemology is fundamentally associationist. The positivist notion of critical inquiry is a naïve misconception of scientific method—what is sometimes called "scientism." Positivists believe that empirical tests yield true facts and that's that; they do not understand that scientists test hypotheses. Underlying all positivist methods and models is a notion of language as, alternately, a set of slots into which we cram or pour our meanings or as a veil that must be torn asunder to reveal reality directly, without the distorting mediation of form. (If that sounds mystical, it's because if you scratch a positivist, you'll find a mystic: neither can tolerate the concept of mediation.) I believe that we should reject this false philosophy, root and branch, and in doing so it is important to realize that we are in excellent company.

We can count as allies, among others, Susanne K. Langer, William James, C. S. Peirce, and I. A. Richards. Mrs. Langer, in the first volume of *Mind: An Essay on Human Feeling* (the very title is important), explains how it is that psychologists have developed no sound theories of mind: when they have seen that to ask, "What is mind?" leads to a futile search for metaphysical quiddities, instead of reconceiving the critical questions that would yield working concepts, they have worshipped the "idols of the laboratory." These are physicalism, mathematization, objectivity, methodology, and jargon. Any teacher who has been intimidated by the false philosophy of such books as Professor Hirsch's should read Dr. Langer's critique every morning before breakfast. And, in resisting the positivists, we will have an ally in William James, a great psychologist by virtue of being a great philosopher. (Alfred North Whitehead listed him as one of the four greatest of all times because of his understanding of the importance of experience.) James, in his typically lively *Talks to Teachers,* warns his audience not to expect insight into the nature of such aspects of thought as attention, memory, habit, and interest to be forthcoming from what he calls the "brass instrument" psychologists. I am just old enough to have studied psychology at a time when those brass instruments were still around, albeit in glass cases lining the walls of the laboratory. Brass instruments were used to measure such phenomena as the fatigue your finger suffered as you tapped it over three hundred fifty-eight times; after you'd had a bit of cane sugar, the psychologist would watch to see the effects on the tapping. If he was very venturesome, he might record the subject's verbal response, though there was no brass instrument to help him in that case. The brass instrument psychologists are with us still, though the instrumentation has changed. Cognitive psychologists carry out their investigations in a clinical atmosphere and feed their data to hungry computers; it could be that psycholinguists wear white coats as they set about discovering the secrets of how the mental encyclopedia is organized by asking such questions as, "What bird is most typical?" The new brass instrument psychologists, like the old, are concerned with what can be factored, plotted, and quantified, and that does not include the things we want to know about—the composing process or the writer's mind or modes of learning and their relationship to kinds of writing.

Our most important ally in rejecting positivism is C. S. Peirce, the philosopher who first conceptualized the structure and function of the sign and invented semiotics (including the term itself). Peirce had an amused contempt for psychologists, who were, in the main, ignorant of logic. He scorned the notion that the study of meaning was of a kind with the study of natural phenomena. In one of his calmer moments, he declared: "Every attempt to import into psychics the conceptions proper to physics has only led those who made it astray."

And, to conclude this short list of allies, there is I. A. Richards, who memorably wrote in *Speculative Instruments:* "The Linguistic Scientist . . . does not yet have a conception of the language which would make it respectable. He thinks of it as a code and has not yet learned that it is an organ—the supreme organ of the mind's self-ordering growth." △ Note the "yet": Dr. Richards, who died last year at 86, always included it in even the gloomiest of his assessments of the state of rhetoric. Our field continues to suffer incursions of those who have no intention of conceiving language as "the supreme organ of the mind's self-ordering growth" and I am not yet sure that we should emulate his patience.

The reason for impatience is simply that we might very well lose the advantage that the novel effort to think about mind could give us. Unless we think philosophically about thinking, what's likely to happen with *mind* is what has already happened with *process:* it will be used and manipulated within the framework of positivist assumptions and thus will not help us develop a pedagogy appropriate to teaching the composing process. To be able to use mind as a speculative instrument, we will have to become authentic philosophers—and quick.

If we are to avail ourselves of that incomparable resource, the minds of our students, we will have to know what we're looking for, to have some philosophically sound idea of the power the mind promises. I believe that for teachers of composition, such a philosophy of mind is best thought of as a theory of imagination. If we can reclaim imagination as the forming power of mind, we will have the theoretical wherewithal for teaching composition as a mode of thinking and a way of learning.

Reclaiming the imagination is necessary because the positivists have consigned it to something called "the affective domain," in contradistinction to "the cognitive domain." You can see the false philosophy at work there, importing conceptions appropriate to neurology and biochemistry into psychics: certainly, there are areas and domains in the brain, but to use the term *domain* about modes of mental operation is to create the same kind of confusion as when the word *code* is used to designate both linguistic form and brain function. The false philosophy cannot account for imagination as a way of knowing or a means of making meaning because it understands imagination as ancillary or subordinate, not as fundamental and primordial. Imagination has famously been defined as "the living power and prime agent of all human perception."[△]Coleridge here, as in so many other instances, is our best guide in developing a philosophy of rhetoric. (Condescension to him on the part of the New Rhetoricians is ridiculous and the allegation that those who believe as he did in the natural powers of mind—"vitalists," we've been called—are therefore opposed to method is an ignorant and self-serving charge.) The imagination is the shaping power: perception works by forming— finding forms, creating forms, recognizing forms, interpreting forms. Let me read you what Rudolf Arnheim, in his superb book *Visual Thinking,* lists as the operations involved in perception: "active exploration, selection, grasping of essentials, simplification, abstraction, analysis and synthesis, completion, correction, comparison, problemsolving, as well as combining, separating, putting in context." Doesn't that sound like an excellent course in writing?

To think of perception as *visual thinking* helps make the case for observation in the composition classroom, not for the sake of manufacturing spurious "specifics" and vivid detail about nothing much, but because perception is the mind in action. Thinking begins with perception; the point is nicely caught in the title of R. L. Gregory's book on perception, *The Intelligent Eye.* A journal of observations—the "dialectical notebook" I've described in *Forming/Thinking/Writing* in which students record observations and observe their observations— affords students the experience of mastery because it exercises pow-

ers we do not have to teach, the natural power of forming in *percep-*
tion and the natural power of *conception*, concept formation, which
in so many ways is modeled on the activities of "the intelligent eye."
Observation of observation becomes the model of thinking about
thinking, of "interpreting our interpretations" (Kenneth Burke),△ of
"arranging our techniques for arranging" (I. A. Richards). The consciousness represented in such circular formulations is not *self* consciousness but an awareness of the dynamic relationship of the *what*
and the *how,* of the reflexive character of language, of the dialectic of
forming. The consciousness of consciousness, which is encouraged by
looking and looking again, is at the heart of any critical method.

Once we give some thought to imagination, "the living power and
prime agent of all human perception," we can see how it is that visualizing, making meaning by means of mental images, is the paradigm of all acts of mind: *imagining* is forming par excellence, and it
is therefore the emblem of the mind's power. Students who learn to
look and look again, to observe and to observe their observations, are
discovering powers they have not always known are related in any way
to the business of writing. If we trust "the intelligent eye," we can
teach our students to find in perception an ever-present model of the
composing process; they will thereby be reclaiming their own imaginations.

Shaping is as important an emblem as visualizing of that forming
which is the work of the active mind. The artist at work—especially
the sculptor—is surely the very image of imagination as the creation
of form, though artists often prefer to speak of their creative activity
as a matter of finding form: Michelangelo famously spoke of liberating the form in the stone. The popular doctrine of art as, simply, the
"expression" of "emotion" leaves out of account forming, shaping,
and thus cannot contribute to a theory of imagination. As an antidote,
let me quote a passage from the autobiography of Barbara Hepworth,
the British sculptor: "My left hand is my thinking hand. The right is
only a motor hand. This holds the hammer. The left hand, the thinking hand, must be relaxed, sensitive. The rhythms of thought pass
through the fingers and grip of this hand into the stone." I like the
echo in Mrs. Langer's title, *Mind: An Essay on Human Feeling,* of Dame
Barbara's phrases, "my thinking hand" and "rhythms of thought,"
and I leave it to you to consider the implications of the fact that neither the philosopher nor the artist considers it paradoxical to speak
of thinking and feeling as a single activity of forming. (And I leave it
to you to consider that both are women.)

That single activity of forming can be carried out in two modes, and
no theory of imagination can be sound which does not recognize

them both. What we call them is a matter of some interest since our
pedagogy will be guided, sometimes surreptitiously, by what we take
as the implications of the terms. I have been arguing that the positivist differentiation of cognitive and affective is wrongheaded and
misleading: indeed, it is the root cause of the widespread failure to
get from so-called personal writing to so-called expository writing,
from informal to formal composition—even from so-called "pre-writing" to writing. This false differentiation creates an abyss, which rhetoricians then spend their time trying to bridge by scotch-taping
together topics and places and modes of discourse, by one or another
innovative strategy, heuristic model, or methodological breeches
buoy. A theory of imagination can help us solve the problem of the
abyss by removing the problem: there is no abyss if composing is conceived of as forming and forming as proceeding by means of abstraction. I will conclude by suggesting how we can differentiate two
modes of abstraction, but let me note briefly why it is that current
rhetorical theory manifests no understanding of forming as abstraction.

That fact must be correlated with the fact that though it's defunct
elsewhere, General Semantics is alive and kicking in the midst of any
assembly of rhetoricians. For General Semantics, abstraction is the
opposite of reality: Cow[1], Cow[2], Cow[3] are real, but *cow* or *cows* are not
real; they are words and they are "abstract." Now, General Seman-
ticists have never understood that Laura, Linda, Louise—all cows of
my acquaintance—are also abstract: the smellable, kickable, lovable,
milkable cow is there: it is recalcitrant, in Kenneth Burke's sense of
that term and the dairy farmer's; it is part of the triadicity of the sign
relationship, in Peirce's terms; but this actual cow, this cow as *event*,
as Whitehead would say, is known to us in the form provided by the
intelligent eye—and the intelligent ear and the intelligent nose. That
form—that percept—is a primordial abstraction.[△] Abstraction is not
the opposite of reality but our means of making sense of reality in
perception and in all that we do with symbolic forms.

Forming is a single activity of abstraction: once we have the genus,
we can then develop the definition dialectically by recognizing the
two kinds of abstraction. There is the *discursive* mode, which proceeds
by means of successive generalization, and the *nondiscursive* or *presen-
tational* mode, which proceeds by means of "direct, intensive insight."
These are Mrs. Langer's terms; they derive from Cassirer and they
are, I think, both flexible and trustworthy. The discursive mode is familiar because it is what rhetoric chiefly describes: generalization is
at the heart of all discourse, and of course it is central to concept formation. But it is not the only mode of abstraction: we do not dream

or perceive or create works of art by generalizing. One of the chief reasons that composition theory is stymied is the dependence on a brass instrument manufactured by General Semantics, *the ladder of abstraction*. Rhetoricians continually use it to explain how we climb from the positive earth to the dangerous ether of concept. But it's that metaphoric ladder itself that's dangerous. We could rename it *the ladder of degrees of generality* to avoid the misleading notion that all abstraction proceeds by means of generalizing, but the ladder metaphor is inappropriate even to the generalizing central to concept formation, because, as Vygotsky points out, conceptualizing is "a movement of thought constantly alternating in two directions":[△] only Buster Keaton could handle that ladder!

When we see a chair, we do not do so by a process of conscious generalizing; when the artist creates or finds the form by means of which feelings and thoughts are to be represented, he (or she) does so not by generalizing but by symbolizing insight—by *imagining*. In perception and in art, forming is primarily nondiscursive, but the point should be made explicitly that both modes of abstraction function in all acts of mind. We can save the term *imagination* to name only the nondiscursive, but having reclaimed it, I think there is much to be said for using it as a speculative instrument to focus on what it means to say that composing is a process of making meaning. The emblems I've discussed—"the intelligent eye" and "the thinking hand"—are images of imagination in the larger sense, that is, as the forming power of mind.

Learning the Uses of Chaos

It is, perhaps, a measure of our sophistication that we English teachers can boldly set about discussing the topic *learning to write,* identifying an issue in nonpretentious terms while realizing that it isn't as simple a matter as it sounds. Holding a conference on the topic suggests an awareness that learning to write is a matter for theoretical consideration, not just recipe swapping; that the difficulties we must confront in teaching students how to write deserve something other than high-minded expressions of dismay. We need theory in order to find out what can be done about teaching composition and to define what it is we think we are doing. No theoretical premise is of greater importance to all the new rhetorics, from "free writing" to tagmemics, than that composing is a process; however, this idea, which is already on the way to becoming conventional wisdom, is not helping us as it should. That is to say, the idea that there is not just *composition* but *composing* is becoming dogma, an idea being handed on to teachers and students alike before the implications it might have for pedagogy and course design have been explored or understood.

What does it mean to say that composing is a process? Why is it important that, at all levels of development and in all grades, students of writing should understand that composing is a process? How do we design courses—sequences of assignments—which can make that understanding something other than received dogma? For unless composing as a process is what we actually teach, not just what we proclaim, the idea cannot be fruitful. In many instances, the language of the new rhetoric is used when there is no correspondingly new attitude towards what we are teaching, to say nothing of how we are teaching it. There may be talk of "pre-writing," but the term is misleading if it is taken to mean getting a thesis statement. (I have seen a writing lab manual for tutors that defines pre-writing as a matter of learning to outline.) A textbook that exhorts students in the first chapter to carry through discovery procedures and in the second discusses the rhetorical modes as they were defined in the eighteenth century has not encouraged students to understand the relationship of earlier and later phases of composing.

A paper read at the annual conference of the Canadian Council of Teachers of English, Carleton University (Ottawa), May, 1979. Published in the collection of conference papers, *Reinventing the Rhetorical Tradition.*

again, watching how the "it" changes. In my view, from my per-
ive, *interpretive paraphrase* is another name for the composing
ss itself. It is the means by which meanings are hypothesized,
fied, developed, modified, discarded, or stabilized. And, fur-
ore, it is the only way I know to teach students how to edit their
ositions. Interpretive paraphrase enacts the dialogue that is at
eart of all composing: a writer is in dialogue with his various
and with his audience. And here is where the classroom hour
tively help us. The composition classroom ought to be a place
the various selves are heard and an audience's response is
—listened to and responded to. Language is an exchange: we
what we've said and what can be understood from it when we
response; we come to know what we mean when we hear what
. It is this critical, reflexive character of language that allows us
k about thinking. Learning to write involves us all in many such
us circles whereby we interpret our interpretations.
rpretive paraphrase—continually asking, "How does it change
aning if I put it this way?"—is, of course, the principal method
critical inquiry, but its importance for us in the composition
om is that it teaches students to see relationships and to dis-
hat that is what they do with their minds. It does not seem so
n: isolation and absurdity, not connectedness and meaningful-
re for our students the characterizing qualities of most expe-
Perhaps it's time to stop when one reaches the point of huge
gical generalization, but I think that this one is true; it is, after
y another way of speaking of the alienation that is recognizably
k of our era. If we can make the composition classroom a fo-
culture circle, a theatre, a version of Tolstoy's armchair
with children questioning, talking, and arguing—if the com-
classroom is the place where dialogue is the mode of making
g, then we will have a better chance to dramatize not only the
language itself changes with the meanings we make from it
its powers are generative and developmental, but also that
indispensable and unsurpassable means of reaching others
ming communities with them. The ability to speak is innate,
uage can only be realized in a social context. Dialogue, that
, is essential to the making of meaning and thus to learning
The chief use of chaos is that it creates the need for that dia-

It is not instructive to talk about "the composing process" unless
we have a conception of the kind of process writing is—or, at least,
the kind of process it is not. Thus writing is *not* like cooking a particular dish; writing may resemble, at one stage or another, some
phase of, say, making a cream sauce, but it is not sequential or "linear"; it is not measurement, followed by amalgamation and transformation. An analogy for writing that is based on culinary experience
would have to include ways of calculating the guests' preferences, as
well as ways of determining what's on the shelf—the cook's and the
grocer's—and what's in the purse. Nor is the composing process like
playing games or developing various motor skills. Such analogies
leave out of account language, or they conceive of it in mechanistic
or merely behavioral terms. But language is not merely a tool; it is
not a set of counters to be moved about nor a set of conventions to
be manipulated in order to express one or another idea. We don't
have ideas that we put into words; we don't think of what we want to
say and then write. In composing, we make meanings. We find the
forms of thought by means of language, and we find the forms of language by taking thought. If we English teachers are to understand
composing as the kind of process it is, we will need a philosophy of
language that can account for this dialectic of forming. A hopeful sign
that this is beginning to happen is that English teachers are beginning
to study Vygotsky, a developmental psychologist who knew that language and thought do not bear one another a sequential relationship,
but that they are simultaneous and correlative.

I believe we can best teach the composing process by conceiving of
it as a continuum of making meaning, by seeing writing as analogous
to all those processes by which we make sense of the world. It is generally a surprise to students to learn that writing has anything in common with anything else they have ever done—and for the very good
reason that, as it has generally been taught them, it has indeed nothing much to do with anything they have ever done. But writing,
taught as a process of making meanings, can be seen to be like taking
in a happening, forming an opinion, deciding what's to be done, construing a text, or reading the significance of a landscape. Thinking,
perceiving, writing are all acts of composing: any composition course
should insure that students learn the truth of this principle, that making meanings is the work of the active mind and is thus within their
natural capacity.

Meanings don't just happen: we make them; we find and form
them. In that sense, all writing courses are creative writing courses.
Learning to write is learning to do deliberately and methodically with
words on the page what we do all the time with language. Meanings

don't come out of the air; we make them out of a chaos of images, half-truths, remembrances, syntactic fragments, from the mysterious and unformed. The most useful slogan for the composition course—along with "how do I know what I mean 'till I hear what I say?"—is *ex nihilo nihil fit:* out of nothing, nothing can be made. When we teach pre-writing as a phase of the composing process, what we are teaching is not how to get a thesis statement but the generation and uses of chaos; when we teach revision as a phase of the composing process, we are teaching just that—reseeing the ways out of chaos.

Our students, because they are language animals, because they have the power of naming, can generate chaos; they can find ways out of chaos because language creates them. Language itself is the great heuristic. Any name implies generalization; any cluster of names implies classification; any classification implies statement. As Kenneth Burke says, to name something *A* is to declare simultaneously that it is not *not-A*. △ All rhetorical functions can be derived from that most profound of linguistic facts, that words, in Vygotsky's formulation, come into being as verbal generalizations. It is the *discursive* character of language, its tendency to "run along," to be syntactical, which brings thought along with it. It is the discursive, generalizing, forming power of language that makes meanings from chaos.

Students can learn to write by learning the uses of chaos, which is to say, rediscovering the power of language to generate the sources of meaning. Our job is to design sequences of assignments that let our students discover what language can do, what they can do with language. Kenneth Koch got poetry out of his youngsters because he gave them syntactic structures to play with; Sylvia Ashton-Warner's "key vocabulary" became what she called "the captions of the dynamic life itself"; Paulo Freire's "generative words" provided the means by which the peasants in his literacy classes—"culture circles"—could name the world. Our students can learn to write only if we give them back their language, and that means playing with it, working with it, using it instrumentally, making many starts. We want them to learn the truth of Gaston Bachelard's observation that "in the realm of mind, to begin is to know you have the right to begin again." Our students cannot learn the uses of chaos if we continue to make assignments appropriate not to these beginnings but to the final phases of the composing process. Beginnings, for instance, should never be graded: identifying mistakes is irrelevant when we are teaching making a start at the process of making meanings.

Now, chaos is scary: the meanings that can emerge from it, which can be discerned taking shape within it, can be discovered only if students who are learning to write can learn to tolerate ambiguity. It is

to our teacherly advantage that the mind do[es] other hand, we have to be alert to the fact th[at] rived at too quickly, the possibility of oth[er] abruptly foreclosed. What we must realize o[r] matically evident to our students is what I. A[.] he calls ambiguities "the hinges of thought."

Learning to write is a matter of learning [to] learning that the making of meaning is a [deter]mined by perspective and context. Meanin[g] about them; statements and events, significa[nces] can mean different things to different pe[ople] Meanings are not prebaked or set for all [time] found, formed, and reformed. Even dicti[onaries] that is a brand new discovery for most stud[ents] history. How we see something—a relatio[nship] idea or object, or between two words or sta[tements] experience, and on our purposes, our persp[ect]ing from." We know reality not directly but [by the meanings] we make. (The role of critical thinking is, o[f course, to re]vise those meanings.) What we know, we [know as per]ceptual or conceptual. We see relationship[s in a] field of other relationships: as a text has a [context] and objects have a "context of situation," [a statement has a context of situa]tion. It is the nature of signifiers to be u[nstable, polyse]mous, ambiguous, until perspective and [context ... I] consider it the most important advance [when a student] moves from "Webster tells us . . ." to "w[hat it means de]pends on how you look at it." *It depends*[: that is to say,] *ex nihilo nihil fit.*

For students to discover that ambi[guities are "the hinges of] thought," we surely will have to move f[rom the kinds of ques]tions that we inscribe in the margins of [their papers, questions] to student readers: "What do you mean[?" and "What are you] trying to say?" Those are not critically u[seful] substantial responses or "I-thought-th[at . . ."] on occasion, students simply cast their [...] focus on the shifting character of meanin[g with perspective] and context, and we can do so by rais[ing such questions as] "How does it change your meaning if y[ou ...] thor is saying *X*, how does that go with [...] the preceding chapter—or stanza?" "W[hat does A mean] in the light of passage *B*?" Students lea[rn that ambiguities are "the] hinges of thought" as they learn to fo[rm ...]

say i[...]
spec[...]
proc[...]
iden[...]
ther[...]
com[...]
the [...]
selve[...]
can a[...]
wher[...]
hear[...]
know[...]
get a[...]
we sa[...]
to thi[...]
unvic[...]

Inte[...]
the m[...]
of all [...]
classr[...]
cover [...]
to the[...]
ness, [...]
rience[...]
sociol[...]
all, on[...]
the m[...]
rum, [...]
aswarr[...]
positio[...]
meanin[...]
fact th[...]
and th[...]
it is th[...]
and fo[...]
but lan[...]
is to sa[...]
to write[...]
logue.

Discovering Limits

Our panel topic is rather less compelling than the convention slogan. The idea of the human mind as the supreme resource is more inspiriting than the notion of one more innovative this or that, and certainly the concept of mind is no more problematic than the notion of "students with learning and language difficulties." Of course, some difficulties are more difficult than others: you can't expect to teach someone to read a paragraph if he can't read a sentence, or a sentence if he can't read words, or words if he can't construe letters or letter groups. And yet that is not to say that we teach reading by teaching the alphabet. I realize that it is casuistry of a sort to stretch the idea of difficulty, but I do want to claim that "students with language and learning difficulties" is a pretty fair description of students entering college. If our freshmen were not burdened with such difficulties, if they encountered no such difficulties, we would not have to labor to teach them to write coherently, to read critically, and to think cogently. I believe that what is good for the best and brightest is essential for students who have difficulties. Those we used to call slow learners need the freedom and the opportunities we trouble to offer our prize students. And, in turn, what is important and worthwhile for disadvantaged students will prove to be useful and valuable for the good readers and the practiced writers.

If we tap this supreme resource, the minds of our students, we will find powerful, profoundly rooted capacities that cannot be identified solely in quantifiable terms and quotients, but which we can learn to identify and train. Mind in this sense is not reducible to what has been called "intelligence" by psychologists looking for something to measure; intelligence is a culture-bound concept as mind is not. Socrates demonstrated his method not with the head of the class but with an illiterate slave boy. Montessori's first school in Rome was for children who had been certified by the state as cretini—morons. It was Brazilian peasants who gained the experience of freedom in attending Paulo Freire's literacy classes. The point from which these great teachers of the disadvantaged begin is the mind's operation, the human mind in action. Now our convention slogan—Let the Minds of

A paper read at the Conference on College Composition and Communication convention, St. Louis, March, 1975. Issued as a cassette recording by NCTE along with other papers from the panel, "Innovative Composition Courses for Students with Learning and Language Difficulties."

Our Students Be the Supreme Resource—is a sound point of departure for the composition teacher because composing *is* the mind in action! The composing process that involves writing down words requires the same acts of mind as the composing process by which we make sense of the world. Jargon like "nonverbal communication" masks the fact that all perception, all communication, takes place in a world built by language. Man is the language animal and the operation of his mind is a linguistic operation, whether words are spoken or not.

It's very refreshing to have the NCTE and its affiliates publicly declaring an interest in mind. It's a welcome change from the pseudoscientific concepts we've grown used to: verbal behavior, communication skills, input and feedback, encoding and decoding. But we should be on our guard against becoming ensnared in the problem of defining what "mind" is; and, be warned, this is the game that psychologists and philosophers who deplore what they call "mentalism" like to play and win. (They do not equally enjoy the game of deciding what is "behavior.") Laboring under the delusion that they are being "scientific," English teachers have all too often asked such questions as, "What *is* creativity?" "What *is* communication?" You may remember that the theme song of the Dartmouth Conference was, "What *is* English?" That kind of questioning gets us nowhere; it is neither pragmatic nor scientific. J. Robert Oppenheimer explains in discussing this misconception of scientific inquiry that Einstein did not ask, "What is a clock?" Rather, he framed questions about how we would measure time over immense distances. We will have to learn to ask not "what *is* mind?" but "what happens when we use our minds in writing that is comparable to what happens when we make sense of the world?" and "what happens in the composing process?" Josephine Miles has entitled one discussion of composition, "What Do We Compose?" and another, "How What's What in the English Language?" Such questions as these will help us develop a working concept of mind. A good name for the mind in action is *imagination:* Coleridge called the imagination "the prime agent of all human perception."△ That is an epistemological concept that English teachers should make their own. I suggest, then, that this panel topic could be restated as follows: *Teaching the composing process by liberating the imagination.*

I will try in this talk to suggest what that might mean when we set about developing "innovative composition courses for students with learning and language difficulties."

The one sure principle of composition, as of imagination, is that nothing comes of nothing; *ex nihilo nihil fit:* nothing can be made from nothing. Recent textbooks in composition have begun to show signs of an interest in the subject of invention, though the process seems still unclear, if not misconceived. The first use of language that a student of composition has to learn, I think, is in the generation of chaos. If we don't begin there, we falsify the composing process because composition requires choosing all along the way, and you can't choose if there are no perceived alternatives: chaos is the source of alternatives. If we are unwilling to risk chaos, we won't have provided our students with the opportunity to discover that ambiguities are, as I. A. Richards has said, "the hinges of thought." △

Once we encourage the generation of chaos, however, we are morally as well as pedagogically bound to present very carefully the ways of emerging from it. Happily, the process of generating chaos provides, itself, the means of emerging from chaos by making something of it. I like to demonstrate how this can be so by having everybody in class name what he sees, what comes to mind in response to, say, a photograph from Steichen's *Family of Man,* with everyone writing down everybody else's word. Twice around the room and there begin to be repetitions; names group themselves like so many birds flocking; three times around the room and the blackboard is full, the sheet of paper covered. (That can illustrate the psychological advantage of having a full page rather than an empty sheet, and it suggests that chaos might be better than nothing.) The chaos begins to take shape: classifying, which is organized comparing, proceeds without the stimulus of prefabricated, loaded "study questions." The primary compositional modes of amalgamation and elimination begin to operate. All this happens more or less without guidance, though if there is a roadblock it can be exploded by asking the only study question anyone ever needs: How does who do what?

The reason that this natural ordering process takes place in the very act of naming is that the mind naturally abstracts. The human mind—but that is a redundancy: the mind naturally orders by comparing and differentiating. (That process of selection apparently goes on in the retinal cells at an electrochemical level.) We see in terms of classes and types; everything we see is seen as an example of a kind of thing. Perception is contingent on the mind's capacity for analogizing.

My point is that we do not have to teach our students *how* to abstract but *that* they abstract. What we do teach is how to listen in on the dialogue in progress when they are looking and classifying in the act of perception. That dialogue is thinking; it is dialectical. *Dialogue* and *dialectic* are cognate: learning to see what you're looking at really means learning to question and questioning is the life of thought.

The composing process, I think we can say, is empowered from beginning to end by the dialectic of question and answer. The way to
bring this fact to life for our students is to encourage writing from the
start—not topic sentences and thesis statements of course, but lists,
class names, questions, and tentative answers and new questions.
This "pre-writing" is writing; a cluster of names is a protoparagraph;
a cluster of clusters is a nascent composition.

To suggest the formal nature of this emergence from chaos I used
to employ rather elaborate schematic devices—bits and pieces of
signs from symbolic logic, tagmemic grids, flowcharts, and so on, but
the trouble is—and it's not a problem peculiar to students with learning and language difficulties—the relationship of the sign to its referent is easily misconceived and the signs themselves become the focus
of interest. I've collected pre-writing sheets covered with diagrams
and charts that bore no relationship to the words employed, with
whatever concepts might have emerged totally obscured by a mass of
lines and boxes. Students have submitted first drafts with the appearance of sketches for a painting of the Martyrdom of St. Sebastian, because they were under the impression that "she likes arrows." Just as
we can't teach reading by simply teaching the alphabet, so we can't
teach composition by laying out unintelligible floor plans.

The alternative, I've come to believe, is a line drawn down the middle of the page. Overschematizing is no more conducive to the definition of choices than the formal outline, but opposition as an
organizing concept, one which has been borrowed from linguistics by
structuralists in all disciplines, can be very helpful to us in teaching
composition. Opposition is a highly generalized term covering juxta-
positions, alignments, echoes as well as antitheses, opposites, and
counterpoint. Figure and ground are in opposition; beginning and
end are in opposition; character and plot are in opposition. The ends
of a scale and the banks of a river represent two kinds of opposition.
It is a concept to think with; it is quickly grasped by all students because it is a name for what they are already doing when they judge
size and distance and degrees of all kinds. Opposition is the principle
informing every phrase they utter, every step they take. I have seen
many a student weighed down with learning and language difficulties
come to life smiling at the brand new discovery that composing has
anything whatsoever to do with anything else he has ever done. Exercises in forming and developing oppositions not only provide the
steps out of chaos; they also become the means of discovering that
composing is a dialectical process: it starts and stops and starts again;
it can proceed in circles; it is tentative, hypothetical, and recapitula-
tive. Our students can learn, when they use the concept of opposition

to think with, that composing means naming, differentiating, comparing, classifying, selecting, and thus defining; that composing means getting it together. Isn't that what we want to teach them?

"A composition is a bundle of parts": that is Josephine Miles' very useful definition.[△] Composing means identifying the parts and bundling them; in the composing process we recreate wholes by establishing relationships between the parts. All our innovative powers in designing composition courses should go to assuring that writing is involved at all stages of this process. The textbooks that warn glibly or sternly, "Don't begin to write until you know what you want to say," ought to be returned to the publishers. The motto of every composition course should be, "How do I know what I mean until I hear what I say?" I'm very fond of that old chestnut; here is a more weighty formulation: I. A. Richards, recalling Plato as usual, declares that "dialectic is the continuing audit of meaning."[△]

Some experienced writers can keep track of what they are saying in that interior dialogue and thus can audit their meanings in their heads, but students with learning and language difficulties should write it down, continually. In that way they can learn to recognize the interior dialogue and keep the dialectic going. Writing at all stages of composition brings to full consciousness the experience of the mind at work, the imagination in action. Writing can counter the notion that ideas fall from heaven, that some people just "have" them and others just don't. Writing at all stages is a way of seeing ideas develop. We want to assure that the student continually discovers that it is his mind that is giving form to chaos; that his language is ordering chaos; that his imagination is just what Coleridge tells him it is, "a shaping spirit."

We encourage that experience of writing and thereby the auditing of meaning by providing linguistic forms, syntactical and rhetorical structures, not for imitation but for use as speculative instruments. Forms are not cookie cutters superimposed on some given, rolled-out reality dough; forms are not alien structures that are somehow made appropriate to "what you want to say." Forms are our means of abstracting; or, rather, forming *is* abstracting. Abstracting is what the mind does; abstracting, forming is the work of imagination. But this can rapidly become more interesting as metaphysics than as pedagogy. I suggest that we think of forms by considering what they do: they provide limits. "A poet," in Allen Tate's definition, "is a man willing to come under the bondage of limitations—if he can find them." Limits make choice possible and thus free the imagination.

Consider what Kenneth Koch calls the "poetry idea" in his experimental writing assignments: that's the conception of form we need.

Koch gets poetry out of his third graders by making forms available to them. He doesn't say, "Tell me what it would feel like to be a geranium in the sunny window." He reads poetry with them and then offers a form that can answer to their experience, their perceptions. "I used to be a_____, but now I am a_____." Or he says, "Talk to something that isn't a person; ask it a question":

> Dog, where did you get that bark?
> Dragon, where do you get that flame?
> Kitten, where did you get that meow?
> Rose, where did you get that red?
> Bird, where did you get those wings?

At first, Koch was apologetic about his dependence on form, but he soon came to see that it was the limits the forms provided that allowed the kids to discover their feelings and to shape their insights.

This conception of form as limit-providing structure can help us see more clearly that throughout the composing process the writer is engaged in limiting: selecting and differentiating are ways of limiting; we limit when we compare, classify, amalgamate, and discard; defining is, by definition, a setting of limits. How we limit is how we form. It is an idea that can help us develop sequences in our innovative composition courses. I. A. Richards has said that all learning depends upon a sequence of "partially parallel tasks." Any composition course should be organized so that learning something about syntactical structure prepares for learning something about paragraph structure. As it is, the new rhetorics every year lay out what the old rhetorics have been explaining since the eighteenth century; that, for instance, there are three modes of writing, called "exposition," "description," and "narrative." Do we create the occasions for our students to discover that argument can take the form of narrative, as in fable? that there is a logic of metaphor, in Robert Frost's sonnets as well as in Donne's? that description and analysis are both essential to definition? How many advanced composition courses incorporate so-called creative writing? It's time our composition courses were themselves composed, that we ask of them unity, coherence, and emphasis.

I have quoted I. A. Richards throughout because he has thought more deeply than anyone I know about the pedagogical implications of a philosophy of mind that stresses the shaping power of imagination. If we let the minds of our students be the supreme resource, it means we will be recognizing that language is "the supreme organ of the mind's self-ordering growth."[△] It is language—not vocabulary or a sophisticated repertory of syntactical structures, though we can work on this; not the students' very own language and not the teacher's—it is language as a form-finder and form-creator that makes possible naming and opposition and definition; it is the power of language as a form that creates order from chaos; it is language that frames the dialectic, limits the field, forms the questions and answers, starts the dialectic and keeps it going; it is language that makes choice possible. That is why we can say that to learn to compose is to discover both the power of the mind and the meaning of human freedom.

Writing and Editing

In the shouting match currently in progress, the hostile claim that "students can't write" is answered by the strident assertion to the contrary. A little casuistry is always helpful in such circumstances; I think we can split writing into composing and editing and give half a cookie to each side: no, students don't know how to edit; yes, students can compose: they are born composers and compose they do, whether they know it or not. I want to claim in these remarks that a theory of composition can help us to understand that differentiation of composing and editing and how to make it work pedagogically.

In a recent seminar on the teaching of composition, I learned from my students who were almost all teachers with four, six, or twelve years experience, that writing in the junior and senior high schools of the Boston area is pretty much limited to *The Book Report* and its variants and a continuing review, semester after semester, of what is still called "grammar." Considering the evidence along with what publishers tell me about the character of manuscripts submitted and the subjects in focus at English conventions, I would guess that what is widely taught as "English Composition" is really editing. Nevertheless, after ten or twelve years of studying correct usage and the conventions of English grammar, those entering as college freshmen are not notably good editors.

One reason is, surely, that no student is going to care very much about learning correct usage, proper agreement, the mechanics of spelling and punctuation and capitalization unless he—or she—cares about the composition being edited. And that is not usually the state of affairs. Another reason is that editing requires a good ear, but the faulty constructions characteristic of our students' writing are there in the first place because they aren't recognized as errors. We may know how to teach the repair of a faulty sentence, once it is recognized, but we do not teach techniques for identifying errors. The symbols we scatter in the margins, the ones listed on the flyleaf of handbooks, keyed to explanatory passages, this red blood is the sign of the English teacher hard at work identifying errors students are then meant to correct. Sometimes the teacher makes both identification and correction of errors. But even the teacher's identification of errors and

This article appeared in a somewhat different form with the title "Composing Is Forming" in *Composition and Teaching*, #2.

the student's correction of them do not teach editing. Nothing can, in my opinion, unless students can themselves be taught techniques of identifying errors.

About the only advice we have on that score is for students to read their papers aloud, straight through. This is an almost worthless tactic, given the propensity of a writer reading his own work for becoming enchanted by the sound of his own voice. The evidence seems to be that interpretive paraphrase in one-to-one conferences is probably the best way to teach error identification and correction. Paraphrasing can bring a student to discover that in writing by the phrase he has failed to see that what he has already written controls in very particular ways the choices available to him as he goes on writing; he can learn that a sentence has, as it were, a will of its own. Interpretive paraphrasing is not a matter of answering the question, "What are you trying to say?" It's a matter of responding to the question, "How does it change your meaning if you put it this way?" That question can lead students who have studied sentence structure at some time in their school careers to locate mixed constructions, faulty agreements, and so forth. What we must aim for, however, is having the student-editor enact that conference dialogue on her own, identifying errors without the help of questions framed and focused by tutor or instructor.

The only tactic I've ever devised for teaching error identification is reading a paper backwards, sentence by sentence. It has always fascinated me that some students can do perfect workbook sheets and turn right around and write sentences in their own papers that make your teeth hurt. It occurred to me that if students could isolate their sentences so that they resembled those in a workbook, they could then locate the errors and edit their compositions more efficiently. Reading backwards focuses attention on the sentence as it is written rather than as a stand-in for what's intended. One of the chief things a writer has to learn is how to hear the difference between what he has intended to say and what he has in fact written. Sentences can be heard more clearly if they are isolated from context a bit: reading backwards, sentence by sentence, can effect this.

There is certainly a lot we have to learn about this matter of teaching editing to students whose auditory imagination is moribund, laid low by toneless public speech, spiritless conversation, and the virtually complete lack of an experience of hearing good prose read aloud expressively. One of the chief uses of a theory of composition should be to help us reclaim the auditory imagination, the capacity to hear form. The other day I was having a student work on interpretive paraphrases of this sentence:

Teachers judge the quality of the student's performance much
like that of the farmer's grading his beef.

And after four versions of the sentence, when she read the original
version aloud, the student, I'm happy to say, grimaced and said: "I
think I could hear the mistake if I tried to sing this sentence." I might
have let this pass as a pleasing whimsy except that I'd just been reading Clara Claiborne Park's account in *The Siege* of learning to communicate with her autistic daughter by means of singing certain phrases.
Also, I had recently heard a young friend talk about how he was using
the Kodaly method of teaching music to youngsters. I'm not quite
ready to teach syntax by means of eurythmic dancing or ritual chanting, but I am ready to read about how such methods are being used
to teach dyslexic students how to deal with print. And I am more than
ever convinced of the usefulness of students reading their interpretive paraphrases aloud.[1]

A theory of composition should remind us continually that the apprehension of linguistic form is analogous to the apprehension of all
other forms. Since learning to edit is in part learning to hear (virtually) the possible differences between the writer's intention and what
is conveyed by the words that have been set down on the page, it will
be useful if we can reclaim the imagination of auditory form—the apprehension of design and cadence, balance and structure—in sentences (actually) heard as they are read aloud. In short, editing
procedures are best carried out when the text is "foregrounded."[2]
Reading sentences in isolation from the sequence of which they are
a part and reading aloud a variety of paraphrases are the best ways
I know to emphasize their formal character.

But editing, as I began by claiming, is not an integral part of the
composing process, and we should not confuse it with revision, which
can, and I believe should, continue through the entire process: rewriting, like pre-writing, is writing. Separating composing and editing, realizing that each offers different pedagogical challenges, is simply
differentiating process and product; it does not mean a downgrading
of editing. I don't think we have to say, "Oh, don't bother about being correct! It's being free and creative that's important." (In fact, I
don't think very many people do say that, although there is a tendency to believe that so-called creative writing has nothing much in common with exposition.) We should rather say, "Don't bother about
being correct *at first,* when you're starting to write, and don't worry
about correcting until you've got a product."

What is not generally understood by many English teachers is that
procedures that are entirely appropriate to editing cannot be easily

adapted to composing and that it is hazardous to try. Furthermore, there is a confusion about what kind of directions and procedures are appropriate for which phases of the composing process itself. Textbooks still urge students not to write until they know what they want to say; teachers in all disciplines ask their students to outline before they begin writing, without understanding that writing can play a heuristic role. To ask students to begin their themes with a clear statement of purpose is, I think, a very misleading piece of advice. If you've already explained to them how to discover topics, to generate chaos and tolerate it in order to find out what their opinions are, to develop perspectives that will allow them to formulate definitions, then of course it's useful to remind them that they need to consider their audience, to ask themselves what their purpose is. But a thesis statement doesn't come first and it can't come first, unless we simply provide it. I recently shared a workshop with the head of a writing program who droned on all morning long about stating purposes, getting a thesis statement, so that students could then compare and contrast OR define OR describe. I asked him at the break where his students got the thesis statement, and he answered without a moment's hesitation: "I *GIVE* it to them!" Directing students to "get" a thesis statement, or giving one to them, is likely to encourage substanceless, directionless assertions, generally in the syntactical form of *the-cat-is-on-the-mat*, the kind of sentence that leads nowhere because the mind of the composer has not been engaged in its formulation.

A theory of composition that allows us to differentiate composing and editing can help us defend ourselves against mechanistic views of writing as a matter of developing somebody else's thesis statement according to rules that are of the same kind as those by which a first grader "draws" a clown by connecting one number and the next with lines. And by reminding us of what it means to say that composing is a process, it can encourage us to devise assignments appropriate to beginning stages, not just to the final stages of revision.

If we take as our chief theoretical principle the idea that composing is forming, then I think we can enjoy the experience of seeing how that idea can help us develop new kinds of writing assignments and rethink old favorites. Visual experience is certainly a commonplace in the composition classroom, but usually it is meant to provide topics or to serve a therapeutic purpose of making students "comfortable." But if we begin with a theory of perception as a means of making meaning—a construing, an interpreting—we can make it available as a model of composing.

A colleague of mine has been having her students keep journals of observation, and when she handed out natural objects to be observed for a week, one woman who'd taken a garlic bud remarked with a heavy sigh "I do NOT see how I'm going to be able to look at this thing for a week! How can I find something to say about it every day? How can I do this when it's not going to change?" After a week she was able to say, "No, it didn't change, but I did." Another student had decided to write about sand dollars. She had a collection of them and finding something to say wasn't going to be a problem, she thought. So she wrote Day 1, Day 2, Day 3, Day 4 . . . and she used up pretty much everything she knew about sand dollars so she decided to sacrifice one of her collection for the sake of Day 5 and break it to see what was inside. She tried to break it and she couldn't. Then she realized that in describing the sand dollar throughout Day 1, 2, 3, 4, she'd assumed as she had all along, that they were fragile and delicate; she discovered that they were tough, or at least that this specimen was. That's thinking, and in the course of following out the process of observing, in challenging the mind's disposition to form structures, writing gets written. And it seems to me that it's likely to be the kind of writing that's worth editing.

Notes

[1]Zoltan Kodaly, friend and colleague of Bela Bartok, developed a method of teaching children to sing based on identifying the rhythmic patterns of one or another culture's folk music. The principles are similar to those of eurythmics, developed by Emile Jaques-Dalcroze as a method of relating ear training to the response of the whole organism to musical rhythms. Like Maria Montessori and Tolstoy, these pedagogues have a great deal to teach us about composing as forming. See Part III.

[2]This term is popular among semioticians because of the current interest in the doctrines of the Russian formalists, but Kenneth Burke made the point long ago (1931) in the notes on form in his "Lexicon Rhetoricae." See *Counterstatement*, 2nd. ed. (Los Altos: Hermes Publications, 1953), pp. 124–30.

3. Instruments of Knowing

The conventional wisdom of rhetoricians, linguists, psycholinguists, and cognitive psychologists is that language is a means of communication. Of course it is, but in teaching the composing process what we chiefly need is a way of thinking about the sources of and the shaping of what we communicate. To understand the relationship of language and thought, we must begin with "the unit of meaning," as Vygotsky puts it. A theory of imagination can guide us in forming the concept of language in such a way that we can turn to account its heuristic powers: Language is fundamentally and primordially our means of making meaning. Language provides the forms which mediate knowing, the forms by means of which we make meaning, the forms which find forms. Once we see composing as a forming activity, the work of the active mind, we can teach writing more intelligently in the context of speaking and listening and reading.

Tolstoy, Vygotsky, and the Making of Meaning

When Leo Tolstoy undertook to teach the children of his newly emancipated serfs to read and write, he discovered a principle of education that keeps getting lost, forgotten, or set aside. Tolstoy discovered there at Yásnaya Polyána what Socrates first taught and what anyone who has won freedom from the conventional wisdom can find out—namely, that the form-finding and form-creating powers of the human mind are the teacher's chief ally, once they are engaged, and that until they are engaged, no genuine learning can happen.

Tolstoy learned to teach by trusting the powers of what he called "the uncorrupted soul," by recognizing the fidelity of the children to

Published in *College Composition and Communication*, October, 1978. Reprinted in *Composition and Its Teaching*, ed. Richard C. Gebhardt (1979).

"artistic truth." Although such language enchanted some of the great educators of the earlier years of our century, we may consider that, from our perspective, there is a great deal of romantic exaggeration in Tolstoy's account of what has been called "the deschooling of Yásnaya Polyána." But there is nevertheless as much to be gained from reading, "Who is to learn to write from whom? Are the peasant children to learn from us? Or, are we to learn from the peasant children?" as in a year's run of monographs, statistical studies, and the speculations of educational psychologists.[1] Despite all the differences between Tolstoy's situation and ours, between his beguiling little *muzhiks* and our students—disaffected and disenchanted when they are not disadvantaged—despite a world of difference and the passage of more than a century, the challenge we face is virtually the same that Tolstoy undertook to meet: the discrimination between sterile and generative pedagogies must be made; the grounds of trust between instructor and instructed must be discovered in common undertakings; the ways and means of liberating the mind's powers must be found.

Tolstoy tells us that he made his discovery only after he had, in his honesty, seen the failure of his other ways. He began, as so many do, with the notion that the simpleminded task is the best point of departure, the best basis for learning control of language. He initially assumed that a simple object in plain view is easy to describe analytically and that mastering that procedure would develop the basic skills, as it were, which could then be exploited. He began, like a good philosopher, with a table. The response to that assignment was dismaying:

> To our great surprise, these demands upon our pupils almost made them weep and, in spite of the aid afforded them by the teacher, they emphatically refused to write upon such themes, or, if they did write, they made the most incomprehensible and senseless mistakes in orthography, language, and meaning. (p. 288)

Tolstoy then offered his pupils "according to their inclination, exact, artistic, touching, funny, epic themes—and nothing worked." When the personal or relevant turned out to be no more inspiring a point of departure than the apparently simple—and how clearly the ticktock of modern pedagogical experimentation is represented in these alternatives!—Tolstoy "unexpectedly hit upon another method":

> The reading of the collection of Snegirév's proverbs has long formed one of my favorite occupations—enjoyments. For every proverb I imagine individuals from among the people and their

conflicts in terms of the proverb. . . . I always imagine a series of pictures, or stories, to fit the proverbs. Once, last winter, I forgot everything after dinner in reading Snegirév and even returned to school with the book. It was a lesson in the Russian language. "Well, write something on a proverb!" I said. (pp. 192ff)

The response was immediate: "What do you mean, 'on a proverb'? What is it? Tell us!" Tolstoy explained, and their interest momentarily waned; they thought the matter was beyond them. But when the master announced that *he* was going to write "on a proverb," the pupils were soon gathering around his chair, anxious to hear and to criticize and contribute. Tolstoy goes on to say,

> All were exceedingly interested. It was evidently new and absorbing to be present while composition was going on and to take part in the process, as nearly all of them did. . . . Their demands had so little of the accidental in them and were so definite that more than once I debated with them, only to give way. I was principally concerned with the demands of a regular structure and with an exact correspondence of the idea of the proverb to the story, while they, on the contrary, were only concerned about the demands of artistic truth.

Tolstoy's new pedagogy required him to provide a choice of themes, certain "literary devices"—heuristics, we might say—and guidance in "how to go about" composing—a method.[2] The imagination is liberated not by the teacher but by "the artistic quality of the themes." An explanation of why the proverbs worked to free the children's imagination is found in this passage in which Tolstoy is commenting on the failure of the assignment to describe simple objects:

> That which forms the favorite description of the schools—the so-called simple objects: pigs, pots, a table—turned out to be incomparably more difficult than whole stories taken from their memories. To the teacher the simplest and most general appears as the easiest, whereas for a pupil only the complex and living appears easy. (p. 289)

The proverbs were complex because they demanded interpretation and provoked interest. By definition, proverbs offer particular examples and general precepts in conjunction; seeing the relationship of the two is as much a lesson in concept formation as it is an opportunity to enjoy poetic form. The proverbs were living because they suggested images of life, both visual and kinetic. (Sémka tended to enact what he was writing; Fédka needed visual details to keep him going, justification for which he discussed with fellow-composer Tolstoy.) The proverbs provided, as any good assignment must, a bridge from the familiar to the unfamiliar; they allowed the children to exercise both the memory and the power of envisagement. Beginning with the proverbs assured that Tolstoy's new students would be actively engaged from the first in the making of meaning, and that is a process which, like the proverbs providing the point of departure, is "complex and living."

Instruction at Yásnaya Polyána took into account the truth that "the relation of the world to the idea and the formation of new ideas is such a complex, mysterious and tender process of the soul that every interference appears as a rude, clumsy force which retards the process of development" (p. 276). But Tolstoy believed that development for development's sake would mean sacrificing the harmony of all aspects of the child's being. The purpose of his method was, therefore, to offer guidance without interference: "It is my conviction that we cannot teach children in general and peasant children in particular to write and compose, especially to compose poetically. All that we can do is to teach them how to go about composition" (p. 222).

Tolstoy's long account of the composing of the story called "A Soldier's Life" is interspersed with comments about the mystery of the children's imaginative powers, but again and again he calls them *natural.* The children's procedures and achievements are awe-inspiring in the same way as all of Nature's works. Citing Rousseau, Tolstoy declares, "Our ideal is behind us, not before us. Education spoils; it does not correct men. The more a child is spoiled, the less he ought to be educated, the more liberty he needs" (p. 222). The pedagogical precept that we should "begin with where they are" is thus allied with the ancient philosophical principle that learning is remembering.

The notion that the teacher is only the facilitator of these innate powers is, probably, the most influential of Tolstoy's ideas on education. Thus when Sylvia Ashton-Warner (who speculates about what Tolstoy would make of what's happening in her infant room) states that she teaches "style, and only style," she is echoing her great predecessor.[3] Another term important for Sylvia Ashton-Warner—central to her own Key Vocabulary—is *organic.* It is a name and a concept that can gather up all that Tolstoy means by "the complex and living"; all that Tolstoy claims for the child's powers testifies to the faith in the organic. To conceive of education as a matter of growth and development, of instruction as nurture, of learning as a natural process of assimilation and accommodation is the philosophical foundation of an organic pedagogy whose aim it is to liberate the innate powers of the mind, to guide the natural bent.

Less familiar in Tolstoy's discussion of what we are to learn from the peasant children is the idea that composition is *conscious*. The claim that the children are conscious of what they are doing is one that Tolstoy makes rather defensively. He anticipates the skeptical responses of those readers who will say that the remarkable creations of the school at Yásnaya Polyána are accidental, if indeed they are not the product of Tolstoy's direction and editing:

> We shall be told: "You are yourself a writer, and, without knowing it, you have been helping the pupils along paths which cannot be prescribed as a rule for other teachers who are not authors themselves." (p. 219)

Tolstoy tries to forestall such criticism by an exaggerated deference to his fellow writers, Fédka and Sémka. In referring to the opening of a story he *had* written, he remarks that anyone with taste or the least amount of "artistic feeling" will "separate this page from the rest as he will take a fly out of the milk" (p. 193). The children's stories, Tolstoy insists, are *conscious* creations; one feels strongly, he says, the *conscious* power of the artists; the *consciousness* of the ideal of harmony, truth, beauty, and goodness is more powerful in the child than in the teacher. In the summary of his way of teaching "how to go about" composing, which he hesitantly calls a method, Tolstoy says that the work of composing consists in selecting, choosing, remembering, and not repeating or omitting—all conscious acts. Further, composing consists "in the ability to combine what follows with what precedes, all the while keeping in mind what is already written down . . . and, finally, in thinking and writing at the same time, without having one of these acts interfere with the other" (p. 223).

Nothing is needed more urgently in the current reassessment of what we think we have been doing in teaching composition than a critical inquiry into this concept of the simultaneity of thinking and writing, of the role of consciousness in composing. Tolstoy's description here is a useful point of departure for that inquiry because it reminds us that composing is both creative and critical and that it is an act of mind: it doesn't just happen; it's conscious. Composing is mysterious, but it isn't supernatural. I think that if we study the relationship of the *conscious* and the *natural* in composing, we will have made a good start towards making Tolstoy's discovery our own—learning, that is, how to trust the forming power of mind, what was once the *imagination*.

Of those who made the pilgrimage to Yásnaya Polyána—actually or metaphysically—Maria Montessori most deeply understood that the natural and the conscious aspects of learning were neither antithetical

nor sequential. "The Montessori Method" proceeds from the exhila-
rating assumption that pupils (and hers, from the Roman slums, were
considered by the state to be at the level of *cretini*) are gifted by Nature and that the chief function of the teacher is to guide the development of those natural powers. The relationship of the conscious
and the natural is defined in Montessori's concept of autodidacticism:
anything that is truly learned is what we teach ourselves. Natural gifts
are realized, brought to consciousness, in what she called a "prepared
environment." If Tolstoy's armchair was the first open classroom, the
second was created when Montessori unscrewed the desks from the
floor. The prepared environment, like Tolstoy's proverbs, assures
that children will encounter "the complex and living"—or is meant
to assure that happening. But any good idea can be ruined in practice,
and when authoritarians took over Montessori's method, seeing the
order that it encourages as structure to be superimposed, not as a
natural heuristic, they were in effect screwing the desks back into
place.

It's a history that should be written: what happens to genuinely innovative pedagogies when they are taken over by the pedestrian and
literal-minded. For our present purposes—to define the soul of Tolstoy's discovery—it would be useful to keep in mind the lesson of this
unwritten history, namely, that if the dynamic of an idea is disregard-
ed, the life will go out of it. Without the dialectic of the simple, which
is "complex and living"; of writing, which is simultaneous with thinking; of composing, which is at once natural and conscious, Tolstoy's
pedagogy is only another version of Romantic child-worship.

One way to keep that dialectic alive and well is to focus on the conception of language implicit in such statements as those I have quoted
above on the relationship of word and idea and of thinking and writing. Language is surely for Tolstoy what it is for I. A. Richards: "the
supreme organ of the mind's self-ordering growth."[4] Now it is impossible to entertain ideas of the heuristic power of language if it has
been reduced to a "communication skill." The concept of verbal behavior has been substituted for that of the making of meaning, and
if that is not the cause of all our woe, it is evil sufficient unto the day.[5]
To develop an organic conception of language requires recognizing
that word and idea are dialectically related and that the place to begin
considering them both is "the unit of meaning."

That phrase is from Lev Vygotsky's *Thought and Language*, published (and promptly suppressed) in the USSR seventy years or so
after the appearance of Tolstoy's articles on the school at Yásnaya Polyána, and now, happily, gaining recognition not only among Soviet
psychologists but also among teachers of English. The influence it

might exert could be a powerful counterweight to the linguistics we have tried to make our own, since most linguists, involved as they are with "structures," have little interest in meaning; and those who do, conceive of it in narrowly positivist and operational terms. And it will be a new experience for English teachers to read a psychologist writing about language who understands the heuristic character of language, the natural gift possessed by poet and peasant alike but not by anthropoid computers or cybernetic chimpanzees.

In his article on the method of studying language and thought, Vygotsky argues that meaning is analogous to the molecule and the cell; it is the unit that retains the properties of the whole. It seems to me that in the following passage we have virtually a gloss on Tolstoy's account of what happened when he "unexpectedly hit upon another method":

> A word always refers not to some single object, but to a whole group or whole class of objects. Therefore, each word is a hidden generalization; each word already generalizes.... The meaning of a word is above all a generalization. But generalization, one can readily see, is an extraordinary verbal act of thought, which reflects reality in an entirely different way than it is reflected in immediate sensations. When it is said that not only the transition from non-thinking matter to sensation, but also the transition from sensation to thought, is a dialectical leap, what is meant is that thought reflects reality in consciousness in a qualitatively different way than does immediate sensation. Clearly, there is every reason to suppose that this qualitative distinction of the unit [of word-thought] is basically and most importantly the generalized reflection of reality.[6]

Tolstoy's proverbs assured that meaning would be the point of departure, assured that the response would be at once critical and creative. The proverbs could start the process of thinking because they clearly reflected reality in consciousness in a generalized way; they were "complex and living" because, unlike pigs and tables or an abstract term like *justice*, they were meaningful to the children from the start. The work of the active mind is making meanings, and that is what the children did as they imagined characters and scenes and both temporal and causal sequences of events: they were making meanings. *The proverbs were understood in terms of pictures that were at one and the same time images and ideas brought to consciousness as symbols created by language.* The proverbs were complex and living—organic, not just "stimulus materials"—and thus could be apprehended as form. For the young storytellers, the proverbs functioned as *speculative instruments,* I. A.

Richards' term for the forms that find forms. The form of the proverbs answered to the symbolic forms that memory and the power of
envisagement brought to consciousness. As soon as the form-finding
and form-creating powers of mind are engaged, purposes are given
shape; intentions are realized; meanings are created.

Meanings are created by seeing relationships in the "complex and
living," as word and idea bring one another to consciousness. To begin with the making of meaning in teaching composition is a pedagogy based on as firm a foundation as we are likely to be able to lay:
the concept that "consciousness and symbolization are simultaneous
and correlative."[7] To begin with meaning is to begin with the imagination—a natural power—which brings forms to consciousness. That
is a fairly good description of pedagogical purpose.

So Paulo Freire holds: the means of *conscientization* in his "pedagogy
of the oppressed" is the creative and critical use of language in the
process he calls (in a typically awkward phrase) "problematizing the
existential situation."[8] It is epistemologically and psychologically
analogous to Tolstoy's use of proverbs. Freire's learners in the "culture circle" (for which Tolstoy's armchair, aswarm with questioning
children, is again the paradigm) name what they see in certain objects
or pictures, accounting for relationships in the process of interpreting
them. A muddy stream used for washing clothes and watering animals
and as a source of drinking water is described, remembered, considered in new contexts. Naming it, interpreting its character, explaining
its uses, accounting for its relationship to human needs transforms
the dirty water so that it is no longer seen as part of a scheme of
things over which the peasants have no control; it is removed from
the category of those things that have to be *(God wills it . . . So gehts
. . . It is man's fate . . . Such is the custom . . .)* to the category of the contingent. The dirty water becomes a political fact; it has been seen as
an emblem of a state of affairs that is, in turn, the creation, in part,
of human choices. Naming thus becomes a revolutionary activity; the
proof is that Freire is in exile. His literacy classes taught Brazilian
peasants not just literacy but the means of bringing to consciousness
the meaning of complex and living reality, thus engaging the power
of mind by which the possibility of changing that reality could be
imagined.

Tolstoy's proverbs, Montessori's prepared environment, Sylvia
Ashton-Warner's key vocabulary (which provides "the captions of the
dynamic life itself"), and Paulo Freire's conscientization provide Archimedean points from which we might move our own theory and
practice of teaching reading and writing. These master teachers have
all struggled against received pedagogies, the conventional wisdom—

Begin with pigs, pots, and tables; No child can think for himself; "See the boat come up the estuary," said Janet to John; ba, be, bi, bo, bu—and in so doing have won a place for humane instruction. If we consider well why they have placed their trust in the imagination—the form-finding and form-creating powers of the mind—we can learn, I think, to do the same.

Notes

[1]All passages quoted below are taken from this "pedagogical article" and "The School at Yásnaya Polyána." Page references in the text are to *Tolstoy on Education* (Chicago: University of Chicago Press, 1968). The translation, by Leo Wiener, has been emended by Rachel B. Douglas.

[2]The term *priyom*, which recurs in the opening of "who should learn from whom . . . ?" means both *literary devices* and *method*.

[3]*Teacher* (London: Secker and Warburg, 1963), p. 103.

[4]*Speculative Instruments* (New York: Harcourt Brace, 1955), p. 9.

[5]"What Behaviorism has chiefly demonstrated . . . is its insufficiency. To substitute Behavior for Meaning has been to miss the point. . . . Behaviorism has discovered a great deal about behavior, but in general has it not shown just this: that the key problems are beyond it?" (I. A. Richards, "Structure and Communication," in *Structure in Art and Science*, ed. G. Kepes. New York: Braziller, 1965), p. 130.

[6]Translation is by Rachel B. Douglas. This and other essays may be found in *Thought and Language*, tr. Eugenia Hanfmann and Gertrude Vakar (Cambridge, MA: M.I.T. Press, 1962).

[7]The formulation is Owen Barfield's in "The Meaning of the Word 'Literal,' " in *Metaphor and Symbol*, ed. L. C. Knights and Basil Cottle (London: Butterworths, 1960), p. 54. Barfield's *Poetic Diction* is the best study I know of the making of meaning. First published in 1928, a third edition (1973) is now available in paperback from Wesleyan University Press.

[8]"The Adult Literacy Process as Cultural Action for Freedom." *Harvard Educational Review*, 40 (May 1970): 218; and Chapter 3 of *Pedagogy of the Oppressed* (New York: Herder & Herder, 1970) offer the best introduction to Freire's pedagogy and its philosophical basis.

Forming Concepts
and Conceptualizing Form

My title is meant to suggest the interdependence of the two conceptual terms, *form* and *concept,* and to draw attention to the fact that they are very tricky words indeed. *Form* has the radical ambiguity typical of centrally important philosophical terms; it has two antithetical meanings, one for nominalists, one for realists: *form* can mean *shape* or it can mean the *essential principle.* It was to avoid precisely this kind of confusion that the word *concept* was first given currency by American philosophers who judged that so many meanings had accrued to the word *idea* that it had become impossible to discern an underlying shape. Burning off the barnacles, those encrusted meanings, seemed a less satisfactory option than deploying a brand new word in the hope—and it is a peculiarly American attitude—that a new word would help us all to return to square one. The Americans who brought *concept* into the world of philosophical discourse little knew that the psychologists—those magpies—would steal the word for their own use, that is, to designate anything that is not "data"; that politicians would use it to mean any ill-defined problem, aim, or program; that undergraduates and admen would use *concept* to mean "what I'm talking about." I have a friend who calls gin and tonic a *concept.*

Rhetoricians, it is to be expected, are more knowledgeable about concepts. We know that a concept is the product of a process of particularizing and generalizing, of that movement of thought that develops the field of a concept's application, what logicians call a *class.* We are teaching concept formation whenever we devise an exercise in classification or assign a paper that calls for definition; indeed, there is scarcely a rhetorical term that does not name a concept important in concept formation: rhetoric is thinking with concepts about forming concepts.

However, it might fairly be said that rhetoricians know more about concepts than they do about forming. We deal chiefly not with *forming* concepts but with concepts *formed.* The logic we teach is the logic of propositions; our rhetoric is, generally speaking, not the rhetoric of motives. Concepts are conceived of as already *there.* New textbooks,

This essay incorporates passages from papers read at the CCCC in Denver (1978) and Minneapolis (1979).

94

especially (alas) those intended for community college students or for the allegedly unmotivated and slow-learning occupants of the remedial sections and writing labs of public universities, still present in the opening chapters the formal outline that is appropriate not to the process of composing, but only to compositions. And the outline is, of course, accompanied by the cautionary slogan, "Don't write until you know what you want to say!" There is no stronger evidence that the conventional wisdom about forming concepts does not include useful, sound conceptions of forming.

In recent years, to be sure, considerable interest has developed in what is commonly called "pre-writing," but the various schemes proffered, the heuristic devices touted, are frequently deployed not to guide invention but to organize what is to be taken prefabricated from the textbook's "study questions" or the instructor's "suggestions." What is called "pre-writing" is often less a matter of forming concepts than it is of moving them around into more "effective" patterns.

We certainly read a lot about the composing *process,* as distinguished from the *product,* but unless there are theoretically sound reasons for the distinction, it can't do much for our pedagogy. When, for instance, a theoretician explains that a writer must carry out two kinds of planning, what he calls "large-scale planning" and "small-scale planning," we might expect that they will be defined and that the ways in which they are interdependent throughout the composing process will be discussed. But what we get is this: "Both in my experience and in that reported by my students, the greatest agony in writing is making the small decisions needed to construct the first version, such as selection of words and grammatical features."[1] Anybody will find composition an "agony" as long as he or she considers that selecting the words and grammatical features is a primary consideration. That there can be no selection of "grammatical features" until there is discourse is a fact that could illuminate not only the quandaries of this professor and his students but those of current rhetorical theory, which, following the lead of modern linguists, continually confuses language and discourse, as well as the analytic methods appropriate to one or the other.

We can only teach the composing process by devising writing assignments appropriate to its different phases; to do that, we should have an understanding of the forming power of mind, of what was once called the *imagination.* To form the concept of forming, we have to think about thinking and this is, of course, a philosophical challenge, one which teachers of English should be prepared to accept. But I see little evidence of a realization that the concerns of rhetoric are profoundly philosophical, that what rhetoricians know and are concerned about is philosophically interesting and complex. Rhetoricians certainly do not see themselves as philosophers of language. Indeed, there is a widespread skepticism about the intellectual respectability of what rhetoricians know and do. I can think of no other reason for the continuing abasement of teachers of English before any psychologist who purports to tell them what they are doing or, more commonly, what they *should* do; any linguist who claims to know what students at any level need to know about the structure and function of language; any sociologist or *Kultur*analyst who declares that he (or she) can explain the inadequacies of students—or teachers—at any level, in any field. English teachers, it seems, will accept almost anything if it is packaged; if it has a memorable name; if it sounds scientific; if it shows promise of lending prestige to our profession. Not only do rhetoricians let other people tell them what they already know, but they are also occasionally willing to listen to what they have surely always known is incorrect or inadequate, misconceived or simply absurd, and, occasionally, to accept it as new, interesting, and true.

The case could be made that what we need is a consumer protection agency; on the other hand, maybe we shouldn't be consumers at all. It would be useful if we could call a temporary boycott of all the social sciences until we have prepared an inventory that could help us decide "what we know about composition and what we need to know."[2] Even without the boycott, I think we should begin to form the concept of rhetoric as a philosophic inquiry, a study that "must take charge of the criticism of its own assumptions and not accept them, more than it can help, ready-made from other studies." That was I. A. Richards' program in *The Philosophy of Rhetoric.* Here's what he went on to say:

> How words mean, is not a question to which we can safely accept an answer either as an inheritance from common sense, that curious growth, or as something vouched for by another science, by psychology, say—since other sciences use words themselves and not least delusively when they address themselves to these questions. The result is that a revived Rhetoric, or study of verbal understanding and misunderstanding, must itself undertake its own inquiry into the modes of meaning—not only, as with the old Rhetoric, on a macroscopic scale, discussing the effects of different disposals of large parts of a discourse—but also on a microscopic scale by using theorems about the structure of the fundamental conjectural units of

meaning and the conditions through which they and their inter-connections arise.[3]

In the forty years after *The Philosophy of Rhetoric,* Richards devel-oped his "new Rhetoric," based on a "contextual theorem of mean-ing" and offering as a method interpretive paraphrase, developed with the help of Basic English. It has been set forth in great detail in seven books: *Interpretation in Teaching, How to Read a Page, Speculative Instruments, So Much Nearer, Design for Escape, Techniques for Language Control,* and *Complementarities.* I list the titles because I suppose they are unfamiliar: what we currently call the new rhetoric has not reject-ed the old new rhetoric; it has not recognized its existence.

So far from taking charge of the criticism of its own assumptions, the new new rhetoric has bought them wholesale from linguistics, be-havioral and cognitive psychology; from information theory and non-directive psychotherapy. So far from developing a contextual theorem of meaning, the new new rhetoric has shown very little in-terest in conceptions of meaning, preferring instead to take its depar-ture from what is called a "theory of discourse"—less theory than taxonomy in presentations I have read, and a question-begging tax-onomy at that. (We don't need a theory of discourse to help us dif-ferentiate *The Joy of Cooking* from *Pseudodoxia Epidemica,* but if we did, the notion of "reference discourse" would not serve us.) The new new rhetoric does not focus on metaphor; indeed, metaphor is con-sidered by some proponents as an aberration of language. Nor does it display any interest, generally, in those powers of language that a study of metaphoric structure might be said to illuminate. There is, however, something new and important going on so far as method is concerned; indeed, it is by its method that the new rhetoric can be defined.

From the Liège Group to Rhode Island, from Michigan to southern California, the new new rhetoricians are committed to a method by which procedures and techniques developed for the analysis of small-er units of discourse (so-called) are adapted to the study of larger units. Thus as the sentence can, in some respects, be analyzed in terms developed for an understanding of words and syntactical struc-tures, so the paragraph can be analyzed, it is alleged, in the light of concepts developed for sentence study. *Beyond the sentence!* is the ral-lying cry of ambitious linguists eager to deploy their wonderfully ma-neuverable equipment in the service, eventually, of discourse analysis.

The case has not been made for this method, so far as its relevance to a teaching of composition is concerned, and the proponents of the

new new rhetoric show little awareness of just how difficult an undertaking that might be. They do not acknowledge the highly problematic character of the most basic assumptions of this method; they fail
to see the consequences of the fact that discourse is not just words
or phrases and is not apprehendable by a linguistically defined unit,
that the sentence has a rhetorical as well as a grammatical character.
(Of course they know this, but do they know what it means?) The new
new rhetoricians take over "models," as they like to say, heedless of
the dangers of analogy. They depend on second and third-hand re-
dactions of theories and arguments, often getting them wrong and
seldom checking the critiques that have been developed of original
studies. A chief source is structuralism, but in freeze-dried form; the
new new rhetoricians add water and serve. The inadequacies of Roman Jakobson's wiring diagram of the communication situation have
been described more than once, but you will find none of that in the
disquisitions of the new new rhetoricians. Piaget is cited over and
over, generally the same handful of texts, but there is no reference
to alternate conceptions, to Heinz Werner, for instance, whose conception of cognitive development as a movement outward from the
undifferentiated self and other might be far more useful to students
of the composing process; nor to Vygotsky's critique of Piaget, his
strong emphasis on the social context of the making of meaning. The
new new rhetoricians do not generally consider the implications of
the theories they latch on to; they suffer, many of them, from a severe
case of what Kenneth Burke once called "methodological repres-
sion": they take step one, but they do not take step two.

The most important resource for rhetoricians, currently, is alleged
by many to be *psycholinguistics.* To see what light is shed by what psycholinguists have to say about concept formation, I have turned to a
book that is highly regarded in this field, *Psychology and Language,* by
Herbert H. Clark and Eve V. Clark (New York: Harcourt Brace Jovanovich, 1977). In a chapter entitled "Uses of Meaning," the authors
begin their consideration of "category names" with this statement:

> Investigators have made little progress in spelling out the se-
> mantic procedures or semantic components for such nouns as
> *bird, furniture, robin, mouse,* and *oak,* which are names of natural
> and man-made categories. It is not hard to see why. No one has
> yet been able to find necessary and sufficient criteria for classi-
> fying something as a bird, a piece of furniture, a robin, a mouse,
> or an oak, and without such criteria, semantic procedures can-
> not be filled out in any detail. Although some natural categories
> have scientific definitions, these seem far from what people ac-
> tually store in their mental lexicons. (p. 462)

The logical confusions in this passage (not to speak of solecisms) are mind-boggling and would take more space to unravel than I have, but it should be noted that this passage, purporting to state what is known about naming and classifying, occurs in a book of 608 pages in which *metaphor* receives no mention.

The authors then turn to a discussion of "the network approach" and "the featural approach," without stopping to comment on the possibility of interdependence. Let's consider for a moment "the featural approach to the study of classification" as it's been developed in the research of cognitive scientists in the past decade.

We are shown eight birds on a wire, depicted in silhouette. The caption for this picture served as the question put to the subjects by researchers: "Which bird is the most typical?" That is a very curious question. Conceivably, it would make sense to ask, with reference to a given geographical area, "What do you think of as a typical bird?" That is framed in the manner of those questions posed by public opinion experts, and it would perhaps elicit some interesting "data" about the relationship of experience and concept formation. But the subjects were asked—and the readers of this textbook are asked— simply, "Which bird is the most typical?" Not typical *of* anything; just *typical.* Birders would find the question unmanageable, even if posed in logically correct terms: "What is a typical heron?" Well, herons are generally rather tall; they stalk their prey in shallow waters, fresh or salt; their flight is leaden, they fly with their necks crooked; but the speciation of the heron is determined by palate formation—not a very useful field mark! To answer the question properly, you would have to know who is asking it.

The question "Which bird is the most typical?" is no more curious than the picture: what purpose could it possibly serve, juxtaposing as it does a starling with three species of swallows, one unidentifiable sparrow, a kingbird, a dove, and a scissor-tailed flycatcher? These are not birds of a feather; they are not comparable in shape or configuration. Though at first glance, the silhouettes seem to be what you would find in a field guide, this assemblage serves no authentic purpose. Field guide silhouettes help the birder to check and fix in mind differences in flight pattern or stance; they provide a handy scale for comparison of sizes and configurations. In Peterson's "Roadside Silhouettes," from which most of these psycholinguistic birds are taken, the starling is next to a grackle so that tails can be compared; the three swallows are together, showing comparable builds and tail shapes; dove and kingbird are shown at favored altitudes, one high, the other low; the flycatcher isn't depicted because it doesn't like to perch in the open. The schema printed in *Psychology and Language* is artificial or fraudulent, depending on your perspective.

"Which is the most typical bird?" You don't have to be a birder to realize how absurd the question is. Substitute the name of any class-concept and the illogical character of the question is clarified: what is the most typical *meal?* which is the most typical *woman?* which is the most typical *disease*—diabetes, chickenpox, cancer, tuberculosis, or ringworm? The paste-up schema is matched by a paste-up question; here is the psycholinguistic finding they led to: "The more typical a category member was, the more easily it could replace the category name. Put another way, the more typical the member, the more similar it is to the prototype of the category" (p. 466). This could be better understood if the central terms weren't misused; but in any case, we can fairly say that these psycholinguists, these cognitive scientists, have no conception of forming concepts.

This absurd bit of "research" illustrates with embarrassing clarity what Richards calls the "Proper Meaning Superstition" (p. 11). Asking "which bird is the most typical?" is simply a version of asking "but what *does* communism—or beauty or truth or education—*really* mean?" (It is entirely consonant with the topic-setting and thesis-statement-getting that passes for teaching composition.) The psycholinguistic birds also illustrate the crudest sort of associationism, the notion that since we develop the concept of bird by seeing many birds, every time we say or hear or read or write the word *bird* it is matched by a mental image—probably a blurred, unidentifiable sparrow, a generalized, *typical bird*. But, of course, there is not necessarily any visual image whatsoever when we say or read or think *bird*. The misconception that for every term there is an active visual image is one that any experienced teacher of poetry will recognize as sophomoric. A concept can be represented sometimes visually or aurally or kinetically (Doris Humphrey, in discussing the limits there, notes that there are no mothers-in-law in dance); by narratives of many forms, from the extended metaphors of fable to novels; by many names and many members of the class. A class is the field of a concept's application and how it is represented in discourse, poetic or otherwise, depends on context and perspective, purpose and intention. The Holstein Breeders' Association might legitimately reject a logo designed for them that featured a Guernsey in profile, but they would have no logical reason—though perhaps a political one—for complaining about a cattle crossing sign designed for general use that depicted a Guernsey or a Highlander or a Walt Disney creation.

These are fundamental and primary principles of logic. Psycholinguists, who proceed with the philosophically inadequate conception of language as a communication medium, and who are used to deploying such question-begging terms as "message," "deep structure," "competence," "semantic component," have little interest in the kind of fundamental inquiry into concept formation as that undertaken by Lev Vygotsky, a cognitive scientist who puts to shame many of those who have been so labeled. Psycholinguists, like many other kinds of linguists, have neither interest in nor method for defining the role of intention, purpose, or context. They have no notion of the dialectic of particularizing and generalizing, of exemplifying and classifying, of naming and interpreting; no notion of the problematic character of all terms used in the discussion of meaning. If they can't see the difference between asking "what behavior is typical of a thrush?" and "which is the most typical bird?" that is symptomatic of more than a failure to understand what *typical* means and what a *species* is; it means that they cannot recognize what Whitehead calls "the fallacy of misplaced concreteness."[4] If they see no need to differentiate between lexical and contextual definitions, or between specification and generalization, that suggests that their methodology is faulty and that they do not understand the principles of taxonomy. That is *their* problem, but we might well conclude that rhetoricians have nothing to learn from them. The point is surely not that the cognitive scientists should simplify their language so that the rest of us can gain access to their findings; it is that without the mystification, it would be obvious that what is looming there on the foggy psycholinguistic horizon is nothing to the rhetorician's purpose.

What is missing in psycholinguistics and in the various new rhetorics that take guidance from cognitive scientists is a philosophical understanding of the making of meaning. The assumptions and presuppositions, the models and methodology of current rhetorical theory derive from behavioral psychology and positivism, both of which entertain views of language as verbal behavior, as a signal code, as merely a system of binary oppositions. These are conceptions appropriate to one or another aspect of language, but they are not conducive to an understanding of how to teach forming concepts, because they cannot account for the forming power of language. Vygotsky's critique of these views, in the opening chapter of *Thought and Language,* was written over forty years ago and it is, like the warning sounded in *The Philosophy of Rhetoric,* very up-to-date.

These new rhetorics cannot do what they claim, which is to provide a method of composing, because their assumptions about language and learning run counter to such an endeavor. They are in especially clear view in the language that is used about language.[5] It is mechanical—or electronic; it derives from information theory, and it is distracting at best, misleading at worst. Here, for instance, is a passage from an article by the distinguished linguist Kenneth Pike, one of the most influential theorists of the present day: "The observer brings to bear on experience a unitizing ability. Without segmentation of events into recallable, nameable chunks, without abstraction of things as figure against ground, without reification of concepts manipulatable as discrete elements by our mental equipment, man would be inept."[6] Man, in such a case, would not be just inept; he would not be man. What is this "unitizing ability," if it is not *forming*? what is "mental equipment," if it isn't *mind*? what is "reification of concepts manipulatable as discrete elements," if it isn't *imagination*? And what is man without the power of forming, without mind, without imagination? This language deadens our sense of man as the *animal symbolicum*, and it actively encourages a conception of language that omits or denies the generative power of language as a symbolic form.

Pike goes on to remark that "these unitizings are an observer imposition on a continuum." *It is this notion of forming as an imposition on something already there that keeps us from forming the concept of forming.* This language encourages the idea that we manipulate the given, that we turn "things" into "figure and ground," whereas the actual state of affairs is that there are apprehendable "things" because we see figure and ground. As Susanne K. Langer observes: "The recognition of structure gives the mind its ability to find meanings."[7] Those structures are brought into being by acts of mind that Coleridge called *imagination*, "the prime agent of all human perception."

Despite the talk of process and the active choices of an engaged composer, the new rhetorics, like the old rhetorics they claim to supplant, conceive of a world "out there" that is to be manipulated by the writer. The initial terms of the new rhetoric are not those "sortings" Richards speaks of, nor the impressions that grow from the mind's "primordial" abstraction,[8] but, as we hear again and again, *raw data*. It is fatuous to go "emic" if the aim is said to be "getting new information" and manipulating the raw data. *Utteremes* and *behavioremes, tagmemes* and *stylemes* are named to sound process-y—the *emic* in opposition to the *etic*—but they are conceptualized as substance-y wads. Alfred North Whitehead once observed that if "you will persist in thinking of the actual world as a collection of passive substances, [the difficulty of explaining how] one such substance can form a component in the make-up of another such substance is not relieved by calling each actual substance an event, or a pattern, or an occasion."[9] The new rhetorics cannot provide a method of composing because they provide no way of thinking of "the actual world" except as "a collection of passive substances."

The alternative to thinking of raw data that is manipulated and of the world "out there" is to form the concept of forming. We form what we see; we can only see what we form. All that we know, we know in some form. In other words, forming is a matter of epistemology: *forming* is a name for knowing. And it is, precisely, the act of knowing, which, as Walker Percy has remarked, "the semioticist leaves unexplained."[10]

Or most "semioticists": there are plenty of philosophers who understand that knowing is integral to all symbol systems, and it is from them that teachers of composition have most to learn—Cassirer, Langer, Richards, Whitehead, Barfield, Peirce, Burke, and Walker Percy himself. Rhetoric can take charge of its assumptions only if it is guided by a philosophy of language that can account for the act of knowing; that is to say, the making of meaning must be seen as contingent on the forming power of the human mind, which is profoundly and essentially the forming power of language.

Piaget observes in a recent essay, "A Structural Form for Tomorrow's Education," that to understand is to invent. I want to suggest that we can improve our understanding of forming and thus of forming concepts if we invent for ourselves some new images of forming, and that theory and pedagogy will follow from them. I believe that thinking with the concept of imagination, reclaiming it for pedagogical purposes, can suggest sources for those images.

What we all have in common is the power of seeing form. (And here "seeing" must be taken metonymically: the fascinating fact is that Soviet psychologists, following Vygotsky's principles, have developed a pedagogy for blind and deaf children in which the sense of touch becomes the medium for the forming power, the shaping spirit, as it was for Helen Keller.) The power of seeing, of forming what we see—we can learn the fundamental laws of imagination by studying the logic of the eye. One sure source of new, fresh images of forming is thus our own minds in action.

What craftsmen say about what they do when they work is another source of images of forming; watching them is even better. I wish some foundation yearning to address itself to "the literacy crisis" would pay for having a lot of old people around the schools making things: whittling whistles, darning socks, crocheting antimacassars, repairing shoes, making bread. The *Foxfire* books are an excellent source of images of forming.

From craftsmen we can learn something about the relationship of pattern and design to forming; from artists we can learn even more fundamental truths about forming—that you don't begin at the beginning, that intention and structure are dialectically related, that the search for limits is itself heuristic, that form emerges from chaos, that you say in order to discover what you mean, that you invent in order to understand, and so on. Another way a foundation could spend some money would be to give English teachers some art books (and art teachers some collections of poems). Listen to these instructions from *The Mustard Seed Garden,* a seventeenth century Chinese manual of painting available in paperback from Princeton University Press:

> From the wrinkled bark of an old plum tree branches grow. In composing the tree from top to roots, space should be left in which blossoms may be added.

> Actually there are things which ten hundred brush strokes cannot depict but which can be captured by a few simple strokes if they are right.

> Drawing must be linked with the idea, for without meaning, the brush cannot function properly.

No theory of an affective domain separate from a cognitive domain—an idea fundamental to current rhetorical theory—could possibly yield such insights.

I think we can also explore ways of making the processes of history alive to our students, as a way of conceptualizing form. The best essay I know on form and forming is Thomas Huxley's "On a Piece of Chalk," given first as a lecture to working men shortly after the publication of the *Origin of the Species.* Geology is a very productive source of images of forming; it provided an important generative metaphor for the early structuralists. History on a different scale was at the heart of an idea Jane Addams had: she thought that if workers could learn the history of the machines they operated, they would come to see themselves in a line of discoverers and inventors. I think we can adopt that idea in teaching the history of words. I send my advanced composition students regularly to the OED and, for most of them, what they discover is a brand new experience: *nobody* at any stage of their schooling has ever taught them that language has a history, that the making of meanings is historical, and that they are in on the process.

To these sources may be added a fourth, my final example of where we might go for images of forming: that is, the experience of observing children at work and play—both our own experience and the accounts given us of theirs by Tolstoy, Montessori, Ashton-Warner, Piaget, Vygotsky—and, I would add, the lively and energetic members of the Teachers and Writers Collaborative. Kenneth Koch is the best known of them, but everybody involved seems to be able to devise projects that continually exercise the form-finding and form-creating powers of mind. One I recommend as a model is an account of a fourth grade project in the Winter 1976 issue of *Teachers and Writers.* It's called "Bugs: One Insect Leads to Another," and it's a fascinating account of forming a concept (see Part III, p. 196). What we can learn from studying the way children go about forming is, for instance, to see certain activities as stages, not mistakes (the formulation of Piaget's); to see that what we might think is simple is not so to a learner, that our points of departure should not be, as Tolstoy wrote, "pigs, pots, and tables," but "only the complex and living." We can learn from children that forming is a dialectic of sorting and gathering, of particularizing and generalizing, of language and thought, as Vygotsky demonstrates over and over.

From all such sources—our own minds, the procedures of craftsmen, the character of historical processes, the ways of artists and children—we can invent images by which to understand that forming is not a mechanical process; it cannot be represented in the language of computer science, not even, I think, if we add to "feedback" I. A. Richards' delightful notion of "feedforward." Forming is not assembling parts into wholes; it is not filling in slots and grids; it is not manipulating discrete elements like chessmen and Scrabble squares.

Forming is best conceived by analogy with organic processes.[11] As geology provides images of structure and history, of permanence and change, so biology can help us invent images of the dialectic of parts and wholes, form and function, order and accident, beginnings and ends. The ancient metaphor of forming as gardening could guide our understanding that forming is a process of growth and development. I know of one course that has been designed according to that model. It is taught by a Danish gardener masquerading as a professor of seventeenth and eighteenth century American literature—Jesper Rosenmeier of Tufts University. The course is called "Roots and Growth"; it's open to everybody—staff, faculty, and students. Everybody in the course has access to the university greenhouse. The continuing composition assignment is a journal of observations in which is recorded the growth and development of what has been planted. I impatiently await the arrival of springtime in Massachusetts, which is slower than it is in the Rockies, to see what images and concepts, to say nothing of radishes and snap beans, will emerge from this course. We got the word *morphology* from Goethe who, in his study of the life of plants, seems to have invented concepts in order to understand images. Composition as morphology, I would say, is a promising image, an image whereby we could come to understand something about forming and thus improve our teaching of how concepts are formed.

Notes

[1]Robert de Beaugrande, "Linguistic Theory and Composition," *College Composition and Communication*, 29 (May 1978): 139.

[2]Guidelines for this enterprise are usefully set forth in the article by Josephine Miles with that title in *College Composition and Communication*, 27 (May 1976): 136–41.

[3]*The Philosophy of Rhetoric* (1936; rpt. New York: Oxford, 1965), p. 23.

[4]*Science and the Modern World* (1925; rpt. New York: NAL, 1948), p. 52.

[5]We should not think that because certain psychologists are now called "cognitive" it means necessarily that their presuppositions are no longer behavioral or that because certain linguists reject some accounts of "verbal behavior" they are therefore free of all mechanistic conceptions. Critical analysis of working concepts, not merely of terminology, is what is needed. Careful examination of behavioral and positivist assumptions may be found in Patricia Bizzell, "Thomas Kuhn, Scientism, and English Studies," *College English*, 40 (March 1979): 764–71; and Carolyn R. Miller, "A Humanistic Rationale for Technical Writing," *College English*, 40 (February 1979): 610–17.

[6]"Beyond the Sentence," in *Tagmemics: The Study of Units beyond the Sentence* (NCTE, 1964), p. 10.

[7]*The Practice of Philosophy* (New York: Holt, 1930), p. 132.

[8]Richards, p. 36.

[9]*Symbolism: Its Meaning and Effect* (1927; rpt. New York: Capricorn, 1959), p. 26.

[10]*The Message in the Bottle* (New York: Farrar, Straus and Giroux, 1975), p. 72.

[11]Richards has this to say in *The Philosophy of Rhetoric:* "The theory of interpretation is obviously a branch of biology—a branch that has not grown very far or very healthily as yet. . . . We shall do better to think of meaning as though it were a plant that has grown—not a can that has been filled or a lump of clay that has been moulded (p. 12)." And Cassirer observes: "In all cultural matters it is the form of growth that enables us to understand the form of the existing product."

Thinking about Language

Since it is our views of language that largely determine our views of composition and how to teach it, we should subject them to a continuing review. What exactly are we saying when we say that language "communicates"? What do we mean by a "communication situation"? What is a "message"? What is entailed in calling language "verbal behavior"? What does it mean to say that we "make meaning"? The questions we raise in this "continuing audit of meaning"△ are only the modern rhetorical version of perennial questions about representation and imitation, the relationship of language and thought, the character of significance and the interpretation of forms. Recognizing them as questions inviting speculation rather than as problems to be solved is the first step towards understanding that the critical review of the language we use about language is a philosophical enterprise. That is to say, we will continually need to rethink as we try to formulate unspoken or unstated assumptions, to test one interpretation against another, to draw out the implications of definitions and propositional statements and metaphors. A philosophical inquiry seeks to identify and define relationships. It is not a matter of renaming; it is no contribution to call meaning a "semantic component" or intention, "deep structure," or to refer to rhetorical constraints as "scenic stipulations." Philosophical inquiry involves us in forming concepts, not in generating new lexical definitions or pseudoscientific taxonomies.

Any critical inquiry concerning language will necessarily be carried out by means of language. When we consider the assumptions implicit in the following statement, for instance, we use language about language.

A well-trained police dog knows four hundred words.

To say that an animal "knows" begs the question of what constitutes knowledge. To define the sense in which he knows these words would involve us simultaneously in defining what "words" means here. Now, if "words" has to cover both what the dog responds to and what human beings know, the conceptual power of the term will be minimal. (If sea anemones are said to "communicate" with one another, that term will have no defining power.) Furthermore, we need to

This is a digest of introductory remarks at workshops I've given at Indiana University; Graduate School of Education, University of Pennsylvania; University of Cincinnati; University of Massachusetts at Boston; Brookline (MA) High School.

know what is meant by "know" in order to interpret the sentence, to determine if it is a sound assertion. If we differentiate *what the dog knows* from *words,* we could arrive at a formulation like this:

> A police dog can be trained to respond to four hundred signals conveyed by voice or gesture.

That is not simply a rewording of the original statement. By substituting *respond* for *know* and *signals* for *words,* we have begun to form concepts of importance in thinking about language.

My aim in this chapter is to set forth very briefly certain propositions that have provided speculative instruments $^\Delta$ I find indispensable in thinking about how to teach the composing process. They have served that function because they illuminate assumptions about how language works. They derive from my reading of critics and others who have written philosophically about language, chiefly Kenneth Burke, Cassirer, Freire, Langer, Richards, and Vygotsky. There are no linguists in the list. I think it is fair to say that modern linguistics offers no guidance to rhetorical theory or composition pedagogy. The reason is that modern linguists are not, generally speaking, able to account for poetic meaning or, indeed, for any kind of meaning: they are not interested in the making of meaning or the meaning of meaning. Some regard the whole subject as metaphysical, beyond the reach of methods of analysis they consider scientific; others consider that they are discussing meaning when they deploy the terms that label the parts of the diagram of the communication system.

Modern linguistics cannot help us because virtually all schools are founded on the notion of the sign relationship as dyadic, constituted by a *signifier* and a *signified.* This two-term Saussurian model is positivist in that it removes intention, purpose, and interpretation from consideration. Positivists are offended by what they see as a vicious circle of language about language about language about. . . . They are impatient with what they see as an infinite regression like the Pet Milk can with the label depicting a cow's head emerging from a Pet Milk can, whose label depicts. . . . Positivists soberly insist that we must deal, rather, with what they call the real world, the raw data, the true facts. The counterinsistence must be that all knowledge is mediated; that our speculative instruments are necessarily linguistic; that what we seek to know is our knowledge of reality, not Reality. Of course, to positivists, this sounds like solipsism, a refusal to deal with the real world. But it could be claimed that acceptance of the fact that we can't get under the net or through the veil of language is a first step towards supplanting those profoundly misleading metaphors.

For what we need are ways of thinking of language not as a barricade but as our means of making meaning. Meaning is not thing-y;

we don't have meanings that we then clothe in words; meaning is not a batter we pour into linguistic molds. We need ideas and images of forming to help us form the concept of language as an instrument of knowing. We can follow Vygotsky's argument about why we should begin our study not with "language" or "thought" but with the nexus of the two, with the "unit of meaning." △ We can study Walker Percy and I. A. Richards, both of whom have demonstrated the inadequacies of the dyadic model of the sign. We can build on C. S. Peirce's formulation that one sign requires for its interpretation another sign. Susanne K. Langer has been exploring for forty years the implications of a semiotics that includes the meaning-maker; we can read, as a starter, *Philosophy in a New Key.* Anything we can do to substantiate the notion that meaning does not subsist in lexical definition but requires context and perspective will help form the concept of triadicity—the idea that the meaning relationship must include the meaning-maker and the idea he thinks with, not just the sign and what it stands for.

Here, then, are five maxims to guide the teacher of composition in thinking about language in a way that is consonant with thinking about composing as forming—seeing relationships and bundling the parts. They are points of departure for thinking about language as an instrument of knowing, a means of making meaning. I will explicate each briefly; the next chapter suggests the pedagogical implications.

〰〰 **Language is the vocal articulation of the tendency to see reality symbolically.**

[Edward Sapir]

Language is not essentially discourse but utterance: modern rhetorical theory, like linguistics-inspired poetics, continually fails to recognize the difference. Language is primordially speech—and what is speech? Speaking requires a stream of air, an appropriate oral cavity, a tongue that can articulate the sound in patterns. However, the patterned sound is a necessary but not a sufficient condition for speech. "Vocal articulation" carries out the mind's activity, which is to transform experience by means of symbols: speech/language is symbolization. Sapir's definition, by making symbolization the genus, encourages us to think of language as analogous to perception, memory, dreaming, and imagining—all acts of mind, all ways of forming by which we "see reality symbolically."

Language continues the work of the active mind in perception, and that activity is meaning-making. Perception is "visual thinking" (Arnheim) and provides the best model for the forming that we do by means of language. Meaning is there from the first: we don't *perceive* and then *conceive.* (As Kant observed, concepts without percepts are empty; percepts without concepts are blind.) We don't see reality and then see it symbolically; our seeing is knowing, and it is a symbolic transformation from start to finish. "The transformation of experience into concepts, not the elaboration of signals and symptoms, is the motive of language." (Susanne K. Langer)

〜〜〜 **The notion of giving something a name is the vastest generative idea that ever was conceived.**

[Susanne K. Langer]

Language gives us the power of naming, but naming is never just designation. When we name, we are implicitly classifying, an act of mind that requires comparing and contrasting, sorting and gathering. To name the little white, fluffy four-legged thing a *lamb* is to do the following: to identify it, to see it as one thing rather than another; to differentiate it from the vaguely similar boulder nearby on the hillside; to see that it is comparable to other such creatures that form a class of which it is a member. Also implicit in classifying is the recognition of the negative. As Kenneth Burke puts it, to declare "this is *A*" is simultaneously to assert that "this is not *Not-A*."△ Aristotelian logic is based on this notion that within a universe of discourse the law of identity must hold; otherwise, no propositions would be possible.

The fact that naming implies the negative is the basis for the ancient claim for language as an instrument of knowing: all acts of mind depend on the power of sorting and gathering that languages gives us, a power that entails recognizing the negative. In the *Cratylus*, Soctates says: "Then a name is an instrument of teaching and of distinguishing natures, as the shuttle is of distinguishing the threads of the web. . . . And the shuttle is the instrument of the weaver?" What the weaver makes provides the radical metaphor of *text:* our instruments are the names by which we differentiate; with those differentiations, those sortings, we weave the fabric of discourse.

The percept itself—the mental image of the lamb in front of us— is an abstraction, but it is not the product of conscious generalizing; it is a "primordial abstraction"△ produced by the autonomous brain. Nor do we go through the process of generalizing in order to call the object, in correlation with the percept, a *lamb*. Both perception and this kind of naming proceed by direct, intensive insight; we grasp the whole as a form. No point about language is more important for the composition teacher to grasp: language represents by abstracting in two modes. Abstraction can be accomplished by generalization, by a dialectical process of forming concepts; or it can be accomplished by imagining—by images of all sorts. The two modes are distinguishable, but in actuality they are interdependent, just as the two halves of the brain are in continual interaction.[1] The two main functions of language—to articulate and to fix—are radically analogous to these two modes of abstraction.

〜〜〜 **A word fixes something in experience and makes it the nucleus of memory, an available conception.**

[Susanne K. Langer]

Like other animals, we have our instincts, but we are rational beings, not creatures of instinct. Rationality entails being able to consider, to contemplate, to "interpret our interpretations."[△] Language stabilizes the images of our experience so that they are available to us as points of reference, sources of the analogies by which we think. Unlike animals, we are historical beings; we are not bound to the particular moment. We are free to REcognize and to envisage alternatives. Language enables us to have knowledge *about,* not just *of.* This power of language to make the fleeting moment recallable, to make experience seem substantial, is called "hypostasis."

〜〜〜 **Language exhibits the principle of discursive thinking.**

Language is an articulation of names: its tendency is to *run along* (the root meaning of *discourse*), bringing thought along with it. We can thus symbolize not just things but their relationships. Syntax is as essential to language as naming. Language can be analyzed as an empty structure, its function of bringing thought along ignored, but semantics is fundamentally inseparable from syntax.

〜〜〜 **Language has two functions. It is converse with another, and it is converse with oneself.**

[Alfred North Whitehead]

Language is the symbolization of thought that is always both public and private, personal and social. The capacity for language is innate, but it must be realized in a social context. The "tendency to see reality symbolically" is a biological necessity: since we are not simply creatures of instinct, we need other, supplementary powers. Language—and all symbol-making activity—is a biological necessity. So is social organization, and language should be seen in this context. This does not mean that we should think of language as "essentially" a communication medium, especially since that theory generally entails the notion that we "have" thoughts, which we then put into language. What it can do for our thinking is to remind us that dialogue is an essential model for the composing process. It is in dialogue that meanings are created and discovered and shaped; it is the foundation of Freire's "pedagogy of knowing": "Dialogue is the encounter between men, mediated by the world, in order to name the world." △

Note

[1]Some psychologists have failed to understand the "data" of their research and have misconceived the "processing" of the brain as being directly analogous to acts of mind. A corrective is supplied by an article by Stephen Grossberg, "How Does a Brain Build a Cognitive Code?" *Psychological Review,* January, 1980.

Speculative Instruments:
Language in the Core Curriculum

I. Critical Thinking

The Ford Seminars have at times been instructive; frequently they have been inspiriting, but they have not, generally speaking, illuminated the immediate problem, which will no doubt be perennial, of how to teach the so-called basic skills in the core curriculum. Of course, coming to cases is not easy in an hour, especially when the subject is writing. Furthermore, recipe swapping is not really useful: the anxieties we all feel—non-English teachers and English teachers alike—cannot be allayed, except temporarily, by offering highly particularized suggestions of "what to do." I will offer a few, but what I want chiefly to do is to assure you that you can teach writing by teaching your subject, and that one of the best ways to teach your subject is by teaching writing.

I want to claim—I won't have time to argue the case—that teaching writing is a matter chiefly of teaching critical thinking. Writing consists of two phases, composing and editing. It is composing that you can teach, not editing. What that comes to, really, is that you can teach paragraphing, not sentence structure. As Gertrude Stein notes in *Narration:* "So paragraphing is a thing that anyone is enjoying and sentences are less fascinating." Composing is a process: it includes both prewriting and rewriting, which are integral to the process—as editing is not. Composing is a matter of forming structures; editing is a matter of identifying and correcting faulty sentences. There are only a couple of things that I'm sure of after teaching composition for thirty years, and one is that teacher identification and teacher correction of error—or even student correction after teacher identification—does not teach editing. Nothing can, in my opinion, unless the mind of the writer is engaged in interpretive paraphrase, something that can best be taught in small groups or one-to-one conferences. I don't believe that it's your job in the core courses to work at the correction of grammatical error—fractured idioms, dangling participles, faulty agreement, and so forth. The correct use of grammar has far more to do with practiced competence, a history of successful performance, than it has to do with thinking.

This paper was delivered at the Ford Faculty Seminars, University of Massachusetts at Boston, December, 1978.

We can all teach writing, insofar as we teach the composing process. We will need to consider writing in the context of the other uses of language: speaking, hearing, and reading. By stressing these other uses of language, I mean to emphasize the hazards of thinking of writing in the core courses as "the composition component." Writing is not like a spark plug or a fan belt; and if we think of it as an element with a definite assigned place in a system, then we lose the chance of learning to make it available as a mode of learning, to use it as a mode of teaching.

Insofar as the core courses introduce students to critical thinking, they should involve them continually in speaking and listening, reading and writing; but I don't think we can learn to do this, to involve students, unless we have on hand several really useful conceptions of critical thinking. Professor Rabb claimed that synthesis and independence are the essential characteristics of critical thinking; but I can't derive pedagogy from that notion, though I suppose he did: what he described sounded like an interesting and teachable course. I think it's more profitable to begin with a down-to-earth operational definition like this: critical thinking is the capacity to see relationships methodically. That's pedagogically useful because, first of all, we can identify relationships: they are spatial, temporal, and causal; they can be classified, defined, rehearsed, rediscovered continually—whatever the topic, whatever the field. We teachers are considering relationships—seeing them—when we discuss parts and wholes, beginnings and ends, ends and means, *now* and *then*, *if* and *then*, and how X is like Y with respect to Z. And we can teach students to do this methodically, once we deliberately consider how it is that we, as scholars in one field or another, make sense of the data, how we organize the knowledge of a field, how we make sense of the world or a universe of discourse. Happily, seeing relationships methodically is as much the defining characteristic of coherent writing as it is of cogent thinking: that's why we can teach critical thinking by means of teaching writing, and vice versa.

In learning to do that, we will need ways to discourage the notion that language is a set of molds into which we pour our incandescent thoughts: language and thought do not bear one another a temporal relationship. But to avoid the metaphysical entanglements that threaten us in considering the relationship of language and thought, it helps in teaching writing to remember that composing is a process of making meaning. Not that "meaning" is easier to define than "language" and "thought," but we don't need to define it! I follow Susanne Langer's advice about the definition of "mind"; what we need is not a definition but working concepts. We need to think of meaning as both ends and means: a principal meaning of meaning is that it is a means to the making of meaning. That circularity does wonders, I think, in helping us imagine ways of using writing throughout the course not just as a final supermold to pour the course into—the term paper—but as an instrumentality for defining and designing and following a course of study.

One of the first and most useful things to learn about teaching writing, and thereby teaching critical thinking, is to learn to ask questions about meaning. "How does it change your meaning if you put it this way?" is a better critical question than, "What do you mean?" "If the author is saying X, how does that go to Y?" is a better question than, "What is the author trying to say?" "What do you make of this passage in light of our discussion of Y?" is a pedagogically more useful opener than, "How does it make you feel?" or "What is the main point here?" That question elicits nothing but a pained expression or a glance heavenward. By focusing on meaning, we will be encouraging attention to what we're looking at, whether it's a poem or a document or a lab report. We'll be teaching how judgments and opinions, generalizations and interpretations, are related to context and perspective. Conceiving of critical thinking as the making of meaning can encourage us to move beyond exhortation to instruction, to discover that it isn't helpful, for instance, to direct students to be specific! if we haven't taught them how to specify.

Teaching critical thinking and writing as the making of meaning can sharpen our sense of the importance of our methods, our pedagogy. Now if the Ford Faculty Seminars have helped, as I think they have, to legitimize an interest in pedagogy, that certainly is to the good. Humanists and scientists have to reclaim pedagogy, to take it away from the educationalists in whose hands it has been corrupted and debased. It amuses me to see the stern announcements from the National Endowment for the Humanities that they are interested in fostering scholarship, not teaching: that their fellowships are for teachers interested in improving their scholarship, not their teaching. Has anyone ever told them, I wonder, that humanism and pedagogy are twins, born in the Renaissance? that dozens of Renaissance texts are pedagogical treatises?

I have never suffered from this particular anxiety, the feeling that teaching is somehow a lesser thing than scholarship. I come from a family of teachers; if the sociobiologists hadn't ruined the metaphor, I could say that teaching is in my blood. More to the point, I was very fortunate in that the early years of my teaching career were spent largely at Bryn Mawr College where there was no differentiation made between scholarship and teaching; both were subsumed under the rubric of *the advancement of learning*. Furthermore, "writing across the curriculum" was not a fad or a program but an assumption. In those years, I learned three important things about the relationship of language use to critical thinking in all fields. To wit.

1. *Observation is central to all disciplines: learning to look and look again is learning to question.*

Careful reporting from the field, in the lab, in close encounters with poems, exercises certain fundamental capacities. A biologist at Bryn Mawr told me that his students were entering freshman biology with excellent backgrounds in biochemistry, but they didn't know how to observe; they didn't know how to look at a frog's leg. (In *The New Yorker*'s current "Annals of Science," Salvador Luria is quoted as saying that "nature study is the enemy of science." I take this to mean an exclusive interest in taxonomy, not the practice of critical examination.) The biologist welcomed the notion that close reading might help to develop habits and strategies of observation. We found support for this idea in the work of T. R. Henn, a Yeats scholar who had been called in to help at Cambridge University shortly after the Second World War when officials became alarmed at—guess what?—the declining writing abilities of the students "doing" science. T. R. Henn lectured on poetry: he analyzed the structure of metaphor in terms of a dry cell battery; meaning is a current between the poles of intention and expression—something like that. He taught argumentation—premises, the development of the opposite case, borderline and model cases, statement of proof—by analyzing a poem by John Donne; he got across the idea of ambiguity—"ambiguities are the hinges of thought," I. A. Richards has remarked △—by means of a close reading of Blake's mysterious little poem, "A Sick Rose." His lectures were published under the title *The Apple and the Spectroscope;* I've often wondered what would have happened if it had enjoyed the popular success of C. P. Snow's polemic dating from the same time— *The Two Cultures,* a book that led to much bitter and fruitless debate. *The Apple and the Spectroscope,* in contrast, suggests over and over again how what the biologist does is comparable to what the poet does, how close looking in the lab is like close reading of a complex poem. There are lessons there for science majors and for English majors. I have always advised English majors to minor in biology, if only because they need an understanding of organic structure as a way of understanding organic imagery. And they need to learn patience.

2. *Learning the special language of a field is a principal way of learning the concepts of that field.*

Another of the biologists at Bryn Mawr used to read to his freshmen Mark Twain's account of discussing a broken wagon without knowing the words: without *whiffletree*, it takes a lot of thingamiggig-ing and pointing to get a point across. He also incorporated in his lectures a structural analysis of the special words for the day. Back then, when Latin was still an entrance requirement, the notion of prefixes and suffixes was not wondrous strange; nowadays, such analysis is extremely important: our students do not realize that words have histories and analyzable structures. We have to work hard to demystify language—all language, but most important, the specialized language of a discipline. George Steiner has recently observed that we will soon have to look up everything; that time is upon us already in some quarters. But there is an opportunity here. I like to remember that Jane Addams, writing in 1902 about the education of immigrants, stressed the importance of providing a historical context for their new lives. She wanted them to know the history of the processes of manufacture they were engaged in. I think that, by analogy, we can provide the history of our disciplines by way of teaching the special language that has developed over time. In any case, learning the terminology required in one or another field of study is a good way of discovering what the chief concepts of the field are. I learned that in working with a microbiologist. I remember a tradeoff: I would learn some of his language if he would learn some of mine. Over the weekend, I struggled with *millepore filters* and *etiology* and *haploid tissues;* what I remember chiefly is that he couldn't use the word *starved* for his mice because the vivisectionists monitor the journals looking for such evidence. I hope he remembers *context, perspective, presuppositions,* and *tone.* I needed to learn some of his language in order to understand the concepts he was deploying so that I could understand the report of his experimentation and thus help him pitch it; he needed my language to understand the critique of his draft, my attempt to help him make himself intelligible to a certain well-defined audience.

3. *The rhetorical concepts of invention and disposition are, as it were, cross-cultural.*

Rhetoric was one of the seven liberal arts, as we rhetoricians continually remind ourselves; Lady Grammar used to run the whole show. What I discovered from talking with art historians, microbiologists, literary historians, archaeologists, chemists, and poets at Bryn Mawr is that we all teach rhetoric whenever we present ideas in context—where they came from and how we use them; we all teach rhetoric whenever we attend to discovering topics, points of departure for the exploration of ideas, the art of *invention;* we all teach rhetoric when we consider the development of ideas, the organization of statements, the art of *disposition.* The answer to the question, "Do we all have to teach English?" is, "You already are." Rhetoric is the study of *how words work*—and all of us use words. The more we learn about one another's languages, the better it will be for all of us. And certainly students gain enormously from the experience of discovering that how words work in one course is relevant to how they work in another. I used to be miffed when a student would say with surprise: "I tried what we've been doing in *history* and it worked!" But I've long since realized that such discoveries are cause for celebration.

Knowing how to observe, and thus to question, understanding the uses of special language, and mastering certain all-purpose procedures in organizing knowledge: these should not, I think, be called "cognitive skills"; they are too complex to be defined in terms appropriate for physical activity. Learning to think critically is not really very much like learning to flip an omelet; learning to see relationships methodically might, perhaps, be appropriate as a description for what a ball player does, but there is a difference between learning skills and learning to think, and that difference is created by the role language plays. "The study of how words work" was the definition I. A. Richards suggested in *The Philosophy of Rhetoric* in 1936; some twenty years later, he arrived at a somewhat more elegant formulation: "There is no study which is not a language study, concerned with the speculative instruments it employs."△ What this means is that we use language about language: we can look back on what we've said, interpreting our interpretations, comprehending our comprehensions more comprehensively. Richards has somewhere defined critical thinking as "arranging our techniques for arranging." I quote from Richards continually because it's from him that I've learned most about pedagogy, but Richards is an appropriate guide for us all, since he invented the core curriculum, as it were: he was the chief author of *General Education in a Free Society*, the response made in 1945 to the then new illiteracy. It is a document that provides, as Professor Muscatine demonstrated, a useful point of comparison with the current conceptions of "the core."

All studies are language studies concerned with the speculative instruments they employ: I want to suggest, now, that we can concentrate on discovering and developing the speculative instruments of each discipline in the core by studying the uses of language in forming concepts. To study, to consider, to learn the uses of language in the four modes of speaking, hearing, reading, and writing is to study critical thinking—which is *not* problem solving, narrowly conceived as guessing riddles; nor is critical thinking the liberation of a higher self or a set of logical tricks: critical thinking is the capacity to think methodically about thinking.

II. The Four Uses of Language

Speaking and hearing, reading and writing, are all related, of course: all have a *dialectical* character because of the reflexive nature of language. I want to suggest how we can take pedagogical advantage of that fact by conceiving of all language use in the core as *dialogue*. (*Dialectic* and *dialogic* are cognate, and the *dia* signals that reflexiveness.) All speakers and writers have listeners and readers, an obvious point that is seldom exploited. I'll consider speaking and hearing first, focusing on lecturing and notetaking.

The lecture was originally a reading (*lectito, lectere*); it developed in answer to the need to share the books. A famous print shows the lector—at Bologna or somewhere—reading to semicircles of humanists, all in their Erasmus hats, listening and *not*, be it noted, taking notes. People in the late Middle Ages and the Renaissance had a more highly developed capacity for remembering more of a phrase, for retaining more complex elements, for keeping more in mind, having developed what they called the art of memory and what modern linguists call, I'm afraid, "short-term retrieval capability." Evidence for this is found in the character of the phrase in the music of the times: there are just more notes to remember than there are in comparable elements of *Lieder*. I believe that one of the chief tasks of modern education, from kindergarten to graduate school, is to reawaken the auditory imagination. And at the college level, I think we can use the lecture to do so. How? By training our students to take notes, a skill tantamount to a kind of conceptual ear training.

Have you recently had a look at your students' notes of your lectures? It can be a harrowing experience. Some years ago when my husband was a visiting professor at the University of California at Berkeley, he learned that notes on his lectures were being sold by a company called Fy-Bate. They gave him a free set to buy him off. (They had failed to ask his permission, and thus were liable for legal action.) He found that full bibliographies had been furnished from very sketchy allusions and whole poems had been printed, from which one or two lines had been cited: on the other hand, what he had said was distorted, to say the least: negatives had been dropped; ironic and skeptical tones had not been registered; contentions that had in fact been discredited were presented as his own.

Notes should enact the dialogue implicit in a good lecture, but students rarely know how to do that; indeed, they often do not know what should be noted. A few weeks ago, I was talking with some Radcliffe undergraduates about this business of note taking. Most students, they said, sit there inertly in a course of the modern novel until they hear a date—and that they immediately take down: "Fitzgerald arrived in Paris in 1925 . . .": *1925, Paris.* What gets noted is what sounds memorable: pat definitions, jokes, formulations, titles, dates, but without context or perspective and without connections indicated. There is a technique which can help train the capacity to organize what is said—at least so that context can be recalled. That is to use law school notebook paper with very wide margins, (or, of course, simply to draw such margins) or, better yet, to use the facing page for recapitulations, summaries, key terms, further study, and *questions.*

That's one thing the student can do. The lecturer can make the argument more explicit, not by numbering the points being made, but by carrying on a virtual dialogue, if the number of students makes actual dialogue impossible. Writing can help us engage students in that dialogue. Five or ten minutes can be set aside at the beginning to hear written questions or summaries of the preceding lecture and discussion. Jim Broderick tells me that Rosemond Tuve used to write down after class the questions which had been raised and would begin the following lecture by alluding to them: "The question Susie raised last Friday was actually a question about the relationship of sensuousness to trope. Let's begin there in undertaking our examination today of *prosopopoeia.*" Susie would feel great; a real bridge would have been set in place; everybody would be caught up in the notion that a dialogue was continuing. If five or ten minutes can be set aside at the end of the class for writing recapitulations or responding to a question the lecturer sets, with everybody including the instructor writing, the notion of dialogue can again be dramatized. If the opening and close of the lecture both expand towards the middle, that is certainly to the good, a way of converting the lecture to a discussion, which is probably the more appropriate mode of teaching in the core course. Short of that, an interrupted lecture is bound to involve students— raising questions yourself if they are not forthcoming, going through the process of answering them yourself, if answers are not forthcoming.

There is a real probability that for some of us this will mean getting off the track, but you can learn to take advantage of that. Recently I found myself discoursing on why it is that lobsters are not returning to Maine waters as they usually have done. The class was considering C. S. Lewis' argument about objective value, and I had no idea how I'd gotten to those lobsters. But we backtracked, the class and I, discovering the route by which I had gone from Lewis' contention that we must learn from the scientists the importance of the temporal dimension in all judgments, to the character of ecological questions that involve future generations, to the case of oil spills, to the fact that oil gums up the organ in their antennae by which the lobsters sense the motion of currents, reading them as signals to go back to where they came from. Getting me back on the track was, I like to think, an occasion for thinking about thinking.

Dialogue, of course, is centrally important to critical reading. In conversation we anticipate, interrupt, question, summarize what is being said; we repeat, deny, take back, and restate: critical reading ought to be like that. To encourage it we should hold a ceremonial burning of all yellow felt markers. An efficient reader talks back to the book by writing, noting, summarizing, glossing—not by making pastel islands on every page. An efficient reader reads not by the letter or the word but by the phrase, and he can do so not because his eyes move efficiently, but because he can anticipate. (*That's* why his eyes move efficiently.) He can do that because he is reading for meaning. When we read for meaning it is *meaning,* you will not be surprised to hear, that provides the *means.* The more we know about what's being said, the meanings that are being made, the more readily will we grasp what will be said next. That's why an hour spent in the close reading of a single complex passage provides better training than the whole of an Evelyn Wood course. It surprises a student to be told that the best way to improve his reading rate is to slow down, but once he's had the experience and can see what it can do for him, you're not likely to have to persuade him of its value. Students certainly need to learn the so-called study skills: preliminary skimming, circling key words, making your own index, noting words to be looked up after a first reading—but they are not enough. When Mortimer J. Adler wrote a book called *How to Read a Book,* I. A. Richards responded with *How to Read a Page.* Our job in the core is to teach critical reading, and that will require both study skills and reading for meaning.

The best way to teach critical reading is by the exhaustive analysis of short, complex passages: the model is sipping whiskey, not diet soda. Now, in these remarks I have been trying not to be opinionated, but at this point I can't avoid opinion, and so I will be explicit: in my opinion, *we cannot teach critical reading by assigning textbooks.* Textbooks—most textbooks—are written in barbarous English with little attention paid to structural or historical analysis of words and meanings. Organization is by typography; there is frequently so little balance of specification and generalization that the reader cannot tell how concepts have been formed; indeed, they frequently have *not* been formed: they are simply laid out. Textbooks are emblematic of what Jean-Paul Sartre has called the *digestive* theory of education: textbooks are feedbags.

At the least, I think we ought to make room in all core courses (all courses, for that matter) for, say, three sessions in a term in which the class can carry out a close reading of a single passage or essay. This can best be done in small groups, once the techniques have been practiced. Such passages can be assigned, and students can keep a reading notebook in which to practice those techniques that are pretty much the same as for taking notes on a lecture. A double-entry journal—what I call a dialectical notebook—allows students to transcribe sentences on the right-hand side and annotate them on the left. In reviewing such a double-entry notebook, you can tell very quickly from the character of the notes and queries, the summaries and parallels noted, just how the student is progressing in learning to think critically, to see relationships methodically, to discover and develop meanings. (May I say in passing that requiring a double-entry notebook is the only way I know to defend yourself against plagiarism, if you want to assign formal term papers. I have never had the nerve to say face-to-face to any colleague, but I will say it now, protected as we are by generality: *anyone who receives a bought paper deserves it.* Assigning papers without monitoring the composing process is not only a waste of time for everybody concerned but also a wasted opportunity to use writing as a mode of learning; it's also asking for trouble.)

Another way of teaching critical reading—aside from the close reading of short, complex, substantial passages—is to assign essays or lectures or addresses that were originally composed by scholars for lay audiences. I don't mean the belletristic effusions of scientists trying to make like humanists or, much worse, linguists and psychologists trying to be scientific; I agree with Martin Green that the study of such works as *The Living Cell* or *The Immense Journey* doesn't teach much about critical writing, or critical reading, for that matter. Rather, what I have in mind are such pieces as these:

Thomas Huxley's "On a Piece of Chalk," delivered to a working men's association, is a popular explanation of geological change that is unrivaled for clarity. It can be dismaying to see how many words Huxley could count on his unlettered audience knowing and, clearly, their auditory imagination was functioning. They had heard the Bible read every day of their lives, and the cadences of the language could help sustain their interest even when they did not, perhaps, understand particular words. Nevertheless, our students can best learn how to listen or read if what they read or have read to them is worth hearing.

Jane Addams addressed the general public in *Democracy and Social Ethics.* Susanne K. Langer spoke to New Yorkers gathered at Peter Cooper Union when she gave the lecture entitled "Man and Animal: The City and the Hive," which to my mind is better than anything we've had from the confraternity of ethologists. Other pieces in her collection, *Philosophical Sketches,* were written for *The Saturday Evening*

Post, the Vassar Alumnae Association, and other nonintellectual forums.

E. H. Gombrich and Kenneth Clark are both wonderful explainers, though they had an easier time in their Mellon lectures explaining sculpture and paintings than philosophers have in explaining ideas.

Robert Oppenheimer is a modern Huxley; again, if only *Science and the Common Understanding* had been the text for debate in the 1950s instead of Snow's silly book, perhaps by now we'd have learned something about how to talk to one another across disciplinary boundaries.

Our students, I firmly believe, have more to learn from reading popular lectures by great scientists, philosophers, theologians, *et al* than they have from textbooks written by mediocre or simply goodwilled technocrats and academics with no wit, no style, no grace, no passion, with very little sense of audience, and hence of dialogue or dialectic. I think there's no doubt that we could gather such lectures and essays for students in the core and share them with one another, testing them in varied contexts.

III. Writing as a Mode of Learning

I hope this lengthy consideration of speaking, hearing, and reading will serve now as a context for a discussion of writing not as a component or a byproduct or simply a long-term goal, but as the chief means of making meanings and thus of laying hold on the speculative instruments of one discipline or another. Writing, if it is supported by other language activity, can in turn lend support to speaking, hearing, and reading.

If you think deliberately of writing as, for instance, a bridge from reading assignments to lecture or from class discussion to reading, you can devise writing assignments spontaneously: those that spring from the Zeushead of classroom discussion are sometimes the most useful. Let me illustrate.

C. S. Lewis calls all moral codes by the name of the Tao, which he takes from one of them. During class discussion, I asked students to define the Tao by analogy, explicitly using the ratio form

$$\frac{TAO}{?} : \frac{?}{?} .$$

One young man wrote, "The Tao is to the people as the ocean is to the fish." We asked him to explain and he said, "Well, the Tao is everywhere and the ocean is everywhere, all around the fish." But that gave us only the genus, and we needed some differentia. (I've been using Andrew Marvell's Aristotelian definition of definition: "Definition always consists, as being a dialectical animal, of a body which is the genus, and a difference which is the soul of the thing defined.") I suggested that we interpret Mao Tse Tung's famous formulation: "The guerrilla lives among the people as the fish lives in the sea." (It always helps, by the way, to convert states to activities: to ask not what *is* something? but what does it *do?* what's it *for?*) And we came to *dependence* as the soul of the definition of that form of relatedness that Lewis is calling the Tao: man can't get outside it and still remain man. The student's definition was better than he knew, since *dependence*, not just *universality*, was implied by the metaphor of the fish in the sea. I like to think that his analogy helped him think about thinking.

Teaching definition is extremely difficult because as you simplify to demonstrate the logical structure, you then are faced with the problem of building the complexity back in. It's the workbook syndrome: students can do 100 percent on drill sheets and turn right around and make the same errors they supposedly had had drilled out of them. Real discourse poses a challenge that drill can't prepare you for. When we crank things down, we have to remember to crank them back up again. Earlier in the course, we'd worked on the problem of how to define *taxation*. We'd all agreed that "taxation is when you collect money" is inadequate. I explained how you can get conceptual terms out of words. We derived a meaning for the root *tax-* in *taxonomy, taxidermy,* and *taxation;* and I asked, then, why a taxicab was called a *taxi:* it was a great pleasure to hear the best student in the class work his way directly to the idea of a scheduled rate, an arrangement beforehand.[1] In this meeting, the class understood definition as a composing process of specifying and generalizing, classifying and categorizing, seeing relationships, the making of meaning; or so I thought. At the next meeting, I asked a student to go over the discussion of definition with another who'd been absent, to use her notes in getting the other student caught up. I overheard her say: "Well I didn't take notes because it was so obvious." I'd forgotten to crank things up again.

I keep forgetting, but the fact is that you don't teach definition just once; you do it over and over again. The same holds true for everything else that has a rhetorical name, from paragraphing to specification. The pedagogical point is not, I think, to have a recipe file of certain assignments which you come to class prepared to do this day rather than that. That might work, but then again, it might not. What you need is to be able to make use of emergent occasions and what can help is having on hand a repertory of *kinds* of assignments adaptable to what's happening. Short, throwaway assignments like the use of ratios in developing a definition by analogy can help you bridge from reading to discussion, and they certainly encourage students to use writing as a way of getting thinking started. Most composition textbooks still say, "Don't write until you know what you want to say." A much better slogan is: "How do I know what I think 'til I hear what I say?" Let me describe a few more heuristics, one that's useful for organization and one that would be good for revision.

Organizing a lot of information—or dredging it up—by means of an image is as useful as metaphor in definition. I have several times taught Colin Turnbull's *The Lonely African* in freshman English—"The Intellectual Confronts the Social and Political Order" was our jazzy title at one point. A sketch of a cotton dress with two columns underneath provides a structure to help organize the facts about the perspectives of the Africans and the British colonists. The cotton dress is seen on one hand as symbolic of one crop economy, a foolish and oppressive morality, a patronizing and manipulative attitude, and just plain irrational; on the other hand, from the point of view of the British, it stands for freedom from subsistence farming, enlightenment, and the civilization of heathen tribes. For most freshmen, the specifications are in narrative and descriptive form, but that's fine: the schema helps to organize an opposition that can generate concepts as particulars are sorted and generalizations are derived. The point is that the image and the line drawn down the middle of the page give us all something *to think with:* they are speculative instruments of a sort that help discover further speculative instruments, the concepts of alienation and oppression, the ideas that make it possible to come to some understanding of the dilemmas of "the lonely African."

The other heuristic involves reading and writing: each student in turn reads the opening paragraph of his or her composition, a short paper assigned on a common topic. Members of the class then write the opening sentence of a feasible second, follow-up paragraph. If we can't do it, the lesson is very clear: there isn't a real introduction. If the writer finds many of our sentences entirely wrongheaded, he will know that he's given inadequate points of departure. And so on. (I've done this as an exam too: I mimeographed the opening paragraphs of fifteen essays in a collection called *Philosophy and History* and then scrambled all the second paragraphs' opening sentences and asked students to match them. One or two are ambiguous; a couple of others could go anywhere, but most are clearly relevant to only one paragraph. A great deal can be learned about organization and revision, about reading and writing from this simple exercise.)

There are many more: almost any logical formulation can be given some kind of visual form that has heuristic value. There is some danger that they will simply remain gimmicks, but that's no reason for not trying to discover ways of using visual thinking in your teaching. In any case, *you*—the instructor—should do all in-class writing; these exercises should not always be responded to; and they never should be graded. As I say, one of the chief things we need to teach our students is that writing is a process and that all processes involve false starts, getting off the track, getting on again. We must persuade them that these are not *mistakes*. I'm very fond of a remark of Gaston Bachelard: "To begin in the realm of mind is to know one has the right to begin again." △

The Ford Faculty Seminars have done a lot to restore collegiality and to help us to rediscover a sense of common purpose; maybe I should speak only for myself, though I've heard others express the same sentiments. I think we have a chance to make our new core curriculum an authentic model for teaching the new student. If we make deliberate use of all the channels of communication—speaking, hearing, reading, and writing—we'll have a chance to create communities of learners in our classrooms. If we consider that whatever subject we teach, we are teaching interpretation—of experience, of texts, of comment, of other interpretations—then I think we'll have a chance to teach our students to think critically. If all studies are language studies, we can borrow one another's speculative instruments, learning from one another by that means. It begins to sound like a university to me.

Note

[1]Three classical philologists have told me that this etymology is incorrect. I hope that error doesn't obscure the point I'm making about the usefulness of the study of roots, even in the manner of the medieval encyclopedists whose principal stratagem was to create "metaphor by mistake."

Part III

Up to
the
Classroom

The classroom, conceived as the philosophical laboratory, deserves that symbolic "Up." Teaching, I've always thought, is scholarship in action.

The essays and passages gathered here are a personal selection: I have chosen comments and accounts and speculations from which I have learned something of central importance about teaching, especially about the teaching of writing (although only two or three are *about* writing). Most were written by people who are not known primarily as teachers, or who are known principally for their contributions in some other role; on the other hand, they have all taught. The fact that half of them belong to history reflects my judgment that we have had on hand for a hundred years at least what we need to know to teach writing. What we really need is not research, as commonly understood, but REsearch of what has been discovered and formulated, learned and taught. There are no "educationists" (defined as taxonomists and theoreticians with no philosophical interest in the nexus of theory and practice), because I have not learned from them, but some writers I have found instructive are not represented only because they are difficult to excerpt, and their books are easily available. Among these are James Britton, Jerome Bruner, J. W. P. Creber, C. S. Lewis *(The Abolition of Man)*, Piaget, and Vygotsky. This is not to say that those I have chosen are adequately represented by these brief excerpts; only that I hope to suggest by them the insights and wisdom which further reading promises.

1. James/Peirce/Whitehead

What these three great philosophers have to say about teaching and learning is illuminating because of their interest in the powers of mind and language. William James' affectionate regard for teachers is matched by Charles Peirce's disdain for everything academic, including academics. Habits of mind, Peirce knows, are not learned according to the examiner's schedule. Whitehead counted James among the four greatest philosophers of the Western world because of his understanding of the importance of experience, but it was actually because of Peirce that he came to that understanding, especially of how experience brings theory to the test.

Nowadays, when most psychologists use language to hide the vacuity of their thought, it's a marvel to read James. Whitehead, in this instance and throughout The Aims of Education, *writes clearly, if not quite so powerfully as in* Modes of Thought *and* Science and the Modern World, *which are both full of interest for teachers. His admonition that "necessary technical excellence can only be acquired by a training which is apt to damage those energies of mind which should direct the technical skill" should be foremost in our minds when we are tempted to think that there is a set of skills to be mastered* first.

William James

(from *Talks to Teachers*)

. . . There is unquestionably a great native variety among individuals in the type of their attention. Some of us are naturally scatter-brained, and others follow easily a train of connected thoughts without temptation to swerve aside to other subjects. This seems to depend on a difference between individuals in the type of their field of consciousness. In some persons this is highly focalized and concentrated, and the focal ideas predominate in determining association. In others we must suppose the margin to be brighter, and to be filled with something like meteoric showers of images, which strike into it at random, displacing the focal ideas, and carrying association in their own direction. Persons of the latter type find their attention wandering every minute, and must bring it back by a voluntary pull. The others sink into a subject of meditation deeply, and, when interrupted, are 'lost' for a moment before they come back to the outer world.

The possession of such a steady faculty of attention is unquestionably a great boon. Those who have it can work more rapidly, and with less nervous wear and tear. I am inclined to think that no one who is without it naturally can by any amount of drill or discipline attain it in a very high degree. Its amount is probably a fixed characteristic of the individual. But I wish to make a remark here which I shall have occasion to make again in other connections. It is that no one need deplore unduly the inferiority in himself of any one elementary faculty. This concentrated type of attention is an elementary faculty: it is one of the things that might be ascertained and measured by exercises in the laboratory. But, having ascertained it in a number of persons, we could never rank them in a scale of actual and practical mental efficiency based on its degrees. The total mental efficiency of a man is the resultant of the working together of all his faculties. He is too complex a being for any one of them to have the casting vote. If any one of them do have the casting vote, it is more likely to be the strength of his desire and passion, the strength of the interest he takes in what is proposed. Concentration, memory, reasoning power, inventiveness, excellence of the senses,—all are subsidiary to this. No matter how scatter-brained the type of a man's successive fields of consciousness may be, if he really *care* for a subject, he will return to it incessantly from his incessant wanderings, and first and last do more with it, and get more results from it, than another person whose attention may be more continuous during a given interval, but whose passion for the subject is of a more languid and less permanent sort.

. . . I must say a word about the contributions to our knowledge of memory which have recently come from the laboratory-psychologists. Many of the enthusiasts for scientific or brass-instrument child-study are taking accurate measurements of children's elementary faculties, and among these what we may call *immediate memory* admits of easy measurement. All we need do is to exhibit to the child a series of letters, syllables, figures, pictures, or whatnot, at intervals one, two, three, or more seconds, or to sound a similar series of names at the same intervals, within his hearing, and then see how completely he can reproduce the list, either directly, or after an interval of ten, twenty, or sixty seconds, or some longer space of time. According to the results of this exercise, the pupils may be rated in a memory-scale, and some persons go so far as to think that the teacher should modify her treatment of the child according to the strength or feebleness of its faculty as thus made known.

Now I can only repeat here what I said to you when treating of attention: man is too complex a being for light to be thrown on his real efficiency by measuring any one mental faculty taken apart from its consensus in the working whole. Such an exercise as this, dealing with incoherent and insipid objects, with no logical connection with each other, or practical significance outside of the 'test,' is an exercise the like of which in real life we are hardly ever called upon to perform. In real life, our memory is always used in the service of some interest: we remember things which we care for or which are associated with things we care for; and the child who stands at the bottom of the scale thus experimentally established might, by dint of the strength of his passion for a subject, and in consequence of the logical association into which he weaves the actual materials of his experience, be a very effective memorizer indeed, and do his school-tasks on the whole much better than an immediate parrot who might stand at the top of the 'scientifically accurate' list.

This preponderance of interest, of passion, in determining the results of a human being's working life, obtains throughout. No elementary measurement, capable of being performed in a laboratory, can throw any light on the actual efficiency of the subject; for the vital thing about him, his emotional and moral energy and doggedness, can be measured by no single experiment, and becomes known only by the total results in the long run. . . .

C. S. Peirce

(from "Vitally Important Topics")

. . . Good instruction in reasoning is exceedingly rare. As for what is taught in the colleges under the name of logic, oh dear, perhaps the less said the better. It is true that mathematics teaches one branch of reasoning. That is, indeed, its chief value in education. But how few teachers understand the logic of mathematics! And how few understand the psychology of the puzzled pupil! The pupil meets with a difficulty in Euclid. Two to one the reason is that there is a logical flaw. The boy, however, is conscious only of a mysterious hindrance.

What his difficulty is he cannot tell the teacher; the teacher must teach him. Now the teacher probably never really saw the true logic of the passage. But he thinks he does because, owing to long familiarity, he has lost that sense of coming up against an invisible barrier that the boy feels. Had the teacher ever really conquered the logical difficulty himself, of course he would recognize just what it was, and thus would fulfill the first condition, at least, of being helpful. But not having conquered the difficulty, but only having worn out the sense of difficulty by familiarity, he simply cannot understand why the boy should feel any difficulty; and all he can do is to exclaim, "Oh, these stupid, stupid boys!" As if a physician should exclaim, "Oh, these horrid patients, they won't get well!" But suppose, by some extraordinary conjunction of the planets, a really good teacher of reasoning were to be appointed, what would be his first care? It would be to guard his scholars from that malady with which logic is usually infested, so that unless it runs off them like water from a duck, it is sure to make them the very worst of reasoners, namely, unfair reasoners, and what is worse unconsciously unfair, for the rest of their lives. The good teacher will therefore take the utmost pains to prevent the scholars getting puffed up with their logical acquirements. He will wish to impregnate them with the right way of looking at reasoning before they shall be aware that they have learned anything; and he will not mind giving considerable time to that, for it is worth a great deal. But now come the examiner and the pupil himself. They want *results,* tangible to them. The teacher is dismissed as a failure, or, if he is allowed another chance, he will take good care to reverse the method of his teaching and give them *results*—especially, as that is the lazy way. These are some of the causes of there being so few strong reasoners in the world.

Alfred North Whitehead

(from *The Aims of Education*)

. . . No president of a large corporation meets his youngest employee at his office door with the offer of the most responsible job which the work of that corporation includes. The young men are set to work at a fixed routine, and only occasionally even see the president as he passes in and out of the building. Such work is a great discipline. It imparts knowledge, and it produces reliability of character; also it is the only work for which the young men, in that novice stage, are fit, and it is the work for which they are hired. There can be no criticism of the custom, but there may be an unfortunate effect—prolonged routine work dulls the imagination.

The result is that qualities essential at a later stage of a career are apt to be stamped out in an earlier stage. This is only an instance of the more general fact, that necessary technical excellence can only be acquired by a training which is apt to damage those energies of mind which should direct the technical skill. This is the key fact in education, and the reason for most of its difficulties.

The way in which a university should function in the preparation for an intellectual career, such as modern business or one of the older professions, is by promoting the imaginative consideration of the various general principles underlying that career. Its students thus pass into their period of technical apprenticeship with their imaginations already practised in connecting details with general principles. The routine then receives its meaning, and also illuminates the principles which give it that meaning. Hence, instead of a drudgery issuing in a blind rule of thumb, the properly trained man has some hope of obtaining an imagination disciplined by detailed facts and by necessary habits.

Thus the proper function of a university is the imaginative acquisition of knowledge. Apart from this importance of the imagination, there is no reason why business men, and other professional men, should not pick up their facts bit by bit as they want them for particular occasions. A university is imaginative or it is nothing—at least nothing useful.

Imagination is a contagious disease. It cannot be measured by the yard, or weighed by the pound, and then delivered to the students by members of the faculty. It can only be communicated by a faculty whose members themselves wear their learning with imagination. In saying this, I am only repeating one of the oldest of observations. More than two thousand years ago the ancients symbolised learning by a torch passing from hand tó hand down the generations. That lighted torch is the imagination of which I speak. The whole art in the organisation of a university is the provision of a faculty whose learning is lighted up with imagination. This is the problem of problems in university education; and unless we are careful the recent vast extension of universities in number of students and in variety of activities—of which we are so justly proud—will fail in producing its proper results, by the mishandling of this problem.

The combination of imagination and learning normally requires some leisure, freedom from restraint, freedom from harassing worry, some variety of experiences, and the stimulation of other minds di-

verse in opinion and diverse in equipment. Also there is required the
excitement of curiosity, and the self-confidence derived from pride in
the achievements of the surrounding society in procuring the advance
of knowledge. Imagination cannot be acquired once and for all, and
then kept indefinitely in an ice box to be produced periodically in
stated quantities. The learned and imaginative life is a way of living,
and is not an article of commerce.

It is in respect to the provision and utilisation of these conditions
for an efficient faculty that the two functions of education and research meet together in a university. Do you want your teachers to be
imaginative? Then encourage them to research. Do you want your researchers to be imaginative? Then bring them into intellectual sympathy with the young at the most eager, imaginative period of life,
when intellects are just entering upon their mature discipline. Make
your researchers explain themselves to active minds, plastic and with
the world before them; make your young students crown their period
of intellectual acquisition by some contact with minds gifted with experience of intellectual adventure. Education is discipline for the adventure of life; research is intellectual adventure; and the universities
should be homes of adventure shared in common by young and old.
For successful education there must always be a certain freshness in
the knowledge dealt with. It must either be new in itself or it must be
invested with some novelty of application to the new world of new
times. Knowledge does not keep any better than fish. You may be
dealing with knowledge of the old species, with some old truth; but
somehow or other it must come to the students, as it were, just drawn
out of the sea and with the freshness of its immediate importance.

2. Addams/Dalcroze/Tolstoy

These three teachers have influenced thousands of others because they discovered pedagogical principles which transcend the particular circumstances in which they taught. Jane Addams was devising "continuing education" programs for immigrants; Dalcroze was inventing a new method of musical training for youngsters; Tolstoy had established a school for the children of his newly liberated serfs. The principle they discovered (anew) is the heuristic, enabling power of imagination—the historical imagination, the kinetic and auditory imagination, the visual imagination.

Jane Addams tirelessly invented ways and means of teaching because she imaginatively entered into the lives of the people for whom Hull House (and its forerunners) was not only a community center but another world. Like so many, she found inspiration in Tolstoy's ideas of education. (See "Tolstoy, Vygotsky, and the Making of Meaning," pp. 85–93.)

Seeing how Dalcroze reasons about where to begin is a way to learn to question prevalent notions about the relationship of the physical and the mental in learning anything.

Jane Addams
(from *Democracy and Social Ethics*)

... Has our commercialism been so strong that our schools have become insensibly commercialized, whereas we supposed that our industrial life was receiving the broadening and illuminating effects of the schools? The training of these children, so far as it has been vocational at all, has been in the direction of clerical work. It is possible that the business men, whom we in America so tremendously admire, have really been dictating the curriculum of our public schools, in spite of the conventions of educators and the suggestions of university professors. The business man, of course, has not said, "I will have the public schools train office boys and clerks so that I may have them easily and cheaply," but he has sometimes said, "Teach the children to write legibly and to figure accurately and quickly; to acquire habits of punctuality and order; to be prompt to obey; and you will fit them to make their way in the world as I have made mine." Has the workingman been silent as to what he desires for his children, and allowed the business man to decide for him there, as he has allowed the politician to manage his municipal affairs, or has the workingman so far shared our universal optimism that he has really believed that his children would never need to go into industrial life at all, but that all of his sons would become bankers and merchants?

... We constantly hear it said in educational circles, that a child learns only by "doing," and that education must proceed "through the eyes and hands to the brain"; and yet for the vast number of people all around us who do not need to have activities artificially provided, and who use their hands and eyes all the time, we do not seem able to reverse the process. We quote the dictum, "What is learned in the schoolroom must be applied in the workshop," and yet the skill and handicraft constantly used in the workshop have no relevance or meaning given to them by the school; and when we do try to help the workingman in an educational way, we completely ignore his everyday occupation. Yet the task is merely one of adaptation. It is to take actual conditions and to make them the basis for a large and generous method of education, to perform a difficult idealization doubtless, but not an impossible one.

... If a workingman is to have a conception of his value at all, he must see industry in its unity and entirety; he must have a conception that will include not only himself and his immediate family and community, but the industrial organization as a whole. It is doubtless true that dexterity of hand becomes less and less imperative as the invention of machinery and subdivision of labor proceeds; but it becomes all the more necessary, if the workman is to save his life at all, that he should get a sense of his individual relation to the system. Feeding a machine with a material of which he has no knowledge, producing a product, totally unrelated to the rest of his life, without in the least knowing what becomes of it, or its connection with the community, is, of course, unquestionably deadening to his intellectual and moral life. To make the moral connection it would be necessary to give him a social consciousness of the value of his work, and at least a sense of participation and a certain joy in its ultimate use; to make the intellectual connection it would be essential to create in him some historic conception of the development of industry and the relation of his individual work to it.

Workingmen themselves have made attempts in both directions, which it would be well for moralists and educators to study. It is a striking fact that when workingmen formulate their own moral code, and try to inspire and encourage each other, it is always a large and general doctrine which they preach. They were the first class of men to organize an international association, and the constant talk at a modern labor meeting is of solidarity and of the identity of the interests of workingmen the world over. It is difficult to secure a successful organization of men into the simplest trades organization without an appeal to the most abstract principles of justice and brotherhood. As they have formulated their own morals by laying the greatest stress upon the largest morality, so if they could found their own schools, it is doubtful whether they would be of the mechanic institute type. Courses of study arranged by a group of workingmen are most naïve in their breadth and generality. They will select the history of the world in preference to that of any period or nation. The "wonders of science" or "the story of evolution" will attract workingmen to a lecture when zoology or chemistry will drive them away. The "outlines of literature" or "the best in literature" will draw an audience when a lecturer in English poetry will be solitary. This results partly from a wholesome desire to have general knowledge before special knowledge, and is partly a rebound from the specialization of labor to which the workingman is subjected. When he is free from work and can direct his own mind, he tends to roam, to dwell upon large themes. Much the same tendency is found in programmes of study arranged by Woman's Clubs in country places. The untrained mind, wearied with meaningless detail, when it gets an opportunity to make its demand heard, asks for general philosophy and background.

In a certain sense commercialism itself, at least in its larger aspect, tends to educate the workingman better than organized education does. Its interests are certainly world-wide and democratic, while it is absolutely undiscriminating as to country and creed, coming into contact with all climes and races. If this aspect of commercialism were utilized, it would in a measure counterbalance the tendency which results from the subdivision of labor. . . .

Emile Jaques-Dalcroze

(from *Rhythm, Music, and Education*)

...No schoolmaster would set a child to draw something with which he was not familiar, and before he knew how to handle a pencil. Nor would he begin to teach him geography before, having learnt to walk and gesticulate, he had acquired an elementary sense of space; nor direct him to draw a map until he could not only handle a pencil and trace lines, but had also acquired both a sense of space and an idea of the lay of the land. No one can exercise several faculties at the same time before he has acquired, however crudely, at least one faculty.

Consciousness of sound can only be acquired by reiterated experiences of the ear and voice; consciousness of rhythm by reiterated experiences of movements of the whole body. Since the practice of music demands the simultaneous co-operation of ear, voice, and muscular system—and it is obviously impossible, in the early stages of music study, to train all these musical media at the same time—the question arises as to which of them should be attended to first.

The movements that produce the voice in all its shades of pitch and loudness are of a secondary order, depending on the elementary rhythm of breathing. We are therefore left to choose between the *muscular system* and the *ear,* confining ourselves to the capacity of each of these—not of forming sound, since this depends on the special muscular activity of breathing, but of executing and perceiving *rhythms.*

The muscular system perceives rhythms. By means of repeated daily exercises, *muscular memory* may be acquired, conducing to a clear and regular representation of rhythm.

The ear perceives rhythms. By means of repeated daily exercises, *sound memory* may be acquired, sharpening and stimulating the critical faculties. This will enable the student to compare the perception of sound rhythms with their representation.

If, at this stage—working on the principle that execution should precede perception and criticism—we compare the functions of the ear with those of the muscular system, we arrive at the conclusion that the first place in the order of elementary music training should be accorded the *muscular system. . . .*

It may be noted that there is an intimate connection between rhythm in all its shades and gesture. A complete musician, to mark a sharp, vigorous accentuation, will shoot out his clenched fist; his thumb and first finger will unite to describe a fine, acute touch; his hands will sway apart to indicate an effect of delicacy and softness. . . . His body is an involuntary medium for the expression of thought. But there are incomplete musicians in whom this capacity for corporal expression requires developing with as much care as would be devoted to the exercising of weak fingers or rigid joints in a piano student. . . .

Observe the movements by which a conductor of an orchestra, endowed with temperament, represents and transmits rhythm. Does he confine himself to movements of the arm alone in seeking to convey to the instrumentalists the image of the rhythm they are to create? By no means. His knees will stiffen, his foot will press against the platform, his back will straighten, his finger and wrist movements harden. His whole body will be seen to co-operate in his representation of the rhythm: each articulation, each muscle, contributing to render the rhythmic impression more intense; the aspect of his whole person becoming, in short, the reflected image of the movement of the music, and animating the executants—his own representation of the rhythm being transmuted to them.

Another example. After my little (or big) pupils have practised eurythmics for a certain time, I give them "exercises in interrupted marching." They will execute a few bars of a rhythmic march, then halt for a bar (later, for several bars), in the position of the last executed bar. The duration of the interruption, the pause, must be estimated and accentuated only in thought; it being strictly forbidden to count out loud, or under the breath, or to move any limb. Yet what do I find? Those who have not yet attained confidence in the faculty they are on the way to acquire (that of *thinking* in rhythm) seek to deceive me (and themselves, too, perhaps) in employing muscles other than those of the leg to execute the rhythm. I catch movements of an eyelid, a nostril, a toe, even an ear, and I have had expressly to prohibit the beating of time with the tongue (while scarcely in a position to control it!) . . . And every musician, by experimenting on himself, will find that, after counting one or two bars mentally, he will feel resonating in his whole organism, so to speak, the *echo* of the time-value, and that, while he appears to be immobile, his muscles are invisibly collaborating with his mental process.

Man instinctively feels rhythmic vibrations in all his conscious muscles; that is why it behoves a teacher of rhythm to train through and in rhythm the *whole* muscular system, so that every muscle may contribute its share in awakening, clarifying, moulding, and perfecting rhythmic consciousness.

Leo Tolstoy

(from "Are the Peasant Children to Learn to Write
from Us? or, Are We to Learn from the Peasant
Children?")

The chief art of the teacher, in the study of language, and the chief
exercise, with the aim of guiding children to write compositions con-
sist in giving them themes, through not so much in furnishing them
as in presenting a large choice, in pointing out the extent of the composition, and in indicating the initial steps. Many clever and talented
pupils wrote nonsense; they wrote: "It began to burn, they began to
drag out things, and I went into the street," and nothing came of it,
although the subject was rich, and that which was described left a
deep impression on the child. They did not understand, above all,
why they should write, or what good there was in writing. They did
not understand the art of expressing life by means of words, nor the
charm of this art.

. . . I tried many different methods of giving them themes to write.
I gave them, according to their inclinations, exact, artistic, touching,
funny, epic themes,—and nothing worked. Here is how I unexpectedly hit upon the present method.

The reading of the collection of Snegirév's proverbs has long
formed one of my favourite occupations,—nay, enjoyments. For every
proverb I imagine individuals from among the people and their conflicts in the sense of the proverb. Among the number of unrealizable
dreams, I always imagine a series of pictures, or stories, written to fit
the proverbs. Once, last winter, I forgot everything after dinner in the
reading of Snegirév's book, and even returned to the school with the
book. It was the lesson in the Russian language.

"Well, write something on a proverb!" I said.

The best pupils, Fédka, Sémka, and others, pricked up their ears.

"What do you mean by 'on a proverb'? What is it? Tell us!" the
questions ran.

I happened to open to the proverb: "He feeds with the spoon, and
pricks the eye with the handle."

"Now, imagine," I said, "that a peasant has taken a beggar to his
house, and then begins to rebuke him for the good he has done him,
and you will get that 'He feeds with the spoon, and pricks the eye with
the handle.' "

"But how are you going to write it up?" said Fédka and all the rest
who had pricked up their ears. They retreated, having convinced
themselves that this matter was above their strength, and betook
themselves to the work which they had begun.

"Write it yourself," one of them said to me.

Everybody was busy with his work; I took a pen and inkstand, and began to write.

"Well," said I, "who will write it best? I am with you."

I began the story . . . and wrote down the first page. Every unbiased man, who has the artistic sense and feels with the people, will, upon reading this first page, written by me, and the following pages of the story, written by the pupils themselves, separate this page from the rest, as he will take a fly out of the milk: it is so false, so artificial, and written in such bad language. I must remark that in the original form it was even more monstrous, since much has been corrected, thanks to the indications of the pupils.

Fédka kept looking up from his copy-book to me, and, upon meeting my eyes, smiled, winked, and repeated: "Write, write, or I'll give it to you!" He was evidently amused to see a grown person write a theme.

Having finished his theme worse and faster than usual, he climbed on the back of my chair and began to read over my shoulders. I could not proceed; others came up to us, and I read to them what I had written.

They did not like it, and nobody praised it. I felt ashamed, and, to soothe my literary ambition, I began to tell them the plan of what was to follow. In the proportion as I advanced in my story, I became enthusiastic, corrected myself, and they kept helping me out. One would say that the old man should be a magician; another would remark: "No, that won't do,—he will be just a soldier; the best thing will be if he steals from him; no, that won't go with the proverb," and so forth.

All were exceedingly interested. It was evidently new and absorbing to be in on the process of creation, to take part in it. Their judgments were all, for the most part, of the same kind, and they were just, both as to the very structure of the story and as to the details and characterizations of the persons. Nearly all of them took part in the composition; but, from the start, there distinguished themselves positive Sémka, by his clearly defined artistic quality of description, and Fédka, by the correctness of his poetical conceptions, and especially by the glow and rapidity of his imagination.

Their demands had so little of the accidental in them and were so definite, that more than once I debated with them, only to give way to them. I was strongly possessed by the demands of a regular structure and of an exact correspondence of the idea of the proverb to the story; while they, on the contrary, were only concerned about the demands of artistic truth. I, for example, wanted that the peasant, who had taken the old man to his house, should himself repent of his good deed,—while they regarded this as impossible and created a cross old woman.

I said: "The peasant was at first sorry for the old man, and later he hated to give away the bread."

Fédka replied that that would be improbable: "He did not obey the old woman from the start and would not submit later."

"What kind of a man is he, according to you?" I asked.

"He is like Uncle Timoféy," said Fédka, smiling. "He has a scanty beard, goes to church, and he has bees."

"Is he good, but stubborn?" I asked.

"Yes," said Fédka, "he will not obey the old woman."

From the time that the old man was brought into the hut, the work became animated. They evidently for the first time felt the charm of clothing artistic details in words. Sémka distinguished himself more than the rest in this respect: the most accurate details poured forth one after the other. The only reproach that could be made to him was that these details sketched only the particular moment, without connection with the general feeling of the story. I hardly could write as fast as they told me the incidents, and only asked them to wait and not forget what they had told me.

Sémka needed primarily objective images: the stiff, frozen bast shoes, and the dirt oozing from them, as they melted out, and the toast into which they were changed when the old woman threw them into the oven.

Fédka, on the contrary, had to evoke the feeling with which he himself was permeated. Fédka saw the snow drifting behind the peasant's leg-rags, and the feeling of compassion with which the peasant said: "Lord, how it snows!" (Fédka's face even showed how the peasant said it, and he swung his hands and shook his head.) He saw the overcoat, a mass of rags and patches, and the torn shirt, behind which could be seen the haggard body of the old man, wet from the thawing snow. He created the old woman, who growled as she took off his bast shoes, at the command of her husband, and the pitiful groan of the old man as he muttered through his teeth: "Softly, motherkin, I have sores here."

Sémka needed mainly objective pictures: bast shoes, an overcoat, an old man, a woman, almost without any connection between them; but Fédka had to evoke the feeling of pity with which he himself was permeated. He ran ahead of the story, telling how he would feed the old man, how he would fall down at night, and how he would later teach a boy in the field to read, so that I was obliged to ask him not to be in such a hurry and not to forget what he had said. His eyes sparkled to the point of tears; his swarthy, thin little hands were cramped convulsively; he was angry with me, and kept urging me on: "Have you written it, have you written it?" he kept asking me.

He treated all the rest despotically; he wanted to talk all the time, not as a story is told, but as it is written, that is, artistically to clothe in words the sensuous pictures. Thus, for example, he would not allow words to be transposed; if he once said, "I have sores on my feet," he would not permit me to say, "On my feet I have sores." His soul, now softened and irritated by the sentiment of pity, that is, of love, clothed every image in an artistic form, and denied everything that did not correspond to the idea of eternal beauty and harmony.

The moment Sémka was carried away by the expression of disproportionable details about the lambs in the door-bench, and so forth, Fédka grew angry and said, "What a lot of bosh!" I only needed to suggest what the peasant was doing, while his wife went to the gossip, when in Fédka's imagination there would immediately arise a picture with lambs bleating in the door-bench, with the sighs of the old man and the delirium of the boy Serézhka; I only needed to suggest an artificial and false picture, when he immediately would angrily remark that that was not necessary.

For example, I suggested the description of the peasant's looks, to which he agreed; but to my proposal to describe what the peasant was thinking while his wife had run over to the gossip, there immediately rose before him the very form of the thought: "If you got in the way of Savóska the corpse, he would pull all your locks out!" He said this in such a fatigued and calmly serious and habitual and, at the same time, good-natured voice, leaning his head on his hand, that the boys rolled in laughter.

The chief quality in every art, the feeling of limit, was developed in him to an extraordinary degree. He writhed at the suggestion of any superfluous feature, made by some one of the boys.

He directed the structure of the story so despotically, and with such right to this despotism, that the boys soon went home, and only he and Sémka, who would not give in to him, though working in another direction, were left. We worked from seven to eleven o'clock; they felt neither hunger nor fatigue, and even got angry at me when I stopped writing; they undertook to relieve me in writing, but they soon gave that up.

It was then for the first time that Fédka asked my name. We laughed because he did not know.

"I know," he said, "how to call you; but how do they call you in the manor?"

I told him.

"Are we going to print it?" he asked.

"Yes."

"Then we shall have to print: Work by Makárov, Morózov, and Tolstóy."

He was agitated for a long time and could not fall asleep, and I cannot express that feeling of agitation, joy, fear, and almost regret, which I experienced during that evening. I felt that with that day a new world of enjoyment and suffering was opened up to him,—the world of art; I thought that I had seen what no one has a right to see—the germination of the mysterious flower of poetry.

I felt both dread and joy, like the seeker after the treasure who suddenly sees the flower of the fern—I felt joy, because suddenly and quite unexpectedly there was revealed to me that stone of the philosophers, which I had vainly been trying to find for two years—the art of teaching the expression of thoughts; and dread, because this art made new demands, a whole world of desires, which stood in no relation to the surroundings of the pupils, as I thought first. There was no mistaking. It was not an accident, but a conscious creation. . . .

No matter how irregular the development of a child may be, there are always left in him the primitive features of harmony. By moderating, at least by not pushing, the development, we may hope to get a certain approach to regularity and harmony. But we are so sure of ourselves, we are so visionarily devoted to the false ideal of nature perfection, we are so impatient with irregularities and so firmly believe in our ability to correct them, we are so little able to comprehend and value the primitive beauty of a child, that we hurry to magnify and paste up the irregularities that strike us: we correct, we educate the child. Now one side has to be equalized with the other, now the other has to be equalized with the first. The child is developed more and more, and all the time departs more and more from the former shattered prototype, and the attainment of the imaginary prototype of perfection becomes ever more impossible. Our ideal is behind us, not before us. Education spoils; it does not correct men. The more a child is spoiled, the less he ought to be educated, the more liberty he needs.

It is impossible and absurd to teach and educate a child, for the simple reason that the child stands nearer than I do, than any grown man does, to that ideal of harmony, truth, beauty, and goodness, to which I, in my pride, wish to raise him. The consciousness of this ideal is more powerful in him than in me. All he needs of me is the material, in order to develop harmoniously. The moment I gave him full liberty and stopped teaching him, he wrote a poetical production, the like of which cannot be found in Russian literature. Therefore, it is my conviction that we cannot teach children in general, and peasant children in particular, to write and compose. All that we can do is to teach them how to go about writing.

If what I did in order to obtain this result may be called method, this method consisted in the following:

(1) Give a great variety of themes, not inventing them specially for the children, but propose such as appear most serious and interesting to the teacher himself.

(2) Give the children children's compositions to read, and give them only children's compositions as models, for children's compositions are always more correct, more artistic, and more moral than the compositions of grown people.

(3) (Most important.) When looking through a pupil's composition, never make any remarks to him about the cleanliness of the copy-book, nor about penmanship, nor orthography, nor, above all, about the structure of the sentences and about logic.

(4) Since the difficulty of composition lies neither in the volume nor the content but in the artistic quality of the theme, the sequence of the themes is not to be determined by volume or content or language, but in the realization, the working out of the matter which consists in selecting one out of a number of ideas; in choosing words, clothing it in words; in remembering it and finding a place for it; not repeating it, not leaving out anything; in combining what follows with what precedes, all the time keeping in mind what is already written down; and finally, in thinking and writing at the same time, without having one of these acts interfere with the other.

Leo Tolstoy

(from "The School at Yásnaya Polyána")

In the first and second class the choice of compositions is left to the students themselves. A favourite subject for compositions for the first and the second class is the history of the Old Testament, which they write two months after the teacher has told it to them. . . .

In the first class we tried compositions on given themes. The first themes that most naturally occurred to us were descriptions of simple objects, such as grain, the house, the wood, and so forth; but, to our great surprise, these demands upon our pupils almost made them weep, and, in spite of the aid afforded them by the teacher, who divided the description of the grain into a description of its growth, its change into bread, its use, they emphatically refused to write upon such themes, or, if they did write, they made the most incomprehensible and senseless mistakes in orthography, in the language and in the meaning.

We then tried descriptions of certain events, and all were as happy as if a present had been given to them. That which forms the favourite topic of the schools—the description of so-called simple objects: pigs, pots, a table—turned out to be incomparably more difficult than whole stories taken from their memories. The same mistake was repeated here as in all the other subjects of instruction: to the teacher the simplest and most general appears as the easiest, whereas for a pupil only the complex and living appears easy.

All the text-books of the natural sciences begin with general laws, the text-books of language with definitions, history with the division into periods, and even geometry with the definition of the concepts of space and the mathematical point. Nearly every teacher, being guided by the same manner of thinking, gives as a first composition the definition of a table or bench, without taking the trouble to consider that in order to define a table or bench one has to have reached a high level of philosophical-dialectic development, and that the same pupil who weeps over the composition on a bench will excellently describe the feeling of love or anger, the meeting of Joseph with his brothers, or a fight with his companion. The subjects of the compositions were naturally chosen from among descriptions of incidents, relations to persons, and the repetition of stories which had been told.

3. Montessori/Ashton-Warner/Freire

Montessori established her Case dei Bambini *in Rome at about the same time that Jane Addams founded Hull House in Chicago. Like her American counterpart, Montessori learned from Tolstoy, among others, to trust the powers of the human mind; the imagination was for her a forming power. From Jean-Marc-Gaspard Itard, the physician who attempted to train the "Wild Boy of Aveyron" to speak, Montessori learned the uses of what she called "didactic materials," physical objects which could mediate the learning process. Montessori was a scientist, the first woman in Italy to receive the M.D. (pediatrics). She aimed for a "scientific method of pedagogy," by which she meant one free of ancient prejudices and informed with the idea that structures and limits are enabling, that form is the means of liberating the imagination. To read* The Montessori Method *is to see how authentic method functions. The book is filled with fascinating narratives of how she came to invent strategies and techniques by which she implemented her central principle, that what we learn we teach ourselves. (I have included as the last line in the excerpted passage the first line of her account of how she came to invent a special alphabet [set of letters] adapted to the kinetic imagination. I hope some readers will be teased into reading the delightful account in* The Montessori Method.*)*

Sylvia Ashton-Warner is temperamentally the antithesis of Montessori and yet she too is a Tolstoyan who has developed a method that is at once scientific (in the sense in which that term is used of Montessori's) and imaginative. Her Key Words— "captions of the dynamic life itself"—are analogous to the "generative words" of Paulo Freire and if we carefully consider the philosophical rationales for each, we will gain for ourselves some very powerful speculative instruments. (Freire and Richards have been for me the most important teachers: I've tried to suggest the kind of insights to be gained from them in "Towards a Pedagogy of Knowing," Part II, pp. 48–60.)

In this selection, Paulo Freire explains how the critical questioning of pictures "problematizes the existential situation" at

*the same time that it generates the words which will then generate
the critical consciousness—the mind in action making meaning.
Freire's notion of the "dialogic action" which constitutes a
"pedagogy of knowing" is consonant with everything Richards
has argued about the centrality of interpretation in teaching.*

It's important to note the differentiation Freire makes between
coding, *which is construing letters, and* codification, *which is
the making of meaning. The interdependence of the two is central
to his method, as in, for instance, the use of the "Card of
Discovery."*

Maria Montessori

(from *The Montessori Method*)

If we study the history of discoveries, we will find that they have
come from *real objective observation* and *from logical thought.* These are
simple things, but rarely found in one man.

Does it not seem strange, for instance, that after the discovery by
Laveran of the malarial parasite which invades the red blood-corpus-
cles, we did not, in spite of the fact that we know the blood system
to be a system of closed vessels, even so much as *suspect the possibility*
that a stinging insect might inoculate us with the parasite? Instead,
the theory that the evil emanated from low ground, that it was carried
by the African winds, or that it was due to dampness, was given credence. Yet these were vague ideas, while the parasite was a definite
biological specimen.

When the discovery of the malarial mosquito came to complete logically the discovery of Laveran, this seemed marvellous, stupefying.
Yet we know in biology that the reproduction of molecular vegetable
bodies is by scission with alternate sporation, and that of molecular
animals is by scission with alternate conjunction. That is, after a certain period in which the primitive cell has divided and sub-divided
into fresh cells, equal among themselves, there comes the formation
of two diverse cells, one male and one female, which must unite to
form a single cell capable of recommencing the cycle of reproduction
by division. All this being known at the time of Laveran, and the malarial parasite being known to be a protozoon, it would have seemed
logical to consider its segmentation in the stroma of the red corpuscle

as the phase of scission and to await until the parasite gave place to the sexual forms, which must necessarily come in the phase succeeding scission. Instead, the division was looked upon as spore-formation, and neither Laveran, nor the numerous scientists who followed the research, knew how to give an explanation of the appearance of the sexual forms. Laveran expressed an idea, which was immediately received, that these two forms were degenerate forms of the malarial parasite, and therefore incapable of producing the changes determining the disease. Indeed, the malaria was apparently cured at the appearance of the two sexual forms of the parasite, the conjunction of the two cells being impossible in the human blood. Morel's theory of human degeneration accompanied by deformity and weakness, inspired Laveran in his interpretation, and everybody found the idea of the illustrious pathologist a fortunate one, because it was inspired by the great concepts of the Morellian theory.

Had anyone, instead, limited himself to reasoning thus: the original form of the malarial insect is a protozoon; it reproduces itself by scission, under our eyes; when the scission is finished, we see two diverse cells, one a half-moon, the other threadlike. These are the feminine and masculine cells which must, by conjunction, alternate the scission,—such a reasoner would have opened the way to the discovery. But *so simple* a process of reasoning did not come. We might almost ask ourselves how great would be the world's progress if a special form of education prepared men for pure observation and logical thought.

A great deal of time and intellectual force are lost in the world, because the false seems great and the truth so small and insignificant.

I say all this to defend the necessity, which I feel we face, of preparing the coming generations by means of more rational methods. It is from these generations that the world awaits its progress. We have already learned to make use of our surroundings, but I believe that we have arrived at a time when the necessity presents itself for *utilising* human force, through a scientific education. . . .

Is it necessary to begin writing with the making of vertical strokes? A moment of clear and logical thinking is enough to enable us to answer, no. The child makes too painful an effort in following such an exercise. The first steps should be the easiest, and the up and down stroke is, on the contrary, one of the most difficult of all the pen movements. Only a professional penman could fill a whole page and preserve the regularity of such strokes, but a person who writes only moderately well would be able to complete a page of presentable writing. Indeed, the straight line is unique, expressing the shortest distance between two points, while any deviation from that direction signifies a line which is not straight. Those infinite deviations are therefore easier than that one trace which is perfection . . . .

I had noticed in the notebooks of the deficient [retarded] children in France . . . that the pages of vertical strokes, although they began as such, ended in lines of C's. This goes to show that the deficient child, whose mind is less resistant than that of the normal child, exhausts, little by little, the initial effort of imitation, and the natural movement gradually comes to take the place of that which was formed or stimulated. So the straight lines are transformed into curves, more and more like the letter C. Such a phenomenon does not appear in the copy-books of normal children, for they persist until the end of the page is reached, thus concealing the didactic [pedagogical] error . . . .

That vertical strokes should prepare for alphabetical writing, seems incredibly illogical. The alphabet is made up of curves, therefore we must prepare for it by learning to make straight lines. "But," says someone, "in many letters of the alphabet, the straight line does exist." True, but there is no reason why we should start with just one of the details of a complete form. We may analyse the alphabetical signs in this way, discovering straight lines and curves, as by analysing discourse, we find grammatical rules. But we all *speak* independently of such rules; why then should we not *write* independently of such analysis, and without the separate execution of the parts constituting the letter?

It would be sad indeed if we could *speak* only *after* we had studied grammar! It would be much the same as demanding that before we *looked* at the stars in the firmament, we must study infinitesimal calculus; it is much the same thing to feel that before teaching an idiot to write, we must make him understand the abstract derivation of lines and the problems of geometry!

No less are we to be pitied if, in order to write, we must follow analytically the parts constituting the alphabetical signs. In fact the *effort* which we believe to be a necessary accompaniment to learning to write is a purely artificial effort, allied, not to writing, but to the *methods* by which it is taught.

Let us for a moment cast aside every dogma in this connection. Let us take no note of culture, or custom. We are not, here, interested in knowing how humanity began to write, nor what may have been the origin of writing itself. Let us put away the conviction, that long usage has given us, of the necessity of beginning writing by making vertical strokes; and let us try to be as clear and unprejudiced in spirit as the truth which we are seeking.

"Let us observe an individual who is writing, and let us seek to analyse the

acts he performs in writing," that is, the mechanical operations which enter into the execution of writing. This would be undertaking the *philosophical study of writing,* and it goes without saying that we should examine the individual who writes, not the *writing;* the *subject,* not the *object.* Many have begun with the object, examining the writing, and in this way many methods have been constructed.

But a method starting from the individual would be decidedly original—very different from other methods which preceded it. It would indeed signify a new era in writing, *based upon anthropology.*

In fact, when I undertook my experiments with normal children, if I had thought of giving a name to this new method of writing, I should have called it without knowing what the results would be, the *anthropological method.* Certainly, my studies in anthropology inspired the method, but experience has given me, as a surprise, another title which seems to me the natural one, "the method of *spontaneous* writing."

While teaching deficient children I happened to observe the following fact: An idiot girl of eleven years, who was possessed of normal strength and motor power in her hands, could not learn to sew, or even to take the first step, darning, which consists in passing the needle first over, then under the woof, now taking up, now leaving, a number of threads.

I set the child to weaving with the Froebel mats, in which a strip of paper is threaded transversely in and out among vertical strips of paper held fixed at top and bottom. I thus came to think of the analogy between the two exercises, and became much interested in my observation of the girl. When she had become skilled in the Froebel weaving, I led her back again to the sewing, and saw with pleasure that she was now able to follow the darning. From that time on, our sewing classes began with a regular course in the Froebel weaving.

I saw that the necessary movements of the hand in sewing *had been prepared without having the child sew,* and that we should really find the way to *teach* the child *how,* before *making him execute* a task. I saw especially that preparatory movements could be carried on, and reduced to a mechanism, by means of repeated exercises not in the work itself but in that which prepares for it. Pupils could then come to the real work, able to perform it without ever having directly set their hands to it before.

I thought that I might in this way prepare for writing, and the idea interested me tremendously. . . .

Sylvia Ashton-Warner

(from *Teacher*)

Creative Teaching

Organic reading is not new. The Egyptian hieroglyphics were one-word sentences. Helen Keller's first word, "water," was a one-word book. Tolstoy found his way to it in his peasant school, while, out in the field of UNESCO today, it is used automatically as the only reasonable way of introducing reading to primitive people: in a famine area the teachers wouldn't think of beginning with any words other than "crop," "soil," "hunger," "manure," and the like.

Not that organic reading is exclusively necessary to the illiterate of a primitive race. True, it is indispensable in conducting a young child from one culture to another, especially in New Zealand where the Maori is obliged to make the transition at so tender an age; but actually it is universal. First words are different from first drawings only in medium, and first drawings vary from country to country. In New Zealand a boy's first drawing is anything that is mobile; trucks, trains and planes, if he lives in a populated area, and if he doesn't, it's horses. New Zealand girls, however, draw houses first wherever they live. I once made a set of first readers on these two themes. But Tongan children's first drawings are of trees, Samoan five-year-olds draw churches and Chinese draw flowers. What a fascinating story this makes!

How can anyone begin any child on any arranged book, however good the book, when you know this? And how good is any child's book, anyway, compared with the ones they write themselves? Of course, as I'm always saying, it's not the only reading; it's no more than the *first* reading. The bridge.

It's the bridge from the known to the unknown; from a native culture to a new; and, universally speaking, from the inner man out.

In July, 1857, Tolstoy wrote in his diary:

". . . and the most important of all: clearly and forcibly the thought came to me to open a school for the entire county."

Only two years later, in the fall of 1859, he came close to realising his dreams. With the same passion with which he did everything, he gave himself to teaching. Almost to the exclusion of all other interests, he gave three years of his life to the peasant children. His work had nothing in common with the standard, well-regulated school systems. Tolstoy wrote that he had a passionate affection for his school.

Under his guidance other young people who helped him in his work developed a similar "passionate affection."

As usual he began by discarding all existing traditions and by refusing to follow any method of teaching already in use. First he must fathom the mind of the peasant child, and by doing away with punishments, let his pupils teach him the art of teaching. In his school his pupils were free to choose their own subjects, and to take as much work as they desired. The teacher considered it his duty to assist the children in their search for knowledge by adjusting his method of approach to the individual child, and by finding the best way of proffering assistance in each case.

These free Tolstoy schools, without programmes, without punishments, without rules, without forcing the will of a child, were remarkably successful. The children spent entire days at their studies and were reluctant to leave the schoolhouse.

And one of the international volunteers in Kabylia in the mountains of Algeria writes:

"About twenty children were sitting in front of the teacher under an ash tree and reading in chorus the name of their village which she had written on a big sheet of paper. They were enormously proud; time and time again they read us the word.

"But the next evening three of the adults came to ask us to teach them to write their names.

" 'Why do you want to write your name?'

"One of them explained: 'To sign at the Post Office. If I can sign my name to collect a registered letter I shall not need to pay the witnesses.'

" 'And do you often get letters like that?'

" 'Sometimes. From my son in France.'

"We went steadily on; but in the evening, instead of resting under the mosquito net, we were all caught up in the fever of fundamental education."

Organic reading for beginners is not new; it's our rejection of it that's new.

The Key Vocabulary

The method of teaching any subject in a Maori infant room [kindergarten] may be seen as a plank in a bridge from one culture to another, and to the extent that this bridge is strengthened may a Maori in later life succeed.

This transition made by Maori children is often unsuccessful. At a tender age a wrench occurs from one culture to another, from which, either manifestly or subconsciously, not all recover. And I think that this circumstance has some little bearing on the number of Maoris who, although well educated, seem neurotic, and on the number who retreat to the mat.

Another more obvious cause of the social failure of Maoris is the delay in the infant room . . . which is due to language as well as to the imposition of a culture. Many children arrive at the secondary school stage too old to fit in with the European group and they lose heart to continue. From here, being too young and unskilled to do a competent job, some fall in and out of trouble, become failures by European standards, and by the time they have grown up have lost the last and most precious of their inheritances—their social stability.

With this in mind, therefore, I see any subject whatever in a Maori infant room as a plank in the bridge from the Maori to the European. In particular, reading. . . .

Children have two visions, the inner and the outer. Of the two the inner vision is brighter.

I hear that in other infant rooms widespread illustration is used to introduce the reading vocabulary to a five-year-old, a vocabulary chosen by adult educationists. I use pictures, too, to introduce the reading vocabulary, but they are pictures of the inner vision and the captions are chosen by the children themselves. True, the picture of the outer, adult-chosen pictures can be meaningful and delightful to children; but it is the captions of the mind-pictures that have the power and the light. For whereas the illustrations perceived by the outer eye cannot be other than interesting, the illustrations seen by the inner eye are organic, and it is the captioning of these that I call the "Key Vocabulary."

I see the mind of a five-year-old as a volcano with two vents; destructiveness and creativeness. And I see that to the extent that we widen the creative channel, we atrophy the destructive one. And it seems to me that since these words of the key vocabulary are no less than the captions of the dynamic life itself, they course out through the creative channel, making their contribution to the drying up of the destructive vent. From all of which I am constrained to see it as creative reading and to count it among the arts.

First words must mean something to a child.

First words must have intense meaning for a child. They must be part of his being.

How much hangs on the love of reading, the instinctive inclination to hold a book! *Instinctive*. That's what it must be. The reaching out for a book needs to become an organic action, which can happen at this yet formative age. Pleasant words won't do. Respectable words won't do. They must be words organically tied up, organically born from the dynamic life itself. They must be words that are already part of the child's being. "A child," reads a recent publication on the approach of the American books, "can be led to feel that Janet and John are friends." *Can be led to feel.* Why lead him to feel or try to lead him to feel that these strangers are friends? What about the passionate feeling he has already for his own friends? To me it is inorganic to overlook this step.... It's little enough to ask that a Maori child should begin his reading from a book of his own colour and culture. This is the formative age where habits are born and established. An aversion to the written word is a habit I have seen born under my own eyes in my own infant room on occasion.

It's not beauty to abruptly halt the growth of a young mind and to overlay it with the frame of an imposed culture. There are ways of training and grafting young growth. The true conception of beauty is the shape of organic life and that is the very thing at stake in the transition from one culture to another. If this transition took place at a later age when the security of a person was already established there would not be the same need for care. But in this country it happens that the transition takes place at a tender and vulnerable age, which is the reason why we all try to work delicately.

Back to these first words. To these first books. They must be made out of the stuff of the child itself. I reach a hand into the mind of the child, bring out a handful of the stuff I find there, and use that as our first working material. Whether it is good or bad stuff, violent or placid stuff, coloured or dun. To effect an unbroken beginning. And in this dynamic material, within the familiarity and security of it, the Maori finds that words have intense meaning to him, from which cannot help but arise a love of reading. For it's here, right in this first word, that the love of reading is born, and the longer his reading is organic the stronger it becomes, until by the time he arrives at the books of the new culture, he receives them as another joy rather than as a labour. I know all this because I've done it.

> First words must have an intense meaning.
> First words must be already part of the dynamic life.
> First books must be made of the stuff of the child
> himself, whatever and wherever the child.

The words, which I write on large tough cards and give to the children to read, prove to be one-look words if they are accurately enough chosen. And they are plain enough in conversation. It's the conversation that has to be got. However, if it can't be, I find that whatever a child chooses to make in the creative period may quite likely be such a word. But if the vocabulary of a child is still inaccessible, one can always begin him on the general Key Vocabulary, common to any child in any race, a set of words bound up with security that experiments, and later on their creative writing, show to be organically associated with the inner world: "Mummy," "Daddy," "kiss," "frightened," "ghost."

"Mohi," I ask a new five, an undisciplined Maori, "what word do you want?"

"Jet!"

I smile and write it on a strong little card and give it to him. "What is it again?"

"Jet!"

"You can bring it back in the morning. What do you want, Gay?"

Gay is the classic overdisciplined, bullied victim of the respectable mother.

"House," she whispers. So I write that, too, and give it into her eager hand.

"What do you want, Seven?" Seven is a violent Maori.

"Bomb! Bomb! I want bomb!"

So Seven gets his word "bomb" and challenges anyone to take it from him.

And so on through the rest of them. They ask for a new word each morning and never have I to repeat to them what it is. And if you saw the condition of these tough little cards the next morning you'd know why they need to be of tough cardboard or heavy drawing paper rather than thin paper.

When each has the nucleus of a reading vocabulary and I know they are at peace with me I show them the word "frightened" and at once all together they burst out with what they are frightened of. Nearly all the Maoris say "the ghost!" a matter which has a racial and cultural origin, while the Europeans name some animal they have never seen, "tiger" or "alligator," using it symbolically for the unnameable fear that we all have.

"I not frightened of anysing!" shouts my future murderer, Seven.

"Aren't you?"

"No, I stick my knife into it all!"

"What will you stick your knife into?"

"I stick my knife into the tigers!"

"Tigers" is usually a word from the European children but here is a Maori with it. So I give him "tigers" and never have I to repeat this word to him, and in the morning the little card shows the dirt and disrepair of passionate usage.

"Come in," cry the children to a knock at the door, but as no one does come in we all go out. And here we find in the porch, humble with natural dignity, a barefooted, tattooed Maori woman.

"I see my little Seven?" she says.

"Is Seven your little boy?"

"I bring him up. Now he five. I bring him home to his real family for school eh. I see my little boy?"

The children willingly produce Seven, and here we have in the porch, within a ring of sympathetic brown and blue eyes, a reunion.

"Where did you bring him up?" I ask over the many heads.

"Way back on those hill. All by heeself. You remember your ol' Mummy?" she begs Seven.

I see.

Later, standing watching Seven grinding his chalk to dust on his blackboard as usual, I do see. "Whom do you want, Seven? Your old Mummy or your new Mummy?"

"My old Mummy."

"What do your brothers do?"

"They all hits me."

"Old Mummy" and "new Mummy" and "hit" and "brothers" are all one-look words added to his vocabulary, and now and again I see some shape breaking through the chalk-ravage. And I wish I could make a good story of it and say he is no longer violent. . . .

"Who's that crying!" I accuse, lifting my nose like an old war horse.

"Seven he breaking Gay's neck."

So the good story, I say to my junior [assistant teacher], must stand by for a while. But I can say he is picking up his words now. Fast. . . .

Out press these words, grouping themselves in their own wild order. All boys wanting words of locomotion, aeroplane, tractor, jet, and the girls the words of domesticity, house, Mummy, doll. Then the fear words, ghost, tiger, skellington, alligator, bulldog, wild piggy, police. The sex words, kiss, love, touch, *haka* [Maori war dance]. The key words carrying their own illustrations in the mind, vivid and powerful pictures which none of us could possibly draw for them—since in the first place we can't see them and in the second because they are so alive with an organic life that the external pictorial representation of them is beyond the frontier of possibility. We can do no more than supply the captions.

Out push these words. The tendency is for them to gather force once the fears are said, but there are so many variations on character. Even more so in this span of life where personality has not yet been moulded into the general New Zealand pattern by the one imposed vocabulary for all. They are more than captions. They are even more than sentences. They are whole stories at times. They are actually schematic drawing. I know because they tell them to me.

Out flow these captions. It's a lovely flowing. I see the creative channel swelling and undulating like an artery with blood pumping through. And as it settles, just like any other organic arrangement of nature it spreads out into an harmonious pattern; the fear words dominating the design, a few sex words, the person interest, and the temper of the century. Daddy, Mummy, ghost, bomb, kiss, brothers, butcher knife, gaol, love, dance, cry, fight, hat, bulldog, touch, wild piggy ... if you were a child, which vocabulary would you prefer? Your own or the one at present in the New Zealand infant rooms? Come John come. Look John look. Come and look. See the boats? The vocabulary of the English upper middle class, two-dimensional and respectable?

Out pelt these captions, these one-word accounts of the pictures within. Is it art? Is it creation? Is it reading? I know that it is integral. It is organic. And it is the most vital and the most sure reading vocabulary a child can build. It is the key that unlocks the mind and releases the tongue. It is the key that opens the door upon a love of reading. It is the organic foundation of a lifetime of books. It is the key that I use daily with my fives, along with the clay and the paint and amid the singing and quarrelling.

It is the key whose turning preserves intact for a little longer the true personality. It is the Key Vocabulary.

MAXIMS
in the preparation of
Maori Infant Reading

The Key Vocabulary centers round the two main instincts, fear and sex.

The Key Vocabulary varies from one locality to another and from one race to another.

Backward readers have a private Key Vocabulary which once found launches them into reading.

The power content of a word can be determined better from a backward reader than from an average reader.

In the presentation of key words to five-year-olds, illustrations are to be shunned rather than coveted.

The length of a word has no relation to its power content.

In all matters in a Maori infant room there is a Maori standard as well as a European one.

Paulo Freire

(from *Education for
Critical Consciousness*)

To acquire literacy is more than to psychologically and mechanically dominate reading and writing techniques. It is to dominate these
techniques in terms of consciousness; to understand what one reads
and to write what one understands; it is to *communicate* graphically.
Acquiring literacy does not involve memorizing sentences, words, or
syllables—lifeless objects unconnected to an existential universe—but
rather an attitude of creation and re-creation, a self-transformation
producing a stance of intervention in one's context.

Thus the educator's role is fundamentally to enter into dialogue
with the illiterate about concrete situations and simply to offer him
the instruments with which he can teach himself to read and write.
This teaching cannot be done from the top down, but only from the
inside out, by the illiterate himself, with the collaboration of the educator. That is why we searched for a method which would be the instrument of the learner as well as of the educator, and which . . .
would identify learning *content* with the learning *process.*

Hence, our mistrust in primers,[1] which set up a certain grouping
of graphic signs as a gift and cast the illiterate in the role of the *object*
rather than the *Subject* of his learning. Primers, even when they try to
avoid this pitfall, end by *donating* to the illiterate words and sentences
which really should result from his own creative effort. We opted instead for the use of "generative words," those whose syllabic elements offer, through re-combination, the creation of new words.
Teaching men how to read and write a syllabic language like Portuguese means showing them how to grasp critically the way its words
are formed, so that they themselves can carry out the creative play of
combinations. Fifteen or eighteen words seemed sufficient to present
the basic phonemes of the Portuguese language. . . .

The program is elaborated in several phases:

Phase 1 Researching the vocabulary of the groups with which one
is working. This research is carried out during informal encounters
with the inhabitants of the area. One selects not only the words most
weighted with existential meaning (and thus the greatest emotional
content), but also typical sayings, as well as words and expressions
linked to the experience of the groups in which the researcher par-
ticipates. These interviews reveal longings, frustrations, disbeliefs,
hopes, and an impetus to participate. During this initial phase the

team of educators form rewarding relationships and discover often unsuspected exuberance and beauty in the people's language.

The archives of the Service of Cultural Extension of the University of Recife contain vocabulary studies of rural and urban areas in the Northeast and in southern Brazil full of such examples as the following:

"The month of January in Angicos," said a man from the backlands of Rio Grande do Norte, "is a hard one to live through, because January is a tough guy who makes us suffer." (*Janeiro em Angicos é duro de se viver, porque janeiro é cabra danado para judiar de nós.*)

"I want to learn to read and write," said an illiterate from Recife, "so that I can stop being the shadow of other people."

A man from Florianópolis: "The people have an answer."

Another, in an injured tone: "I am not angry (*não tenho paixão*) at being poor, but at not knowing how to read."

"I have the school of the world," said an illiterate from the southern part of the country, which led Professor Jomard de Brito to ask in an essay, "What can one presume to 'teach' an adult who affirms 'I have the school of the world'?"

"I want to learn to read and write so I can change the world," said an illiterate from São Paulo, for whom *to know* quite correctly meant *to intervene* in his reality.

"The people put a screw in their heads," said another in somewhat esoteric language. And when he was asked what he meant, he replied in terms revealing the phenomenon of popular emergence: "That is what explains that you, Professor, have come to talk with me, the people."

Such affirmations merit interpretation by specialists, to produce a more efficient instrument for the educator's action. The generative words to be used in the program should emerge from this field vocabulary research, not from the educator's personal inspiration, no matter how proficiently he might construct a list.

Phase 2 Selection of the generative words from the vocabulary which was studied. The following criteria should govern their selection:

(a) phonemic richness;

(b) phonetic difficulty (the words chosen should correspond to the phonetic difficulties of the language, placed in a sequence moving gradually from words of less to those of greater difficulty);

(c) pragmatic tone, which implies a greater engagement of a word in a given social, cultural and political reality.

Professor Jarbas Maciel has commented that "these criteria are contained in the semeiotic criterion: the best generative word is that which combines the greatest possible 'percentage' of the syntactic criteria (phonemic richness, degree of complex phonetic difficulty, 'manipulability' of the groups of signs, the syllables, etc.), the semantic criteria (greater or lesser 'intensity' of the link between the word and the thing it designates), the greater or lesser correspondence between the word and the pragmatic thing designated, the greater or lesser quality of *conscientização* [conscientization] which the word potentially carries, or the grouping of sociocultural reactions which the word generates in the person or group using it."

Phase 3 The creation of the "codifications": the representation of typical existential situations of the group with which one is working. These representations function as challenges, as coded situation-problems containing elements to be decoded by the groups with the collaboration of the coordinator. Discussion of these codifications will lead the groups toward a more critical consciousness at the same time that they begin to learn to read and write. The codifications represent familiar local situations—which, however, open perspectives for the analysis of regional and national problems. The generative words are set into the codifications, graduated according to their phonetic difficulty. One generative word may embody the entire situation, or it may refer to only one of the elements of the situation.

Phase 4 The elaboration of agendas, which should serve as mere aids to the coordinators, never as rigid schedules to be obeyed.

Phase 5 The preparation of cards with the breakdown of the phonemic families which correspond to the generative words.

A major problem in setting up the program is instructing the teams of coordinators. Teaching the purely technical aspect of the procedure is not difficult; the difficulty lies rather in the creation of a new attitude—that of dialogue, so absent in our own upbringing and education. The coordinators must be converted to dialogue in order to carry out education rather than domestication. Dialogue is an I-Thou relationship, and thus necessarily a relationship between two Subjects. Each time the "thou" is changed into an object, an "it," dialogue is subverted and education is changed to deformation. The period of instruction must be followed by dialogical supervision, to avoid the temptation of anti-dialogue on the part of the coordinators. Once the material has been prepared in the form of slides, film-strips, or posters, once the teams of coordinators and supervisors have been instructed in all aspects of the method and have been given their agendas, the program itself can begin. It functions in the following manner:

The codified situation is projected, together with the first generative word, which graphically represents the oral expression of the object perceived. Discussion of its implications follows.

Only after the group, with the collaboration of the coordinator, has exhausted the analysis (decodification) of the situation, does the coordinator call attention to the generative word, encouraging the participants to visualize (not memorize) it. Once the word has been visualized, and the semantic link established between the word and the object to which it refers, the word is presented alone on another slide (or poster or photogram) without the object it names. Then the same word is separated into syllables, which the illiterate usually identifies as "pieces." Once the "pieces" are recognized, the coordinator presents visually the phonemic families which compose the word, first in isolation and then together, to arrive at the recognition of the vowels. The card presenting the phonemic families has been called the "discovery card." Using this card to reach a synthesis, men discover the mechanism of word formation through phonemic combinations in a syllabic language like Portuguese. By appropriating this mechanism critically (not learning it by rote), they themselves can begin to produce a system of graphic signs. They can begin, with surprising ease, to create words with the phonemic combinations offered by the breakdown of a trisyllabic word, on the first day of the program.[2]

For example, let us take the word *tijolo* (brick) as the first generative word, placed in a "situation" of construction work. After discussing the situation in all its possible aspects, the semantic link between the word and the object it names is established. Once the word has been noted within the situation, it is presented without the object: *tijolo*.

Afterwards: *ti-jo-lo*. By moving immediately to present the "pieces" visually, we initiate the recognition of phonemic families. Beginning with the first syllable, *ti*, the group is motivated to learn the whole phonemic family resulting from the combination of the initial consonant with the other vowels. The group then learns the second family through the visual presentation of *jo*, and finally arrives at the third family.

When the phonemic family is projected, the group at first recognizes only the syllable of the word which has been shown:

(ta-te-*ti*-to-tu), (ja-je-ji-*jo*-ju), (la-le-li-*lo*-lu)

When the participants recognize *ti*, from the generative word *tijolo*, it is proposed that they compare it with the other syllables; whereupon they discover that while all the syllables begin the same, they end differently. Thus, they cannot all be called *ti*.

The same procedure is followed with the syllables *jo* and *lo* and their families. After learning each phonemic family, the group practices reading the new syllables.

The most important moment arises when the three families are presented together:

ta-te-ti-to-tu ⎫
ja-je-ji-jo-ju ⎬ THE DISCOVERY CARD
la-le-li-lo-lu ⎭

After one horizontal and one vertical reading to grasp the vocal sounds, the group (*not* the coordinator) begins to carry out oral synthesis. One by one, they all begin to "make" words with the combinations available:[3]

tatu (armadillo), *luta* (struggle), *lajota* (small flagstone), *loja* (store), *jato* (jet), *juta* (jute), *lote* (lot), *lula* (squid), *tela* (screen), etc.

There are even some participants who take a vowel from one of the syllables, link it to another syllable, and add a third, thus forming a word. For example, they take the *i* from li, join it to *le* and add *te: leite* (milk).

There are others, like an illiterate from Brasília, who on the first night he began his literacy program said, *"tu já lê"* ("you already read").[4]

The oral exercises involve not only learning, but recognition (without which there is no true learning). Once these are completed, the participants begin—on that same first evening—to write. On the following day they bring from home as many words as they were able to make with the combinations of the phonemes they learned. It doesn't matter if they bring combinations which are not actual words—what does matter is the discovery of the mechanism of phonemic combinations.

The group itself, with the help of the educator (*not* the educator with the help of the group), should test the words thus created. A group in the state of Rio Grande do Norte called those combinations which were actual words "thinking words" and those which were not, "dead words."

Not infrequently, after assimilating the phonemic mechanism by using the "discovery card," participants would write words with complex phonemes (*tra, nha,* etc.), which had not yet been presented to them. In one of the Culture Circles in Angicos, Rio Grande do Norte, on the fifth day of discussion, in which simple phonemes were being shown, one of the participants went to the blackboard to write (as he said) "a thinking word." He wrote: "*o povo vai resouver os poblemas do Brasil votando conciente*"[5] ("the people will solve the problems of Brazil by informed voting"). In such cases, the group discussed the text, debating its significance in the context of their reality.

How can one explain the fact that a man who was illiterate several days earlier could write words with complex phonemes before he had even studied them? Once he had mastered the mechanism of phonemic combinations, he attempted—and managed—to express himself graphically, in the way he spoke.[6]

I wish to emphasize that in educating adults, to avoid a rote, mechanical process one must make it possible for them to achieve critical consciousness so that they can teach themselves to read and write.

As an active educational method helps a person to become consciously aware of his context and his condition as a human being as Subject, it will become an instrument of choice. At that point he will become politicized. When an ex-illiterate of Angicos, speaking before President João Goulart and the presidential staff, declared that he was no longer part of the *mass*, but one of the *people*, he had done more than utter a mere phrase; he had made a conscious option. He had chosen decisional participation, which belongs to the people, and had renounced the emotional resignation of the masses. He had become political.

The National Literacy Program of the Ministry of Education and Culture, which I coordinated, planned to extend and strengthen this education work throughout Brazil. Obviously we could not confine that work to a literacy program, even one which was critical rather than mechanical. With the same spirit of a pedagogy of communication, we were therefore planning a post-literacy stage which would vary only as to curriculum. If the National Literacy Program had not been terminated by the military coup, in 1964, there would have been more than 20,000 culture circles functioning throughout the country. In these, we planned to investigate the themes of the Brazilian people. These themes would be analyzed by specialists and broken down into learning units, as we had done with the concept of culture and with the coded situations linked to the generative words. We would prepare filmstrips with these breakdowns as well as simplified texts with references to the original texts. By gathering this thematic material, we could have offered a substantial post-literacy program. Further, by making a catalog of thematic breakdowns and bibliographic references available to high schools and colleges, we could widen the sphere of the program and help identify our schools with our reality.

At the same time, we began to prepare material with which we could carry out concretely an education that would encourage what

The following drawings represent some of the "situations" discussed in the culture circles. Freire's comments accompany them.

FIRST SITUATION

MAN IN THE WORLD AND WITH THE WORLD, NATURE AND CULTURE

Through the discussion of this situation—man as a being of relation-ships—the participants arrive at the distinction between two worlds: that of nature and that of culture. They perceive the normal situation of man as a being in the world and with the world, as a creative and re-creative being who, through work, constantly alters reality. By means of simple questions, such as, "Who made the well? Why did he do it? How did he do it? When?" which are repeated with regard to the other "elements" of the situation, two basic concepts emerge: that of *necessity* and that of *work;* and culture becomes explicit on a pri-mary level, that of subsistence. The man made the well because he needed water. And he did it because, relating to the world, he made the latter the object of his knowledge. By work, he submitted the world to a process of transformations. Thus, he made the house, his clothes, his work tools. From that point, one discusses with the group, in obviously simple but critically objective terms, the relations among men, which unlike those discussed previously cannot be either of domination or transformation, because they are relations among Sub-jects.

THIRD SITUATION

UNLETTERED HUNTER

The debate is initiated by distinguishing in this situation what belongs to nature and what belongs to culture. "Culture in this picture," the participants say, "is the bow, it is the arrow, it is the feathers the Indian wears." And when they are asked if the feathers are not nature, they always answer, "The feathers are nature, while they are on the bird. After man kills the bird, takes the feathers, and transforms them with work, they are not nature any longer. They are culture." (I had the opportunity to hear this reply innumerable times, in various regions of the country.) By distinguishing the historical-cultural period of the hunter from their own, the participants arrive at the perception of what constitutes an unlettered culture. They discover that when man prolongs his arms five to ten yards by making an implement and therefore no longer needs to catch his prey with his hands, he has created culture. By transferring not only the use of the implement, but the incipient technology of its manufacture, to younger generations, he has created education. The participants discuss how education occurs in an unlettered culture, where one cannot properly speak of illiterates. They then perceive immediately that to be illiterate is to belong to an unlettered culture and to fail to dominate the techniques of reading and writing. For some, this perception is dramatic.

FIFTH SITUATION
THE HUNTER AND THE CAT

With this situation, the participants discuss the fundamental aspects which characterize the different forms of being in the world—those of men and of animals. *They discuss man as a being who not only knows, but knows that he knows; as a conscious being (corpo consciente) in the world;* as a consciousness which in the process of becoming an authentic person emerges reflective and intent upon the world.

In regard to the preceding series, I will never forget an illiterate from Brasília who affirmed, with absolute self-confidence, "Of these three, only two are hunters—the two men. They are hunters because they make culture before and after they hunt." (He failed only to say that they made culture while they hunted.) "The third, the cat, does not make culture, either before or after the 'hunt.' He is not a hunter, he is a pursuer." By making this subtle distinction between hunting and pursuing, this man grasped the fundamental point: the creation of culture.

The debate of these situations produced a wealth of observations about men and animals, about creative power, freedom, intelligence, instinct, education, and training.

Aldous Huxley has called the "art of dissociating ideas"[7] as an antidote to the domesticating power of propaganda.[8] We planned film-
strips, for use in the literacy phase, presenting propaganda—from
advertising commercials to ideological indoctrination—as a "prob-
lem-situation" for discussion.

For example, as men through discussion begin to perceive the deceit in a cigarette advertisement featuring a beautiful, smiling woman
in a bikini (i.e., the fact that she, her smile, her beauty, and her bikini
have nothing at all to do with the cigarette), they begin to discover
the difference between education and propaganda. At the same time,
they are preparing themselves to discuss and perceive the same deceit
in ideological or political propaganda;[9] they are arming themselves to
"dissociate ideas." In fact, this has always seemed to me to be the way
to defend democracy, not a way to subvert it.

One subverts democracy (even though one does this in the name
of democracy) by making it irrational; by making it rigid in order "to
defend it against totalitarian rigidity"; by making it hateful, when it
can only develop in a context of love and respect for persons; by closing it, when it only lives in openness; by nourishing it with fear when
it must be courageous; by making it an instrument of the powerful in
the oppression of the weak; by militarizing it against the people; by
alienating a nation in the name of democracy.

One defends democracy by leading it to the state Mannheim calls
"militant democracy"—a democracy which does not fear the people,
which suppresses privilege, which can plan without becoming rigid,
which defends itself without hate, which is nourished by a critical spirit rather than irrationality.

Notes

[1]I am not opposed to reading texts, which are in fact indispensable to developing the visual-graphic channel of communication and which in great
part should be elaborated by the participants themselves. I should add that
our experience is based on the use of multiple channels of communication.

[2]Generally, in a period of six weeks to two months, we could leave a group
of twenty-five persons reading newspapers, writing notes and simple letters,
and discussing problems of local and national interest.

Each culture circle was equipped with a Polish-made projector, imported
at the cost of about $13.00. Since we had not yet set up our own laboratory,
a filmstrip cost us about $7–$8. We also used an inexpensive blackboard. The
slides were projected on the wall of the house where the culture circle met
or, where this was difficult, on the reverse side (painted white) of the blackboard.

The Education Ministry imported 35,000 of the projectors, which after the
military coup of 1964 were presented on television as "highly subversive."

[3]In a television interview, Gilson Amado observed lucidly, "They can do this, because there is no such thing as oral illiteracy."

[4]In correct Portuguese, *tu já lês*.

[5]*resouver* is a corruption of *resolver; poblemas* a corruption of *problemas;* the letter *s* is lacking from the syllable *cons.*

[6]Interestingly enough, as a rule the illiterates wrote confidently and legibly, largely overcoming the natural indecisiveness of beginners. Elza Freire thinks this may be due to the fact that these persons, beginning with the discussion of the anthropological concept of culture, discovered themselves to be more fully human, thereby acquiring an increasing emotional confidence in their learning which was reflected in their motor activity.

[7]*Ends and Means* (New York and London, 1937), p. 252.

[8]I have never forgotten the publicity (done cleverly, considering our acritical mental habits) for a certain Brazilian public figure. The bust of the candidate was displayed with arrows pointing to his head, his eyes, his mouth, and his hands. Next to the arrows appeared the legend:

You don't need to think, he thinks for you!
You don't need to see, he sees for you!
You don't need to talk, he talks for you!
You don't need to act, he acts for you!

[9]In the campaigns carried out against me, I have been called "ignorant" and "illiterate," "the author of a method so innocuous that it did not even manage to teach him how to read and write." It was said that I was not "the inventor" of dialogue (as if I had ever made such an irresponsible affirmation). It was said that I had done "nothing original," and that I had "plagiarized European or North-American educators," as well as the author of a Brazilian primer. (On the subject of originality, I have always agreed with Dewey, for whom originality does not lie in the "extraordinary and fanciful," but "in putting everyday things to uses which had not occurred to others." *Democracy and Education,* New York, 1916, p. 187.)

None of these accusations has ever wounded me. What does leave me perplexed is to hear or read that I intended to "Bolchevize the country" with my method. In fact, my actual crime was that I treated literacy as more than a mechanical problem, and linked it to *conscientização,* which was "dangerous." It was that I viewed education as an effort to liberate men, not as yet another instrument to dominate them.

4. Richards/Freund/Frye

Literacy must soon come to be seen as the province of all scholars; otherwise, there will be nobody to sit in their classes— nobody capable of reading literature or law or medicine. I have gathered here two literary critics and a law professor writing about thinking and its relationship to reading and writing in a manner representative of the kind of concern I mean.

Since Richards is the principal source of the ideas about method I've tried to articulate in this book, I will introduce this selection simply by noting that it comes from a book called How to Read a Page, *published shortly after the appearance of Mortimer J. Adler's* How to Read a Book. *Richards would certainly have agreed with Montessori that to civilize is to multiply needs (of a certain sort). The civilizing effect of all his books is that we discover the needs of the critical reader—of any meaning-maker.*

Paul Freund makes as neat a case as I've seen for stressing the continuity of what is taught in the schools and what is to be learned in professional training. Northrop Frye shows how the challenge of curriculum design can only be met by marshalling everything we may know about language and literature and the way the forming powers of mind grow and develop.

I. A. Richards

(from *How to Read a Page*)

No one can justly or successfully discover the nature of any one thing in that thing itself, or without numerous experiments which lead to farther inquiries.

SIR FRANCIS BACON

We may now pause to consider what, so far, in the process of reading as we have been observing it here in our minds, offers any suggestion toward a technique for improving reading. A number of points seem worth noting. I believe most readers will confirm them.

1. When eye reading alone does not give us a clear sense of the grammar and of the logical structure, we tend to switch speaking and hearing on. We can do this in two ways which are, as it were, degrees of realization or actualization of the sentences.

(a) We read it in imagination—producing *images* of the speech movements and of the sound of the words.
(b) We really utter the words faintly or out loud.

Vocal reading can aid in giving structure to the argument. It is an experimental manipulation, a testing procedure on trial-and-error lines. . . . While noting that reading a thing out loud may be a great help, we should not forget that it can be a great hindrance. As the name "trial and error" (rather than "trial and triumph") suggests, there are likely to be more errors than successes. The eye is a more neutral agent than the voice. Or, to put it more fairly, the voice, if there has been failure, can easily add a very persuasive garb or garble of rhythm and intonation to support the misinterpretation. This commonly happens when the cause of the misinterpretation has been prejudice—the interference of some sentiment. Nothing is easier than to make words ring out or fall flat as we please, to our own ears—especially if we don't know we are doing it. So the chances of our detecting the twist we are giving in our reading are much reduced. When other people read things to us, we often think, "So long as you read it *that way* you can't possibly understand what it says!" We should more often be saying the same thing to ourselves. In particular, a certain querulous questioning tone—"What *can* it mean?"—is an enemy of comprehension. Read it as though it made sense and perhaps it will.

2. In addition to reading the words on the page to ourselves in various ways and with various tones, we can add to them—anything from ejaculations, delighted or derisive, to an analytic commentary. Some people do no little talking to themselves while reading. For them, it is very much a part of the reading process. With argumentative matter the reader should talk back as much as possible unless he is merely fighting, talking for a victory there will be no one but himself to award. Though debate is silly, reasoning is still dialogue, as Plato said.

This touches a large theme—the different modes of reading suited to different types of writing. I will make only one comment here. It is absurd to read everything—poetry, prose, pulp—alike, especially to read it all as *fast* as possible. Whom are they fleeing from, these running readers? I fear the only answer is, "Themselves." Anything that is worth *studying* should be read *as slowly* as it will let you, and read again and again till you have it by heart. Only so will the persistencies be repeated frequently enough for a power of systematizing them to develop. But "Let us not pass an act of uniformity against poets," said Coleridge. I would add, "or against readers either." Still most of us read too fast rather than too slowly. This opinion goes bang in the teeth, I know, of the massed professional teachers of the reading art, those who are telling one another so often that they are failing to teach it. They will brandish their figures to show that the fastest readers get most. Their conception of comprehension, however, and of the aim of reading is so very different from that presented in these pages that I am not daunted. One may still ask: How do you know they would not have got something of another order if they had not sped so fast? Have their speeding teachers themselves got quite enough out of their reading to be able to judge? And these are things which no "comprehension test" yet devised can measure. . . .

3. From internal dialogue to rephrasing is a small step. Most people find that having two versions of a passage before them opens up the task of exploration immensely. This is true even when one version is clearly very inferior; its presence still throws the implications of the other into relief. So a black-and-white reproduction of a picture can make us see what the color in the original is doing. A better parallel, perhaps, is with photographic surveying. Two versions are like two views from slightly different angles. If we can fit them together, each tells us much about the things seen in the other. . . .

These effects are striking enough to promise (if we can study them successfully) some real improvement in reading. And tradition in teaching backs up this hope. Translation work has been the main technique of literary education in the past. Now no one who knows how translation—whether from Latin into English or back again or with French or German either way—is ordinarily done and has ordinarily been done in the past will see in that dreary and largely mechanical routine any saving virtue. It is only in the best translation work, which comes after the mechanics of the strange tongue have been mastered, and only in the hands of teachers who are themselves exacting readers, that the incessant comparisons required between different ways of saying more or less the same thing become any royal road to good reading. *Thorough* mastery of a foreign language, no doubt, always improves our understanding of the mother tongue in some degree. Getting a smattering does not. Even the first steps in a foreign tongue *can* be made a profitable study of our own language, but current practice fails to do this; and the grim toil which follows consists mainly in replacing, one by one, words we hardly understand at all with words we have not time to consider—or vice versa. So my reference here to translation as a method of improving reading will not cheer up anyone to whom translation means primarily that. But there is an altogether different sort of translation in which both languages, as to the routine handling of their mechanics and the pocket-dictionary senses of their words, are fully grasped. The task then can become a deep exploration of meaning, a perfect exercise for developing resource and justice in interpretation.

The same merits can be possessed by English—English translation, if we put certain controls on it which bar out synonym trading and glosses which dodge or veil the difficulties. . . .

Comparison seems to be the key to all learning of this type. Learning to read is not fundamentally different from learning to be a good judge of wine, or of horses, or of men. Persistence of effects must be repeated frequently enough to become systematized. And, for progress to be rapid, effects whose similarities and differences—their sameness amid difference rather—are instructive should persist together. Some people can compare things across wide intervals of time. They go ahead faster than the rest of us. Others cannot make subtle comparisons between things which do not overlap in their effects. Everything depends, of course, on what things are being compared by whom. What I have just been saying applies chiefly to first comparisons between somewhat novel things in somewhat novel respects. . . . The more any body of perceptions becomes systematized, the easier it becomes to span vast stretches of time in comparing examples within it. A real expert can identify a wine and its condition even though he has not tasted any similar wine for years. But that is only because his experience became well systematized in the bygone days when he was tasting such wines. And then, no doubt, his comparisons were not very widely spaced apart.

Now, if reading is a matter of organized comparisons between meanings, as it certainly is, it should not be difficult to arrange things so that the best opportunities for the growth of this organization or systematization are secured. What we have to do is put the materials for distinctions and connections about which we are not clear enough *together,* so that the universals can develop through comparison. And we will do this best by using different ways of saying "the same thing" in close collocation.

But four very important qualifications must be made or this program will lead us into nothing but folly:

(a) We must know which are the important distinctions and connections.

(b) We must be very much on our guard with the phrase "the same thing."

(c) We must respect the fundamental conditions of interest.

(d) We must recognize that failure to see an important distinction or connection is most often due to our not *wanting* to see it.

I will take these up in turn. . . .

(a) . . . The most important ideas (and an idea here is a form of distinction and connection) are the *necessary* ones in the sense that we cannot do without them. They enter inevitably into all our thinking, for thinking is just another name for the operation of these ideas. Typical among them are the ideas covered by *same, different, change, cause, thing, idea, part, whole, abstract, concrete, general, special, form, implies, matter, quality,* and *relation.* Language has an inexhaustible variety of ways of expressing these ideas, and we may easily fail to notice that they are serving still as the structure of our thought. Sometimes, too, we may handle them better through language which does not make them prominent by using these bald and somewhat formidable words. More often, though, we miss a point or confuse an argument by failing to see that under the attractively novel phrasing, and behind its special graces, we have to do with the same familiar joints and muscles and bones.

To say we cannot do without these ideas may seem to get us into a difficulty. If we have them and use them all the time already, what is the point of working up great programs for teaching ourselves about them? The point is that no one is as skillful with them as he might be, and that much of the inefficiency of thought and language comes from needless blundering with these ideas. But here again we must note that skill with them is not in the least the same thing as being able to propound even the best theories about them. A first-rate authority on the foundations of mathematics might well be a poor mathematician. And so it is throughout. Our aim will not be improved theory of language but improved conduct with it.

If we can improve our conduct of these ideas, our reward is everywhere. That is why time given to the words which can handle them least confusingly is better spent than time given to distinctions and connections which are only locally useful.

If we open a dictionary of synonyms we are faced with thousands of subtle problems. The early nineteenth-century compilers used to attempt to *state* distinctions between usages—with all but uniformly absurd results. The only thing that will show us what these different implications are is watching them at work. And only then, when we see with the help of all around it what a word is doing, can we fruitfully attempt to state this, or by experiment explore differentiations. When we do so we discover that there is a certain limited set of words which we use most in such attempted elucidations. They form a language within a language—the words needed in explaining the rest of the language. The ideas these words cover are fewer than we suppose, though there is something very artificial about pretending that we can *count* such things as ideas. All we can say is that the meanings of words are relatively compound or simple, and that careful analysis *in contexts* can as a rule break down a complex meaning into simpler ideas acting together in a certain form. It is the simpler ideas (and the words which handle them best) that are the most important for us to study if we are to improve our reading. No one will pretend, of course, that an improved understanding of these ideas will by itself teach us what different things different complexes of them will do. For that we need experience of the complexes themselves at work. But better knowledge of the simples will certainly help to form that experience of complexes at work.

(b) We have now to take a look at some of the problems behind the innocent-seeming words "say the same thing." Both "say" and "same" need our best attention. Their meanings are closely intertwined.

When something is *said,* words are uttered (whether through waves in the air or patterns of rays from the surface of paper does not matter here) which have certain effects. How widely and generally, or how narrowly and specifically, are we to take these effects? Looked at closely enough, they are never the same for two readers or for the same reader twice. Looked at undiscriminatingly enough, they are much the same always. (What other words come with them, what the situation is, and so on, must, of course, be kept in mind throughout.) Whether for practical purposes we account them *the same* depends upon two things: upon our purpose and upon the respects in which they are the same and different. . . .

All this, which is wearing to write out and still more wearing to read, we all know in a sense very well already. Yet we endlessly talk and frequently (alack) think as if in forgetfulness of it. We assert that two phrases say the same or that they do not, as if that were something which turned on the phrases alone—in utter independence of who reads them and when and why and within what setting. Probably when we do this we are assuming a host of things: including a standard reader with some sort of normal purpose and a standard setting and range of situations. We would be very hard put to it, indeed, if we had to be specific about these assumptions. But we are rather suspiciously careful not to explore them. We take them for granted and people are only too ready, in fact, to grant them. We seem even to suffer from a fear that questioning these assumptions will lead to no good, will shake the foundations of communication perhaps and let anyone with any word mean anything he pleases.

This background fear is empty, though its roots are perhaps deep in man's first speculations about language when he first began to experience its magical powers. Nobody perhaps, after reflection, now believes that words have their meanings in their own right, as our bodies have their minds. We have replaced that old belief with another which looks much more plausible but is as groundless. It is the belief in a sort of compact or agreement between all good users of the language to use words only in certain limited ways.[1] It is true enough that we do behave with words *as if* some such compact ruled their uses. But the explanation in terms of usage agreement is wrong. The stability of the language has other causes. It comes from our experience of the ways in which words are tied up with one another. A language is a fabric which holds itself together. It is a fabric which, for the most part brokenly and confusedly but sometimes with startling and heartbreaking clarity, reflects the fabric of universals which is our world.

There is no risk whatever, then, in questioning the assumptions which make us say two phrases must or can't mean the same. And to be able to question them—not as a piece of linguistic theory but in practice as they come up—is a large part of the art of reading. We ought to be incessantly ready to ask of two phrases which seem "more or less to mean the same" just wherein (and for whom) are their effects alike and wherein different. And to decide whether—for the purpose in hand, which is what the whole passage is swayed by—the differences are relevant. If they are not, we can be indifferent to them. But with a slight change in the purpose they might become very important. Any ruling on such points which does not take the purpose into account *is* an attack on language. We ought to fear pedants who cry, "But that *isn't* the meaning of the word," much more than any rash or wanton innovator.

One other quirk in our behavior with phrases said to mean the same is also perhaps connected with remnants of magical beliefs. My Basic English version of the Aristotle passage, for example, says, *more or less,* what the Oxford translation says. In comparing two versions our minds sometimes perform this antic: instead of regarding them as two sets of words which in some ways have similar outcomes in other ways different, we may suddenly find ourselves thinking, of one, "So *that* is what he was trying to say!" We are then likely to follow it up with, "It's a pity he didn't say it!" In extreme cases (and none such will probably occur in this instance) what happens is that the reader then identifies the thought with the *words* of the version he prefers. They become for him what the other passage is (inefficiently) saying, and he makes no comparison between meanings. He is helped in this by the chief regular systematic ambiguity of *say:* We say certain words and then *they* may say more than we are saying with them. These three *say*'s say very different things—as we see if we replace them with more explicit phrases: We *give voice to certain words* and then they *may be taken to mean* more than we *have in mind.*

(c) There are few important words which are not in varying patterns systematically ambiguous; *say* is typical. These *regular* shifts of sense as a rule give us little trouble in reading. Later I distinguish them as Part-Whole Shifts. But all untechnical words also *change* their meanings from place to place in discourse under the pressures of the purpose and the setting. And these Sense Content Changes, because they are so closely related to the purpose, are specially important to follow. We need not *notice* them and usually do not; but we must submit to them if we are not to misread. But because they are made against the resistance of the word's normal relations with other words, the likelihood of misreading is considerable. If we accept the change we will probably never be aware that it occurred. If we don't, then we will either boggle at the passage and find discontinuity or nonsense in it, or more probably we will go on happily assured of a meaning which a better reader would see was not intended. If an author's purposes lead him to change the meanings of too many words, people do not go on reading him. He becomes too hard to follow—unless he is so great a writer and so adroit in relating his changes to one another that he reshapes language for us. Shakespeare is the great example. The interest of what he is doing has made us accept an experimental handling of language which otherwise would have been unreadable. He wrote, though, for an audience which was very skillful in interpretation. Thus language protects itself.

It is possible to collect examples of important words pushed out of their normal uses by various pressures. The great dictionaries contain such collections in an early, as yet little organized, stage of development. By drawing on these collections and appending paraphrases to show how words which in one place say one thing in another say another, tables and exercises affording unlimited opportunities for comparisons can be prepared. It might well be thought that these would provide the best means of improving reading. The traditional grammar books, however, by failing to teach the lessons they intended, have taught us another; of more value perhaps. We do not learn linguistic points from tables and examples; we learn through using the language—not in exercises but in the pursuit of a meaning we are seeking for a specific not a general purpose. In other words, the desire to improve our reading, worthy though it is, won't help us unless it operates through the work of puzzling out a passage because we care what it says. The persistencies of effects—no matter how well we make them overlap—will not systematize themselves into experience (knowledge that returns as power) unless they are heated by an immediate sustaining interest.

(d) But interest, the great weldor (as the weldors spell it now, a *welder* being a machine: compare *actor* and *sailor*) of universals, is also the great logic-breaker. If we want to, or if something in us wants to establish something, we grow blind to any thwarting idea, however familiar it is or however obvious it might otherwise be; we deform our distinctions and connections to meet our aim, commit every sort of injustice and make the very word "argument" a term of derision. Mercury, the interpreter and messenger of Heaven, was also the patron god of rogues.

Most mistakes in reading look willful—not only to the man in the other camp but to the impartial eye. Few of them are, but it is harder to be fair-minded in reading than we know, and a passion for the truth is misinterpretation's favorite guise. . . .

Notes

[1] I have written at some length and in detail about this doctrine of usage in my *Interpretation in Teaching*, Harcourt Brace, New York, 1938. See Chapter XVI. Also in my *Philosophy of Rhetoric*, Oxford Press, New York, 1936, Lecture III.

Paul A. Freund

("The Law and the Schools")

If you were to look at a book on law and the schools, the chances are that you would find a discussion of the contract rights of teachers, tax exemption of school property, disciplinary powers over pupils, and similar issues on which lawyers might give advice to school administrators. Law, that is, comes in from the outside, and is to be left, a useful but esoteric art, in the hands of the professionals. It is as if science were relevant to the schools only as the basis for the design of buildings, or government only as the source of administrative regulations. The root cause of this comparative neglect of law as an appropriate subject for general education is, I believe, that law is regarded as a system of rules to be mastered by those self-doomed to work with them, and not, like science or government, as an enterprise, an ongoing process, whose study contributes to an enlarged understanding of, and participation in, the world around us.

In the colleges, to be sure, law as a subject of undergraduate study is receiving increasing attention. Surprisingly, perhaps, the most heavily subscribed kind of undergraduate course in law is that in business law. The older and still prevalent form of such a course is one devoted to rules: the requirements of valid contract, the liability of the various signers of a check, and the like—a how-to-keep-the-lawyer-away, or what-to-do-till-the-lawyer-comes sort of exposition. Happily, there is growing dissatisfaction with this conception of legal study, and the younger generation of business-law teachers is striving to give the subject the intellectual content and stimulus that could warrant its place in a university curriculum.

In liberal arts programs, a variety of approaches is taken, often conditioned by the departmental niche to which the course is allotted and by the general orientation of the department itself. Law In Society is a familiar offering in sociology. It has the virtues and the hazards of any such over-view. It has the virtue of seeing law as more than simply a system of punishments designed to keep order in society. Rather, it shows law to be a system that facilitates organization, association, transactions; that resolves conflicts or deliberately leaves a certain amount of friction; that operates as an educational force; and that can yet be dysfunctional in some of its operations. The hazard of the course is that any attempt at a systematic, functional analysis may compress too much into too few or too general categories and may, as in anthropology, require more refined differentiations. A political-science oriented approach can take a variety of forms. Law may be brought within the fold, domesticated and subdued, as it were, by the pressure-group theorist who assimilates the judicial process to the legislative; or it might be captured by the operations analyst who equates understanding with predictive power and so, programming judicial decisions, gets out of a computer, as from a major premise, all that was put into it, elaborating the obvious by methods that are obscure. These are caricatures, of course, though it is hard to avoid the impression that the work of some of the grimmer practitioners of behavioralism is a caricature of itself. There are partial insights to be gained from all these approaches, and from others; what is intolerable is the claim of any of them to constitute the one true faith, the only road to intellectual salvation. Their tactical legitimacy may well depend on the polemic context in which they are employed: to insist that a pitcher is half full or half empty may turn on whether you are combating the illusion that it is completely empty or completely full.

Aside from these rather special approaches, there is a view of law from the inside of the process that seems to me highly fruitful for general education, whether at the university or the school level. What I have in mind is more than a view: it is a vicarious participation in the process of legal thinking through immersion in some of the problems and the literature of the common law.

There is probably no more systematic literature of justification than the reports of decided cases extending back for several hundred years, with conflicting claims and interests laid bare and judgments rendered in the light of reasoned opinions and dissenting opinions, taking account in varying measure of precedent, analogy, logic, history, custom, morality, and social utility. For educational purposes the problem is to extract from this abundant quarry a set of materials that will be intrinsically interesting and comprehensible to particular age groups, that will link themselves to the students' own range of experience and observation. The problem is not as formidable as it may seem, inasmuch as the stuff of law can be related to such normal experiences of schoolchildren as association in clubs, disciplinary proceedings, engaging in simple commercial transactions at the neighborhood shops, and reading facts, opinions, gossip, and untruths in newspapers. The art is to hold the legal materials in a double focus: to see them as significant for their own sake, developments in the rationalizing of certain areas of human experience, and also as exemplifications of the rational process itself, with a wider significance for the developing intellectual style (to use a too pretentious phrase) of the student.

Let me try to be more concrete, setting out in summary form certain modes of thought that are almost inescapably called for in legal reasoning, together with sectors of the law that might appropriately evoke these responses.

1. Dialectical Thinking

There is a built-in dialectic in law, not merely because of the adversary procedure in litigation but because of the nature of the issues. When Justice Holmes would jauntily enter his study, fling his hat on the rack, and turn to his law clerk with the challenge, "State any proposition and I'll deny it," he was embodying the spirit of the common law, the rubbing of blade against blade in the scissors of the mind, making a truer and finer line. When Columbia University, a decade ago, celebrated its bicentennial, the theme of the celebration was "The Right to Knowledge and the Free Use Thereof." It is a noble theme, but one that challenges the legal mind to produce countervailing nobilities. Does it matter how the knowledge is acquired, whether by resort to eavesdropping or unauthorized search and seizure of private papers? Does it matter how the knowledge is used, whether by plagiarism or indiscriminate tale-tattling? The legal problems of illegal search and seizure and interference with a right of privacy call for accommodations of a sensitive sort; these are richly documented in the literature and hardly beyond the appreciation of the schoolboy.

In this connection, it seems to me that courses in the Bill of Rights, admirable as they are in intent, lose much of their value unless they are conceived in a dialectical way. Granted that it is important to know about the guarantee of a fair trial under the Fifth Amendment and the guarantee of a free press under the First. What is more important is to see the two in confrontation, in the context of the problem of press coverage of pre-trial investigations and trial reporting, and to try to resolve the clash by more refined principles than either of them alone. It is important pragmatically if we are to learn to mute the clangor of clashing isms; it is important for learning because we do not really "know" a principle until we know its opposing principles and reshape them all in the process. Better that students be encouraged to feel this implicitly, kinesthetically, than that they be taught from outside, as it were, the theories of scholasticism, Hegelianism, or Morris R. Cohen's principle of polarity.

2. Contextual Thinking

Questions like "What caused the Civil War?" are a staple of the schools. Would it be thought an impertinence if a student, before responding further, were to put a question of his own: "What exactly do you mean by 'caused'?" or "Why should we want an answer to that question?" This kind of response, pertinent or impertinent, is endemic in legal analysis. Consider, for example, the problem of legal cause in the law of torts. If a child is drowning offshore while two observers watch passively on the beach, one the child's nursemaid and the other a stranger, has either "caused" the child's death? If an intoxicated man, having been served by a too compliant bartender, playfully slaps the head of a companion who has an abnormally thin skull, who or what caused the resulting injury to the victim? It will surely be evident that to answer the question some decision on the purpose of the inquiry will have to be taken. The question may be asked of a lawyer, a moralist, a sociologist, or a physician, and the answer may vary accordingly. Was the question asked to assess legal liability, to affix moral blame, to promote understanding of human actions, or to aid in taking corrective or preventive measures? In the process, such concepts as concurrent cause, proximate cause, cause versus condition, and purposive identification of cause will have emerged without their formidable labels. Ideally, a discussion of this kind could end with this interchange between teacher and student: "Have you ever heard of Mill's theory of cause in history?" "No sir." "Well, you've just discovered it."

3. *Ethical Thinking*

The concept of commutative justice is central to much of our treatment of social issues. It is also central to that great corpus known as the law of contracts, which deals essentially with the making, keeping, and breaking of promises. What kinds of promises should be binding and what not binding? What circumstances should qualify as excuses for non-performance? What remedies should be available in case of breach?—these are the major classes of issues raised in this branch of the law. In considering them, the student will have to consider questions of public policy regarding illegal or odious undertakings, the extent to which supervening unforeseen events ought to release one from an undertaking, and the rationale of enforcing promises at all, as reflected in the law of damages—whether it be based on the reliance by the promisee upon the expected benefits that performance by the promisor would bring him, or on the promisor's having received a *quid pro quo* for his promise. The meaning of just expectations, on which the social order ultimately rests, can here be explored in considerable depth, without ranging beyond the students' personal field of reference.

4. *Genetic Thinking*

The responsiveness of the social organization to changes in modes of production, distribution, and labor is a recurring theme in social studies. The pace, the pains, and the progress in this adaptive process are documented in quite human terms in the law reports. The subject of industrial accidents is a notable example, moving from the plight of the injured worker whose claim would be defeated by the employer's defense—either of the worker's contributory negligence, his assumption of the risk of the job, or the causative conduct of a fellow-employee—through the abolition of these defenses by legislation, to the provision for workmen's compensation as a cost of the business irrespective of the negligence of employer or employee. A comparable evolution emerges from a study of the manufacturer's liability for defective products in the hands of the consumer, a progression that eventually enabled the consumer to sue the remote manufacturer and that has tended to supplant the criterion of proof of negligent manufacture with an implied absolute warranty on the manufacturer's part. These responses to changing patterns of industrial and commercial life give point to the remark of the late Professor Hocking, the Harvard philosopher, that to teach social studies without law is like teaching vertebrate anatomy without the backbone.

5. *Associative Thinking*

Movement occurs not only through organic institutional changes but through the adaptive and assimilative processes of the mind. We live by metaphor; we advance by simile; we rise by concepts. The legal right of privacy is a fairly recent notion, which can be traced, in one sense, from protection against eavesdropping (itself a metaphor), through offensive shadowing (a metaphor but also "like eavesdropping"), to the gossip sheet and unauthorized use of name or photograph (the general concept of privacy). Related to this process is the human addiction to fictions, to thinking "as if" one thing were another, an addiction particularly strong, no doubt too strong, in the law. Legal fictions (the "white lies of the law," von Jhering called them) can be looked at in many ways, but for the purposes of comparing them with fictions elsewhere two categories suggest themselves: (a) normative fictions, like models or ideal types: the "reasonable man," or "everyone is presumed to know the law"; (b) categorizing fictions, whereby the new is assimilated to the familiar, the tribute that change pays to continuity—for example, the protection of interests of personality, such as privacy, as if they were "property rights," and the treatment of corporations as if they were legal "persons."

The conspicuousness of fictions in the law may serve to point to their prevalence in other more respectable disciplines—political science or economics or the natural sciences—and to suggest their uses and abuses and their relation to hypotheses and myths.

6. *Institutional Thinking*

Perhaps the most distinctive feature of a legal system is the central position of a procedural framework, with specialized organs and ways of operation, underscoring the interrelation of ends and means. The amenability of a given problem to resolution by codified rules, or by generalized principles and *ad hoc* decision, or by unstructured nonlegal methods, is an inquiry that serves to sharpen an understanding of the problem itself. Given an apparent agreement in the abstract on an issue, say, of mercy-killing or the right of privacy, the effort to put the agreement into an institutional form with attention to who decides disputes, by what procedures, under what standards, with what sanctions, may uncover some latent differences and some consequent reshaping of the ends themselves. The effort may, at the same time, suggest some ways of resolving or by-passing initial differences through agreement on procedures. A simple exercise in negotiating and drafting an uncomplicated contract can prove illuminating for an understanding of international disputes and constitution-making.

7. *Self-Critical Thinking*

Occasions arise when old doctrine has been so radically reinterpreted, when fictions have become so attenuated, that an abandonment of the old in favor of a fresh formulation seems inescapable. The phenomenon of judicial overrulings is familiar enough and is almost always accompanied by a reasoned articulation. The factors that lead judges to reach such conclusions are not very different, *mutatis mutandis,* from those that lead theoretical scientists to opt, at a certain point, for change over continuity. Every experiment, we are told, implicates in principle not only the postulate under investigation but the whole system of postulates of which this one is a part; and so it is with the novel case in law. The decision whether to continue the process of assimilation and adjustment or to abandon antecedent positions is in either field a quasi-ethical judgment. The elements that ought to enter into such a choice can be analyzed in notable episodes of the judicial, no less than the scientific, process.

If these seven intellectual traits, or some of them, seem worthy of more deliberate cultivation in the schools, and if the law appears to offer some particularly apt opportunities in this direction, the mechanics of the educational enterprise (the preparation of teachers, the assembling of materials and their sequential use) can be explored by teachers and lawyers together. I should confess, finally, that this essay, like the approaches to which I alluded at the outset, should be taken in a polemic context: that the cardinal sin of our classrooms is one-dimensional thinking, all warp and no woof, making for glibness of mind that knows the answers without really knowing the questions. It is the cardinal sin, I would maintain, because it characterizes some of the most academically successful products of the system. What I have tried to suggest is essentially an antidote to glibness, that can be ingested without tears.

Northrop Frye

(from *Design for Learning*)

... In all learning there is a radical pioneering force and a conservative supporting force, a learning that explores and a learning that consolidates. It seems to me that there are three main phases in the relationship of these two forces, three main turns of the spiral: a primary phase, a secondary phase, and a tertiary phase, which correspond roughly, if not exactly, to the elementary, secondary, and university levels of education.

In the primary phase the consolidating or conservative force is memory. Children seem to have good memories, and many children enjoy the power of using them: like the poets of primitive societies, they have an affinity for catalogues of names, accentual verses, and lists of all kinds that can be delivered in the chanting rhythm of a child's speech. Behind whatever I know of the social and cultural effects of the Norman Conquest is a primitive mnemonic chant of "William the First, William the Second, Henry the First, and *Stee*-phen!" I remember encountering a small girl in California who had just "taken Canada" in school, and who saw in a Canadian visitor an approaching captive audience. She backed me into a corner and recited the names of the provinces of Canada, complete with capitals, quite correctly. A question or two revealed that she had no notion where any of these provinces were. It was unlikely that she had been so badly taught; much more likely that she had simply remembered what interested her, the roll-call of strange names, and tuned out what did not, such as their location in space. Perhaps much the same thing was true of the lad in the Social Science report, with whom I have a good deal of sympathy, who remembered the three voyages of Captain Cook but not the fact that he was an emissary of eighteenth-century British imperialism.

Perhaps in our justified distrust of "mere" memorization we underestimate the power in it that can be harnessed to education. What we are apt to underestimate, in a civilization which is almost compelled to identify education with book-learning, is the role still played in memory by oral and visual experience. Many a boy who cannot remember what countries are in South America can tell the year and make of an automobile a hundred yards away, a feat mainly achieved within what literary critics call the oral tradition. A comic strip recently made an extremely shrewd comment on such extra-curricular learning. Two children in Kindergarten are out for recess; a plane flies overhead; one calls it a jet, the other disagrees, and a quite technical discussion follows on the difference between jet and piston planes. The recess bell rings, and one of them says, "Come on, Mike: we gotta go back and string them beads." What is true of sensational learning is even more obviously true of practical learning, especially in practical skills and sports, where memory develops into motor habit. Elementary science has to be deductively taught, but it does not follow that children should be discouraged from experiment at first hand; and learning to write and to speak intelligible English are practical skills also. There is a core of truth in the principle of learning by doing, as long as "doing" is not assumed to exclude reading and thinking, and as long as motor activity is not thrust into studies where it has no business to be.

The difference between a good and a mediocre teacher lies mainly in the emphasis the former puts on the exploring part of the mind, the aspects of learning that reveal meanings and lead to further understanding. In English, this means ensuring that a child knows the meaning of what he reads as well as the mechanics of reading; in social and historical studies it means understanding why things happened instead of merely that they happened; in science it means understanding central principles illustrated by what without them would be a bewildering variety of unrelated phenomena. Unless there is reason and system to give direction to the memory, education burdens the memory; and however resilient a child's memory may be, nobody is going to keep a burden in his mind an instant longer than he is compelled to do. What is merely learned is merely forgotten, as every adult knows. Those who never get psychologically beyond the primary phase of learning are apt to retain a conviction all their lives that total recall is the same thing as intelligence. Until some scandals, which however regrettable were extremely useful to educators, changed the fashion, there was a widespread belief that the "smartest" people were those who proved on television programmes to have the largest stock of information on non-controversial subjects. But it was the sense of how much they themselves had forgotten which gave their audiences a superstitious reverence for those who had been unable to forget.

It is important to realize that the pioneering element in the primary learning process has to do with the reasonable and the systematic, with what makes learning continuous and progressive. It is not a matter of arousing interest or stimulating a student, even to the pitch of enthusiasm. Civilized people respond readily to intellectual stimulation all their lives. Those who speak at businessmen's luncheons and women's clubs, from pulpits on Sunday morning or through the microphones of the CBC, find intelligent and receptive hearers. But these activities, however valuable in other ways, are not strictly educational. The sense of continuity, of one step leading to another, of details fitting gradually into a larger design, is essential to education, and no sequence of individually isolated experiences can possess this. The fact that all three reports [which constitute *Design for Learning*] stress the genuinely educational aspect of teaching, rather than the psychologically attractive aspect of it, is one of their most distinctive features. They do not, like so much writing in this field, fail to distinguish between interest and concentration.

Because memory is the more passive element in the learning process, mediocre students tend to rely on their memories, and even good students do so for the subjects in which they are less interested. Mediocre teachers, similarly, and examinations where the marking-schemes have been ossified by a desire to make them mechanically accurate, are also apt to stress memory at the expense of intelligence. Sometimes attempts are made, especially in science, to simplify the grasp of structure into a methodology, but we note that the authors of the Science report, like most scientists, have very little to say about "the scientific method." A scientist enters into the structure of his science, and then uses the same mixture of hunch and common sense that any other mental worker would use. Literature, like mathematics, is practically all structure, and the attempt to master it by memory forces the student to grapple with a pseudo-content, something not really there at all. A teacher who boasted of his ability to get his students through Grade 13 English, would, when teaching Browning's *Epistle* of Karshish, ask his students how many letters Karshish had written (the poem contains the line "And writeth now the twenty-second time"). He admitted that remembering this number was not very central to understanding the poem, but, he argued, unless students had something definite to learn they just gave you a lot of boloney on their examinations. This is the kind of thing I mean by pseudo-content, and its victims are strewn all over the first-year university results in English.

In the secondary phase of learning the pioneering and consolidating forces become more conceptual. The former is now the power of understanding that asks the radical questions: What good is this? How true is it? Could we get along without it? The latter asks the conservative questions: What does this mean? Why is it there? Why has it been accepted? It is particularly in the social sciences that these questions seem relevant. . . . Even with things admitted to be bad, such as slavery or persecution, it is worth asking conservative questions about why the human race has practised them so widely and with such enthusiasm; and even with things admitted to be good, such as religion and democracy, it is worth asking radical questions about what would happen if we did not possess these things, or possessed them in a different form. In literature the student is now advanced enough, not simply to listen to stories, but to inquire within them for real motivation and imaginative causality. Hence his questions here also fall into similar patterns: Why does the author say this? Would this kind of thing really happen? and the like.

Thus the secondary phase of learning revolves around the problem of symbolism. There are realities, and there are appearances related to them. Some appearances represent the reality, as a thermometer represents the temperature or, in a different way, as a drama represents a certain kind of human conflict. Some appearances partly conceal or disguise a reality, like the appearance of the sun "rising" in the east. And some appearances masquerade as reality, like the appearance of lofty intentions in a government about to grab someone else's territory. Learning to sort out these various relationships, or in other words developing what is in the broadest sense a critical intelligence, is the main preoccupation of students on the verge of becoming adult citizens.

In education properly so called, radical and conservative questions are asked within the subjects themselves. If a student asks, "What use is the conception of gravitation or relativity to physics?" or "What was the point of fighting the Crusades?" or "Why did Shakespeare put a ghost into *Hamlet*?" it is possible to give him a scientific, a historical, and a literary answer respectively. Asking questions about the relation of the subjects themselves to ordinary life is another matter. With young children the educational process competes on fairly even terms with the social one: the young child is interested in everything, and he might as well be interested in his education. But as he gets into his teens the growing power of his social adjustment, where he feels the immediate response of possession, and does not have to be in the humbler position of questioner and seeker, begins to fight against the learning process. This is the stage at which we may see some highly intelligent fourteen-year-old firmly closing his mind to further education, while parents and teachers stand helplessly by, knowing how much he will regret it later on, unable to make the slightest impression on him now. This is the stage too at which many questions are likely to take the form of: "What good is this subject to me when it has no place in the kind of life I now think I want to live?" or "Why should I study science (or history, or literature) when I don't particularly want to study anything?" It is impossible to give a student real answers to such questions, and the weary and helpless

answers he does get (e.g., without science we couldn't kill our ene-
mies with bombs or our friends with automobiles) have nothing to do
with the actual "good" of these subjects.

We can now see, perhaps, how serious the confusion between social
and educational standards, on which the old "progressive" theories
foundered, really was. It is because so many intellectually stunted
lives result from it that all three reports speak out sharply about every
aspect of the confusion that comes to their attention. The Social Science report attacks the "rosy cosy" view of society, of giving a child
his own situation (if it *is* his own situation) in the ideal form of a Bla-
kean song of innocence before he has any song of experience to compare it with. The point is that presenting the child's society to him in
the form of a superego symbol is deliberately weighting social standards at the expense of educational ones. The English report says
much the same thing about primary readers, and the Science report
insists on the difference between science and technology, on the im-
propriety of calling by name of science the various devices for providing the North American middle class with the comforts of home.
I remember a word recognition test given to children in a school
which drew from a middle-class group, a lower-middle-class group,
and an "under-privileged" group. One of the words was "gown."
Children of the first group said a gown was what mummy wore when
she went to a party; children of the second group said it was what
mummy wore when she went to bed; children of the third group had
never heard of the word. Such intrusions of class distinctions into
tests of learning and intelligence are not always easy to spot, and may
in themselves seem very trifling. But the more fundamental problem
of weeding social standards out of educational ones is something that
requires constant vigilance and astute criticism. The principle involved is the most important in the whole process of education.

Secondary learning, we suggested, revolves around the relation of
appearance and reality. What education as a whole deals with is the
reality of human society, the organized forms of intelligence, knowledge and imagination that make man civilized. The middle-class
twentieth-century Canadian world the student is living in is the appearance of that society. Education, freedom, and nearly all happiness
depend on his not mistaking it for the real form of society. The young
student needs to be protected from society, protected by literature
against the flood of imaginative trash that pours into him from the
mass media, protected by science against a fascination with gadgets
and gimmicks, protected by social science against snobbery and com-
placency. The crisis of his education comes when he is ready to attach
himself to the standards represented by his education, detach himself

from his society, and live in the latter as a responsible and critical citizen. If he fails to do this, he will remain a prisoner of his society, unable to break its chains of cliché and prejudice, unable to see through its illusions of advertising and slanted news, unable to distinguish its temporary conventions from the laws of God and man, a spiritual totalitarian. Whether he has voluntarily imprisoned himself or whether he has been betrayed by educators under the pretext of adjusting or "orienting" him, he cannot live freely or think freely, but is pinioned like Prometheus on his rock, oriented, occidented, septentrionated, and australized. . . .

The university is concerned specifically with the third phase of learning, where the conservative aspect is the consciousness of the presence of one's own society, with all its assumptions and values, measured against the radical criticism of that society by the standards of accuracy, profundity, and imaginative power to be found in the arts and sciences. The detachment required for this is symbolized in a four-year physical withdrawal from full participation in society. The very small number of university graduates who really achieve such detachment, along with those who achieve it outside the university, are enough to keep our society's head above water. One hardly dares speculate about what might happen if the number were suddenly to increase.

The reports that follow are witty and pointed, sharply critical, and fearless in their expression of criticism. This does not mean that the educational system they discuss is ridiculous or that the authors consider it to be so. They are criticizing something to which they themselves are completely committed. One's vision of life, like the units of one's elementary understanding of science, is a metaphor, and the natural metaphor for any responsible man's job is that of a complex machine, likely to be smashed up in incompetent hands. Contempt for the amateur critic is built into all professions: it is a part of . . . the bias of communication. And those who have places of trust in education must often feel, when reading books intended to stir up public resentment, like a farmer seeing his crops trampled and his fences broken by a hunting pack in clamorous pursuit of an enemy that he could have disposed of quickly and quietly with his own shotgun. But these reports have not been written by amateurs, and they are not indictments but specific and sympathetic suggestions. The real power that drives the educational machine, or, in our other image, the final twist on the "spiral curriculum," is the power of self-criticism in teachers, which means the renewing of the vision of the subject they teach. It is such a renewing of vision that is here presented to the public.

5. Teachers and Writers Collaborative/Schoolboys of Barbiana

Tolstoy lives: the idea of a community of learners who teach one another continually generates pedagogy which, if we are alert, we can make our own. So far as the search for an understanding of how theory and practice are related is concerned, the grade level is irrelevant. Plato can guide the nursery school teacher; Piaget, the director of the PhD dissertation. Montessori is adaptable to the seminar; the seminar, to the kindergarten. A seminar is (by way of seminary*) a place where seeds are kept; a garden is where they grow.*

Foxfire *brought youngsters together with their elders in dialogue, which probably did more to help them become readers and writers than a thousand hours of sentence-combining could have done. The Bay Area Writing Project, which gathers teachers of writing together to write themselves, "problematizes" the existential writing situation so that writing teachers can return to their classes to teach writing as writers. Any teacher of English, at any level, could learn a lot about how communities of learners are formed from Kenneth Koch. He has shown better than anybody I've read how reading and writing belong together. He invites the children to help him devise the writing assignment, which stems from "the poetry idea," itself generated by a communal reading of a real text (e.g., Blake's "The Tyger"). Kenneth Koch understands the true nature of "collaborative learning" because he understands the centrality of "interpretation in teaching."*

Teachers and Writers Collaborative, in operation in New York City for ten years or so, has put poets and painters in the classroom with the aim of encouraging students in drawing and carving, building and constructing—making meaning all the way. Transformation *is the generative idea: dreams become stories; stories become plays; drawings become puppets; observations become notes, which become biographies, reports, meditations. This kind of change will always make meaning because the active mind is engaged in asking* what's happening? what am I doing? what do you think? how would I know? *Of his own experiment, Bob Sievert writes: "Everyone was able to do it—the triumph of teaching form rather than trying to evoke emotion." Sievert's "basic bug" is a delightful demonstration of how the two modes of abstraction actually function: the children create in the image of what they think a bug really is; then they generalize (in dialogue) so that a basic bug is created; finally, the basic bug is recreated in individual interpretations. If I had to choose between Chapter 5 of Vygotsky's* Thought and Language *and Bob Sievert's "Bugs: One Insect Leads to Another" as a text to explain the dynamics of concept formation, I would take Sievert.*

In the mid-fifties, the parish priest of a tiny Tuscan village named Barbiana gathered the sons of shepherds and dirt farmers in their own after-school school. Public schooling had left them illiterate, on purpose: Don Lorenzo Milani began their schooling as an inquiry into that purpose. He did not, apparently, know Freire's work, but his convictions about the interdependence of learning skills and making meaning are in many ways analogous. (Comment I have read from British critics suggests that this book is not so much the work of the schoolboys themselves as it is the testimony of Father Milani, his interpretation of their voiceless experience. Such doubts were also expressed by those who read what Tolstoy claimed his schoolboys had written. Tolstoy troubled to counter those criticisms; Milani died before Letter to a Teacher *was published abroad.) It may be that Milani, like his countryman Danilo Dolci, will in the final analysis have had more influence on teachers and reformers everywhere on earth than he has had in Italy. But perhaps the invention of a school which is not a school, with teachers who are not teachers, will return to his homeland in the guise of a foreign innovation: Martin Luther King discovered the doctrine of nonviolence in reading Gandhi, who had learned it from Henry David Thoreau.*

Teachers and Writers Collaborative
(Bob Sievert)

Bugs: One Insect Leads to Another

It started as an insect project in the Bronx. Debbie Kantor, Assistant Principal at C.S. 232 in the Bronx, introduced me to Wendy Branch, who taught a fourth grade. We discussed ways in which we might work together. I suggested we do a project that would tie in with something the class was doing and help illuminate it with a visual art element. We talked over social studies and science projects. The idea of insects kept circling around, until finally we decided it had to be an insect project.

The project led in unexpected directions. After three weeks it was going so well that I started a second insect project in Selma Benjamin's third grade class at P.S. 84 in Manhattan. In each group there was a different momentum, and each achieved something different. Both groups made fantastic papermaché insects. At the end, Wendy's class had made a giant mural; Selma's had produced a film in which the school is menaced by a horde of insects from Mars and the teacher devoured (to the class's delight) before their eyes.

During the week that followed my first talk with Wendy, I had found a book on ants with some pretty good pictures in it. I realized that if I taught ant anatomy, it would serve as an introduction to all insects, since insects seem to me to be variations on the same form. I made a "basic insect drawing" and brought it to Wendy's class.

At the first session I drew the insect on the board, naming each part as clearly as possible. I explained that millions of different kinds of insects had these parts, although some of them varied greatly: whereas butterflies had large, feathery wings, beetles had hard shell-like wings.

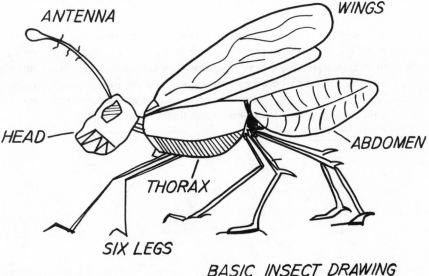

BASIC INSECT DRAWING

After the ant was drawn, we made a list of insects on the board and tried to sketch them. Butterflies, dragonflies, cockroaches, and·bees all had the basic form. After the board was covered with drawings, I passed out paper and crayons and had everyone draw the basic form. Everyone was able to do it (the triumph of teaching form rather than trying to evoke emotion). Each child did a very personal rendition of the drawing, and I let them spend the rest of the period drawing all the insects they could think of. We cut them out and hung them on the wall. It was exciting to see the work, and the class responded with great enthusiasm.

Throughout the first half of the project, pretty much the same format was used. I would come in with some material about insects and explain it with drawings on the board. The class would draw from the board and make up their own drawings about the materials presented. Some of the topics were: insect life cycle, insect homes, social insects, and beetles.

Wendy got meal worms for all the children. They watched them grow and change from larvae to pupae to adult beetles.

I began the second project with Selma's class at P.S. 84 to see if it would meet with equal enthusiasm. A student teacher thought the class needed three-dimensional work, and she and Selma suggested making models. Wendy had also asked about making models, so I thought about it for a while and finally sat up one night playing with wire, papermaché, string and plaster and came up with this recipe:

> heavy wire, string, wallpaper paste, newspaper, and masking tape = basic insect.

For the first model-building session, an armature is fashioned. Three loops of wire, representing the head, thorax, and abdomen of the insect, are put together. The body loops should be about three inches long. Then three wires are twisted into the joints (one between the head and thorax, two between the thorax and abdomen) for the six legs. Antennae are fastened to the head.

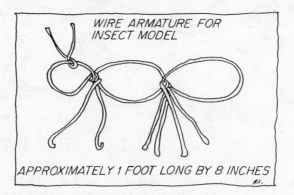

WIRE ARMATURE FOR INSECT MODEL

APPROXIMATELY 1 FOOT LONG BY 8 INCHES

After the wire armature was completed, I had them stuff newspaper into each wire loop, which was then held in place with masking tape.

This made a rough model that could be covered with papermaché during the second session.

Most students were able to build the armature independently; some needed help. In projects like this, I always give as much support as possible, without doing the work for them.

One girl in Wendy's class had us do as much for her as possible. When we got tired, she took it into a back corner of the class. With patience she worked on her almost completed version until suddenly, using wild destructive energy, she crushed it shapeless and came screaming across the room holding the mangled form.

"Oh, God, I've killed it. It's dead. I've killed it," she yelled.

Immediately everyone rushed to revive the crumpled bits of wire and string.

In the second model-building session, we took the armature stuffed with wadded newspapers and covered it with two or three layers of papermaché. We smeared wallpaper paste on medium-size pieces of newspaper (envelope size) and fixed them one at a time to the armature. Each leg and antenna was carefully wrapped. After this "rough" coat was on, we began to mold and shape it.

Ricardo, a boy in Wendy's class, revealed himself to be a gifted artist at this point. While most of the children had relied on the basic insect form to convey the image, Ricardo's insect had definition and personality. It was a bright, cheerful praying mantis, with a wonderful sense of form and life. However, at some point Ricardo became frustrated and smashed it. I was shocked.

"Don't you want to fix it?" I asked.

"No. Why do I need that junk!" he said.

It scared me to see him reject his talents so easily.

In the third session, we applied several more coats of papermaché, until the dried insects had the feel of stiff cardboard. The coats of maché became easier and easier to apply. Once it was stiff and dry (after three weeks) we painted the insects in bright colors, and found we had a wonderful series of insects crawling about both classrooms. In Wendy's class we attached clear plastic wings, but the plastic was not heavy enough and the wings never seemed substantial.

Wendy and I were both very happy with the results, and we moved on to working with plant forms for a while—also a good project. I brought in a giant piece of "seamless" photobackground paper (9 ft. by 12 ft.) on which we painted a huge mural of insects and flowers.

However, in Selma's class, everybody was still getting off on insects. They hovered about the room in eerie inspiration. They had to be realized more deeply. So we decided to make a movie using the insects. The whole class was to make the film.

I showed them how to make a story board for a film, and Selma assigned them to bring in a story the next day. It was amazing how similar the stories were. In most, the lovely insects were cast in the role of hostile monsters that attack the class and kill poor Selma. Every time a new story was read with Selma's end, the class went wild cheering. Selma seemed to enjoy it as much as the children.

I made a storyboard that was an editorial digest of all the stories. We rehearsed as a group two or three times and finally shot the film on the hottest day of early June. The heat made everybody very business-like and professional. No one wanted to waste energy.

The film was shot with a Super 8 movie camera that Marie Charney, a P.S. 84 corridor teacher, lent us. It had a single-frame device, so that we could film live action scenes and then, when the insects were supposed to "act" we placed them in position and shot four to six frames. Then we advanced the insects barely an inch and shot a few more frames. The insect shots were hard to control because each child had the responsibility of moving his own insect. I worried a lot about the quality of various shots. The scene in which the insects devour Selma was shot in the classroom under hot lights, an awfully demanding situation, but the class was up to it.

The finished film was a delight. With no editing, we managed a very believable fifty-foot, three-minute horror film. The scenes with the children running in terror juxtaposed with the mechanical scurrying of the insects were perfect. Only in one or two places did the visual line of the film break credibility.

We were all pleased, and at some point during this year, we plan to let the two groups at the two schools see each other's work.

Schoolboys of Barbiana
(from *Letter to a Teacher*)

Comments

One subject is totally missing from your programs: the art of writing. It is enough simply to see some of the comments you write at the top of your students' compositions. I have a choice collection of them, right here. They are all nothing more than assertions—never a means for improving the real work.

"Childish. Infantile. Shows immaturity. Poor. Trivial."

What use can a boy make of this sort of thing? Perhaps he should send his grandfather to school; he's more mature.

Other comments: "Meager contents. Poor conception. Pale ideas. No real participation in what you wrote." The theme must have been wrong, then. It ought not to have been assigned.

Or: "Try to improve your form. Incorrect form. Cramped. Unclear. Not well constructed. Poor usage. Try to write more simply. Sentence structure all wrong. Your way of expressing yourself is not always felicitous. You must have better control of your means of expression." You are the one who should have taught all that. But you don't even believe that writing can be taught; you don't believe there are any objective rules for the art of writing; you are still embalmed in your nineteenth-century individualism.

Then we also meet the creature touched by the hands of gods: "Spontaneous. Rich flow of ideas. Fitting use of your ideas, in harmony with a striking personality." Having gone that far, why not just add: "Blessed be the mother who gave you birth"?

The Genius

You returned one of my compositions with a very low grade and this comment: "Writers are born, not made." Meanwhile you receive a salary as a teacher of Italian.

The theory of the genius is a bourgeois invention. It was born from a compound of racism and laziness.

It is also useful in politics. Rather than having to steer through the complex of existing parties, you find it easier to get hold of a de Gaulle, call him a genius and say that *he* is France.

This is the way you operate in your Italian class. Pierino has the gift. I do not. So let's all relax about it.

It doesn't matter whether or not Pierino reflects on his writing. He will write more of those books that already surround him. Five hundred pages that could be reduced to fifty without losing a single idea.

I can learn resignation and go back to the woods.

As for you, you can go on loafing behind your desk and making little marks in your grade book.

School of Art

The craft of writing is to be taught like any other craft.

But at Barbiana we had to argue this question among ourselves. One faction wanted to describe the way we go about writing. Others said, "Art is a serious matter, even if it uses simple techniques. The readers will laugh at us."

The poor will not laugh at us. The rich can go on laughing all they want, and we shall laugh at them, not able to write either a book or a newspaper with the skill of the poor.

Finally we agreed to write down everything for readers who will love us.

A Humble Technique

This is the way we do it:

To start with, each of us keeps a notebook in his pocket. Every time an idea comes up we make a note of it. Each idea on a separate sheet, on one side of the page.

Then one day we gather together all the sheets of paper and spread them on a big table. We look through them, one by one, to get rid of duplications. Next, we make separate piles of the sheets that are related, and these will make up the chapters. Every chapter is subdivided into small piles, and they will become paragraphs.

At this point we try to give a title to each paragraph. If we can't it means either that the paragraph has no content or that too many things are squeezed into it. Some paragraphs disappear. Some are broken up.

While we name the paragraphs we discuss their logical order, until an outline is born. With the outline set, we reorganize all the piles to follow its pattern.

We take the first pile, spread the sheets on the table, and we find the sequence for them. And so we begin to put down a first draft of the text.

We mimeograph that part so that we each can have a copy in front of us. Then, scissors, paste and colored pencils. We shuffle it all again. New sheets are added. We mimeograph again.

A race begins now for all of us to find any word that can be crossed out, any excess adjectives, repetitions, lies, difficult words, overly long sentences and any two concepts that are forced into one sentence.

We call in one outsider after another. We prefer that they not have had too much school. We ask them to read aloud. And we watch to see if they have understood what we meant to say.

We accept their suggestions if they clarify the text. We reject any suggestions made in the name of caution.

Having done all this hard work and having followed these rules that anyone can use, we often come across an intellectual idiot who announces, "This letter has a remarkably *personal* style."

Laziness

Why don't you admit that you don't know what the art of writing is? It is an art that is the very opposite of laziness.

And don't say that you lack the time for it. It would be enough to have one long paper written throughout the year, but written by all the students together.

List of Sources for Part III

*William James, from chapters on attention and memory, *Talks to Teachers* (1899).

Collected Papers of Charles Sanders Peirce, six volumes, edited by Charles Hartshorne and Paul Weiss (Cambridge: Harvard University Press, 1931–35), 1.657.

*Alfred North Whitehead, from "Universities and Their Function," *The Aims of Education* (1929; rpt. N.Y.: Macmillan, 1957), pp. 96–98.

*Jane Addams, from "Educational Methods," *Democracy and Social Ethics* (1902).

*Emile Jaques-Dalcroze, from "The Initiation into Rhythm," *Rhythm, Music, and Education* (1921).

*Leo Tolstoy, from "Are the Peasant Children to Learn to Write from Us? or, Are We to Learn from the Peasant Children?" and "The School at Yásnaya Polyána." (A new translation of Tolstoy's papers on education will shortly appear in Britain, edited with an introduction by Michael Armstrong.)

*Maria Montessori, from "Teaching Reading and Writing." *The Montessori Method* (Tr. Anne E. George from the original, *Il Metodo della Pedagogia Scientifica applicato all' educazione nelle Case dei Bambini;* N.Y.: Frederic A. Stokes, 1912), pp. 254–55; 259–61.

*Sylvia Ashton-Warner, from "Creative Teaching," *Teacher* (N.Y.: Simon and Schuster, 1963), pp. 27–42.

*Paulo Freire, from "Education as the Practice of Freedom," *Education for Critical Consciousness* (N.Y.: Seabury Press, 1973), pp. 48–58; pp. 62–63; 66–67; 70–71.

*I. A. Richards, "To Learn, Compare," from *How to Read a Page* (1942; rpt. Boston: Beacon Press, 1959), pp. 40–56.

*Paul Freund, "The Law and the Schools," *Harvard Educational Review* (40) 1966, 470–76.

*Northrop Frye, from the Introduction to *Design for Learning: Reports submitted to the Joint Committee of the Toronto Board of Education and the University of Toronto,* ed. Northrop Frye (Toronto: University of Toronto Press, 1962), pp. 11–17.

*Bob Sievert, "Bugs: One Insect Leads to Another," *Teachers and Writers Collaborative Newsletter* (7), 1976, pp. 32–35.

*Schoolboys of Barbiana, from *Letter to a Teacher,* Tr. Nora Rossi and Tom Cole (N.Y.: Random House, 1970), pp. 118–22.

Additional Readings

Every teacher of writing should own a copy of *Teaching Writing: Essays from the Bay Area Writing Project* (Boynton/Cook, 1983) and get from BAWP (School of Education, University of California, Berkeley, CA 94720) a copy of Josephine Miles's indispensable "Working Out Ideas: Predication and Other Uses of Language."

I have not included articles from the two principal journals in the field of composition pedagogy, *College English* and *College Composition and Communication*, since they are easily available. But I would like to note several from the last decade or so which I have found useful because of their methodological focus, the illumination of theory by practice, or vice versa, which they provide.

H. Eric Branscomb, "Turning the Corner: Story to Meaning in Freshman Composition Class," *College English*, March, 1976.

Phyllis Brooks, "Mimesis: Grammar and the Echoing Voice," *CE*, November, 1973.

Francis Christensen, "The Course in Advanced Composition for Teachers," *College Composition and Communication*, May, 1973.

William E. Coles, Jr., "An Unpetty Pace," *CCC*, December, 1972.

Congressman Robert F. Drinan, "The Rhetoric of Peace," *CCC*, October, 1972.

Anne Ruggles Gere, "Writing Well Is the Best Revenge," *CCC*, October, 1978.

May Newman Hallmundsson, "Teaching Remedial English: The Dictionary as Textbook," *CE*, October, 1976.

Joan E. Hartman, "Teaching Poetry: An Exercise in Practical Criticism," *CE*, October, 1973.

Philip Keith, "Burke in the Composition Class," *CCC*, December, 1977.

Lou Kelly, "Is Competent Copyreading a Violation of the Students' Right to Their Own Language?" *CCC*, October, 1974.

Alan K. Lemke, "Writing as Action in Living," *CCC*, October, 1978.

Andrea A. Lunsford, "What We Know—and Don't Know—About Remedial Writing," *CCC*, February, 1978.

A. E. Malloch, "A Dialogue of Plagiarism," *CE*, October, 1976.

Lewis Meyers, "Texts and Teaching: Basic Writing," *CE*, April, 1978.

Carolyn Miller, "A Humanistic Rationale for Technical Writing," *CE*, February, 1979. Further comment in *CE*, March, 1980.

Sidney P. Moss, "Logic: A Plea for a New Methodology in Freshman Composition," *CCC*, October, 1969.

Jean Pumphrey, "Teaching English Composition as a Creative Art," *CE*, February, 1973.

Ann Raimes, "Writing and Learning Across the Curriculum: The Experience of a Faculty Seminar," *CE*, November, 1980. Further comment in *CE*, November, 1980.

John Rouse, "The Politics of Composition," *CE*, September, 1979; "Knowledge, Power, and the Teaching of English," *CE*, January, 1979; further comment in *CE*, April, 1980.

Ira Shor, "Learning How to Learn: Conceptual Teaching in a Course called 'Utopia'," *CE*, March, 1977.

Bernard Van't Hul, "Yet the Sea Is Not Full," *CE*, December, 1975.